WILLIAM GODDARD, NEWSPAPERMAN

WILLIAM GODDARD, NEWSPAPERMAN

WARD L. MINER

DUKE UNIVERSITY PRESS Durham, North Carolina 1962

© 1962, Duke University Press

Library of Congress Catalogue Card number 62-14873
Cambridge University Press, London N.W. 1, England

Printed in the United States of America
by the Seeman Printery, Inc., Durham, N. C.

To my Mother

This book has been published with the assistance of funds from a grant to the Duke University Press by the Ford Foundation.

PREFACE

THERE ARE always mixed feelings when any scholar sits down to write his preface, faced as he is with the galley proof of what will soon turn into a printed book. Seeing the long sheets results in sighs of mingled satisfaction and relief. Yet this very awareness of perspective prevents a too complacent satisfaction and relief. No matter how individual one's own research is, its existence depends on the help of so many others. The "Note on Sources" at the conclusion of this book is therefore, in so many ways, an extension of this preface, the citations not only suggesting guide lines for the reader but also expressing gratitude for what others have done.

First, I would like to express my appreciation for financial assistance. I was able to travel to the appropriate libraries and secure microfilms, photostats, and the like—in other words, do the basic research—under a research grant from the American Philosophical Society. Later, a grant from the Graduate Council of the University of Kansas made possible the typing of a portion of the manuscript of this book.

For their many courtesies I want to indicate my gratitude to members of the staffs of the New-York Historical Society, Manuscript Room of the New York Public Library, National Archives, Hall of Records of Maryland, Manuscript Division of the Library of Congress, Library of the American Philosophical Society, Enoch Pratt Free Library, Library Company of Philadelphia, Department of Records of the city of Philadelphia, Connecticut State Library, New Haven Colony Historical Society, Henry E. Huntington Library, Massachusetts Historical Society, Yale University Library, University of Pennsylvania Library, Vassar College Library, Historical Society of Pennsylvania, Rhode Island Historical Society, American Antiquarian Society, New London County Historical Society, Maryland Historical Society, and John Carter Brown Library, Brown University. Individuals I would like to name who have contributed much include Clarence S. Brigham, Clarkson A. Collins, III, Lois V. Given, Hope Goddard Iselin, Dwight C. Lyman, Fred Shelley, Neda Westlake, and Lawrence C. Wroth.

For permission to quote from unpublished manuscript material in their possession may I express my thanks to the following institutions: American Antiquarian Society, Rhode Island Historical Society, American Philosophical Society, Salem County Historical Society, Hall of Records of

Maryland, Maryland Historical Society, John Carter Brown Library of Brown University, Historical Society of Pennsylvania, National Archives, Providence Public Library, Library Company of Philadelphia, New-York Historical Society, New York Public Library, and Yale University Library. The 1774 letter of John Foxcroft is unpublished Crown copyright material in the Public Record Office, London, and has been reproduced by permission of the Controller of H. M. Stationery Office.

I will deposit an annotated copy of this book in the John Carter Brown Library, Brown University, where it may be consulted.

Words can never state the gratitude and the debt I owe for the many patient hours so lovingly given by my wife, Thelma.

Feb. 4, 1962
Youngstown University

Notes on sources will be found on pages 209 ff.

The index will be found on pages 215 ff.

WILLIAM GODDARD, NEWSPAPERMAN

WILLIAM GODDARD was not the most important of the many printers who operated in the colonies after Stephen Daye set up the Widow Glover's press in Cambridge. Nor was he unimportant. In the heyday of his career other printers published more books than he did. James Parker started numerous magazines; Goddard did not, perhaps because of his intimate knowledge of Parker's failures. Nor did Goddard occupy the public prominence of Franklin, who to the end of his life regarded diplomacy and public service as mere avocations compared to the not only primary, but *the* vocation—printing. Yet the public contributions of William Goddard are noteworthy and distinguished. John Peter Zenger made, perhaps unwittingly, a special legacy to all succeeding printers as a result of his famous trial in 1745; but freedom of the press as a fundamental principle had no more staunch defender than William Goddard. And he understood, believed in, and practiced the principle long before Baltimore mobs placed the Goddard press in jeopardy.

After all has been said about what Goddard was not, there remain the very positive qualities of his personality and the positive contributions he made both to our printing and to our political history. Yet when these qualities and contributions have been presented, what stands out most about his career is—William Goddard, newspaperman. In a period when a newspaper was subordinate in the mind and purse of the average printer to the almanacs, broadsides, pamphlets, and workaday ephemeral publications of the colonial print shop, Goddard printed the almanacs, broadsides, pamphlets, and other ephemera, but they were subordinate for him to the regular publication of a newspaper. A careful perusal of the published Franklin and Hall workbooks will show that the financial success of Franklin was based not so much on the *Pennsylvania Gazette*, though that helped, as on Poor Richard, on the printing of the provincial assembly's laws, on the wholesale business in printing supplies that Franklin was so successful in conducting among the printers of all the colonies, on his various partnerships, and on the thousand and one items that made up the total output of the colonial printing establishment. Another financially success-ful contemporary was Isaiah Thomas, in later life a close friend of Goddard. Yet, ironically when we look at the business of printing in the twentieth century, Thomas made far more money from his books—Bibles, spelling books, and books of all sorts—than from his different newspapers. Today fortunes are made from news-papers, and fortunes are spent publishing books. Only a little over a hundred and fifty years ago we find the wealthy book publishers Isaiah Thomas and Mathew Carey and the struggling newspaper-man William Goddard. And the struggling is true in spite of his twice being the owner of the newspaper with the largest circulation in the colonies and in the new country. Once, at Philadelphia, such a "mass-circulation" newspaper ended by Goddard's going through bankruptcy proceedings in the local courts; the other news-paper, at Baltimore, ended by Goddard's selling out and retiring to live not just off those proceeds, however, but off the income and properties owned by his recently married wife. And so we find the newspaperman William Goddard well-nigh forgotten by later generations while the Franklins, Thomases, and Careys continue to attract both popular and scholarly attention.

Being a newspaperman in the 1760's, 1770's, and 1780's was much different from being one today. The closest parallel to the newspapers of those days is the weekly paper often found in rural areas of this country. Many of these weeklies are edited, written, set up, and run through the presses under the immediate super-vision of one man, who also acts as advertising and circulation manager. And it was much like this for all the printers before and just after the Revolution. Printer's ink soiled the hands of those men and women. Much is revealed of the lives of the colonial printers when we note that Goddard's son, William Giles Goddard, was one of the first newspaper editors who had not been trained in the composing room; he entered the newspaper business from the editorial room. But he did not begin his journalistic career until twenty years after his father had retired. Appropriately I have without thinking used the word *journalist* to describe the son's occupation and reserved the words *printer* and *newspaperman* for the father. A useful distinction is thereby made between the two activities. Today our thinking of journalism as a profession and printing as a trade has succeeded only in making both aspects of the newspaperman tawdry. The eighteenth century would have been horrified at this attitude. Imagine that gravestone in the small cemetery at Fifth and Arch Streets in Philadelphia reading Benjamin Franklin, Journalist.

In 1928 Michael Kraus in *Intercolonial Aspects of American Culture on the Eve of the Revolution* stressed the unifying forces in colonial society in contrast to the divisive forces conventionally emphasized. Among these unifying elements are the colonial newspapers and printers. Much has been said about how the newspapers contributed to the "intercolonial" attitudes Kraus speaks of—in their dissemination of news, in the editors' clipping of articles from each other (John Dickinson's "Letters from a Pennsylvania Farmer" first published in Goddard's *Pennsylvania Chronicle* appeared in all but three of the colonial newspapers), and in the selectivity, the emphasis implied in the work with the scissors. But it is the second of these two elements I should like to talk about here—the printer, well illustrated by Franklin's activities as a printer, long before he became involved in public affairs. His apprenticeship and first practice of his trade as a journeyman were in Boston. He worked as a journeyman and as master of his own shop in Philadelphia. A familiar passage in the *Autobiography* narrates his flight from Boston. He first sought employment in New York at the shop of the elder William Bradford, who referred him to the shop in Philadelphia of his son, Andrew Bradford. Even as early as the 1720's colonial printers and their journeymen thought it natural to move from colony to colony in pursuit of their trade. And the workmen in each shop knew much about the activities and personnel of the other shops. After Franklin got his printing business well under way, among his first actions was the financing of other printing establishments throughout the colonies as far away as South Carolina and later Jamaica. I have, in another connection, mentioned the wholesale business for other printers that Franklin conducted. One reason for his success in this was Philadelphia itself, its geographical location, its commercial enterprises. The central location of Penn's "green country town" among the original thirteen colonies is apparent from the most casual glance at a map. More important to Franklin's wholesale business in printing supplies was the role of Philadelphia and vicinity in paper-making and in a smaller way the making of the ingredients for printing ink. Appropriately enough the first paper mill in the colonies was started in 1690 by William Rittenhouse on a branch of the Wissahickon. Though mills were established throughout the colonies, the mills of Philadelphia and Germantown continued to produce most of the paper made on this side of the Atlantic until early in the nineteenth century. Lawrence C. Wroth in *The Colonial Printer* gives these figures for 1787: of a total of eighty or ninety mills in operation in all the states forty-eight were in Pennsylvania alone. It was not very difficult for Franklin with his keen business sense to step in as a middleman and supply other printers with their much-needed paper. Of course, we must add to the reasons for Franklin's success as a wholesaler his London connections, particularly his lifelong friendship with William Strahan, one of the leading printers in London.

The career of William Goddard also illustrates the "intercolonial" contributions of the printers just in following their trade. He started his apprenticeship as a printer in New Haven, after growing up in New London. Before he had finished his training he was working in New York. Goddard's first printing establishment was in Providence. Later, for about a year he worked in New York with a sojourn in New Jersey long enough to print a single issue of a newspaper (more properly treated as a broadside). For several years he published a newspaper in Philadelphia. On a small scale, while publishing the *Pennsylvania Chronicle*, he sold paper to the printer John Holt in New York and perhaps to others. He ended his activities as a printer by an almost twenty-year stay in Baltimore. As a silent partner, though very much financially involved, Goddard helped set up the first press in Alexandria, Virginia. At various times he contemplated financing presses in Norfolk, Virginia, and in Jamaica. This same pattern is evident in the careers of many printers. Isaiah Thomas worked from the Carolinas to Nova Scotia before settling in Worcester. Another lesser known example is Benjamin Mecom, the dapper, ne'er-do-well nephew of Franklin. Mecom worked in several of the colonies (at one time for Goddard in Philadelphia) and had his own shop for short periods in places as separated as New Haven and Jamaica. Goddard's seeming peripatetic career as a printer should not be thought of as unusual in any sense. Practitioners of his trade thought of themselves as printers first and New Yorkers or Virginians afterwards.

And so we come to the career, the life, the personality of William Goddard—in many ways typical of his period and his profession. Like other colonial printers he moved around; yet unlike most others it was a tempestuous moving around. Difficulties with the postal system affected all the newspaper editors as well as Goddard; however, he did not merely complain about the vagaries of the colonial postmasters and postriders—he did something. Typical, yes, untypical, yes; sometimes strong, sometimes weak; sometimes great-minded, sometimes small-minded. All add up to a very human William Goddard.

THE antecedents of William Goddard are in no way unusual for his time and place, both his paternal and maternal ancestors being from New England. Who the first Goddard was to emigrate from England is somewhat in doubt, but probably it was Giles Goddard (*ca.* 1648-*ca.* 1729) found in Boston and Brookline by 1678. His son William (other records say that it was a brother Joseph), born in 1678, married Miss Elizabeth Fairfield in 1697. The son of William (or Joseph) was again named Giles, and this Giles was the father of William, the subject of this biography.

Giles Goddard was born between 1703 and 1705. In 1725 he was in the vicinity of New London, Connecticut. The first entry in the parish records of the local Episcopal Church attests this: "Colony Connecticott, June 6, 1725. Wee the subscribers doe oblige ourselves to pay to the Rev. Mr James McSparran, or to his substitute, he being Treasurer, the particular sums annexed to our names for the building and erecting a Church for the service of Almighty God, according to the Liturgie of the Church of England as by law established." Twelve names follow with sums ranging from £3 to £50. The last is "Giles Goddard £5." Giles was evidently not the richest person in New London, but only a well-to-do citizen of 1725 could have afforded £5. Ten years later we find: "December 11th 1735, Doctor Giles Goddard of Groton in Connecut viz the Town of Groton was married to Mrs Sarah updike at the House of her Father Capt. Lowdowick Updike by Mr McSparran." (Groton, it might be explained, is just across the river Thames from New London.) We can picture the young doctor, a confirmed Anglican as his descendants to the present day have remained, getting himself established in his profession in Groton and New London. By 1735 he was successful enough in his practice to be able to put down the social roots of marriage. There must have been a warm friendship for the Reverend Mr. McSparran, by 1735 pastor at Narragansett, Rhode

Island, for the Updikes to go to the trouble to secure his services for the marriage ceremony in the home.

New London of this period was fortunate in having had an industrious and careful diary keeper in the person of Joshua Hempstead. The diary's first entry mentioning Doctor Goddard is dated March 26, 1735, and the last February 1, 1757, the day after Giles's death. Altogether there are fourteen references. Unfortunately Hempstead is not the kind of diarist to characterize either his neighbors or the events he mentions. Usually the entry will be a laconic "I was up to Doctr Goddards in the middle of the Day," the one for October 17, 1754.

But several of the entries in the Hempstead diary do concern the medical activities of Doctor Goddard. Where he got his training we have no idea, but most likely he served his apprenticeship with an older practitioner before hanging out his own shingle. The medical treatment of those days can be seen: "I sent for Doctor Goddard & he came & considered my Case and Says tis the Same Distemper that hath of late prevailed among Children & Directs to a drink of Strong Tea made of the bark of Sassafrax Roots boiled with Lignum vitia Saw dust." Sassafrass roots and sawdust—and yet Hempstead got well.

We catch a glimpse of the personality of the doctor in the *Itinerarium* of Doctor Alexander Hamilton, an Annapolis physician who traveled to Portsmouth, New Hampshire, in 1744. "26 August 1744 New London I stayed att home [Duchand's at the sign of the Anchor] most of the forenoon and was invited to dine with Collector Lechmere [Nicholas Lechmere, naval officer stationed at New London], son of the surveyor att Boston. There was att table one Dr. Goddard and an old maid whom they called Miss Katy, being a great fat woman with a red face, as much like an old maid as a frying pan. There sat by her a young, modest looking lady dressed in black whom Mr. Lechmere called Miss Nansy, and next her, a walnut coloured, thin woman, sluttishly dressed and very hard favoured. These ladies went to meeting after dinner, and we three sat drinking of punch and telling of droll storys." The picture of the two doctors and the naval officer drinking punch and telling droll stories (that the ladies were not to hear) is a pleasant one. We may be sure the punch was potent.

Probably not too long after his marriage Giles Goddard moved across the river from Groton to New London. Hempstead speaks of doing some surveying at Groton for him on March 26, 1735. The marriage record in December of the same year reveals him still in Groton. All later references in the diary imply residence in New London. We know that he lived finally on Bradley Street in a house originally built by Jonathan Gardiner, later buying it, for in 1743 he sold part of this lot to Charles Jeffery.

In 1752 he became involved in a lawsuit with Richard Durfey. What the suit was about is now impossible to tell. Under the May proceedings of the Connecticut Colony Assembly there is this summary remark: "On the petition of Richard Durfey of New London, vs. Giles Goddard of New London, on file: The question was put, whether anything should be granted on the said petition: Resolved by this Assembly in the negative. *Cost allowed respondent is £10 10s. 8d. old tenour. Ex. granted July 21st, 1752.*" Like all colonial legal matters this took a long time to be settled. More than two years later Hempstead writes: "I was att home foren[oon], & in Town in the aftern[oon] att Doctor Goddards to settle the Difference between him & Capt. Durfey & Compleated it with the assistance of Justice Perkins & I Recd of Ms Goddard 40s." Let us hope that the affair was *compleated.*

By the time the dispute with Captain Durfey was settled to the satisfaction of Joshua Hempstead if not of Goddard, the doctor was already partially incapacitated by gout, which was soon to force him to his bed and to his death, January 31, 1757. "Doctor Giles Goddard Died yesterday morning aged between 50 & 60. he hath been decriped [decrepit] with the Gout &c Several years & of late Confined to his house & Bed." The widow and two children were left with an estate evaluated at £780, a considerable sum for 1757. Thus the affable doctor suffered the fate of so many eighteenth-century drinkers of strong punch and tellers of droll stories—gout. The dinner session with Doctor Hamilton was obviously not the only such convivial bout that found Giles Goddard an active participant.

In 1635 a physician named Gysbert op Dyck emigrated from Wesel, Germany, to Lloyd's Neck, Long Island. Shortly his medical practice was shoved into the background, and we find him in 1638 employed by the Dutch as Commander of Fort Hope, situated at what is today Hartford. In 1643 in New Amsterdam he married

Katherine Smith, whose family was prominent among the early settlers of Rhode Island. Her grandfather, Richard Smith, owned on the west side of Narragansett Bay 30,000 acres, called Cocumscussuc. A son of Gysbert, born in 1646 and named Lodowick, in 1664 moved from New Amsterdam to Kingston, Rhode Island, anglicizing his surname to Updike. Somewhat later he married Abigail Newton (1654-1745). (One of Lodowick's descendants was Daniel Berkeley Updike, the famous printer of Merrymount Press.) Lodowick died about 1737, leaving one son and five daughters. The son, Daniel, later served for several years (1731-32, 1743-57) as attorney-general of the colony of Rhode Island. According to a descendant, Wilkins Updike, "Daniel was educated in his father's house, by an able French instructor [probably Daniel Vernon] in the Greek, Latin and French languages, and his sisters, in the Latin and French." Such an education bespeaks a household with financial means and intellectual interests far beyond the average. One of the five sisters, Esther, on June 29, 1720, married Doctor Thomas Fosdick, like Giles Goddard, of New London.

Sarah, another of the five sisters, was born, probably not too long after 1700, at Cocumscussuc. Isaiah Thomas says of her: "She received a good education, acquired an acquaintance with several branches of useful and polite learning." In her youth she is alleged to have spent some time in Boston. Probably Sarah met Giles during visits to her sister Esther and therefore did not come as a total stranger to New London after her marriage on December 11, 1735. As the well-educated wife of a local physician she must have contributed a good deal to the little seaport. But her duties as a colonial housewife who must bear children went on apace. Her first child, Catherine, died at the age of two months on January 15, 1736/7. The next child, Mary Katherine, was born June 16, 1738 (frequently the date is given as 1736, but that is evidently a confusion with the other Catherine), while the family may have been still living in Groton. Two years later the family was in New London, where William was born October 20, 1740. Another child is recorded as having died (September 19, 1742) though no age or sex is mentioned. To have half of the children live to adulthood was in those days a reasonable average.

Though we can readily verify the date of William Goddard's birth, we have no further specific record of him until 1755, but our imaginations can be of some help to us in filling in the fifteen years. We have seen that the father regularly practiced his medical profession in the community, had prospered, and enjoyed the amenities of comfortable, perhaps even luxurious, living. The mother had had an education possessed by only a few of the local seagoing citizenry. After 1742 she was able to devote her energies to her family uninterrupted by childbearing. She herself probably taught Mary Katherine and William to read and write, to cipher (living in a seaport community would have shown the necessity for this), and to enjoy the beauties of Shakespeare and of Pope, Swift, and the other eighteenth-century writers later quoted so frequently by the printer. More than likely William attended a dame's school in New London or its vicinity. Unfortunately we do not know where he went or for how long this formal education lasted. We only know that years later William mentioned reading Latin authors and learning Roman history at school. But outside of school hours undoubtedly the young boy and his sister played with the neighboring children in the long sunny days of summer and found all kinds of pleasure in the winter snow and the ice of the Thames River. And the profession of the father would have given the children an acquaintance with adult townspeople. Surely they frequently heard stories of sea voyages on the New England triangular route to the West Indies, to Africa, and thence back to the home port, New London. Many an evening the convivial doctor and other men must have finished their Teneriffe and Madeira and rejoined the family in front of the fireplace as a guest recounted his experiences storming Louisburg. The vicissitudes of colonial New England found their way into that household, but the amenities of comfortable living, of social pleasures, of aesthetic satisfactions would have done much to ameliorate the lives of the Goddards.

In 1755 the round of play on the docks, studies alongside his sister, and hearing each Sunday the sermons of the Reverend Samuel Seabury were interrupted for William. His father may have already been forced to be not quite so active in his practice and his mother to take over an increased proportion of the family responsibilities. Sending William out of the family circle to apprentice himself to the printing trade would have been favorably regarded by Giles Goddard; in fact, we can recognize his active participation in the choice of the shop in which William was to work. As postmaster of New London the father would have had correspondence with and perhaps have met James Parker, then postmaster in New Haven and owner of a press there. Thus it is not surprising to find young William sent to serve as a printer's apprentice in New Haven. We may add another surmise about William's apprenticeship. Likely a family in the financial circumstances of the Goddards had in mind from the very beginning that their only son should have his own establishment. Possibly discreet inquiries were made by the parents about the cost of a press, of fonts of type, and of the other paraphernalia necessary for the maintenance of such a business.

James Parker, in whose shops William was to work as an apprentice until he was twenty-one years old, was born in 1714 in Woodbridge, New Jersey. He learned his trade in the print shop of William Bradford in New York. In 1742 Benjamin Franklin became a silent partner in the Parker enterprises, and thereafter the two corresponded regularly until Parker's death in 1770. Parker's affairs prospered after the financial support of Franklin was infused into his business. In 1743 he became public printer in New York replacing his former mentor, William Bradford, and started a newspaper, the *New-York Weekly Post-Boy*. In the 1750's he became postmaster of Woodbridge, New Jersey, and New Haven, where John Holt served as his deputy. Under Franklin he was also comptroller-general of the entire colonial postal system. He was at times public printer to the colony of New Jersey and printer to Yale College. During much of the 1750's and 1760's Parker's attention was taken up by printing establishments in Woodbridge and Burlington, New Jersey. At these plants Parker tried his hand at magazine publishing, none of his ventures lasting more than a few months. He was a good printer for his day, better than William Bradford and probably better than Franklin. He was aware, as few colonial printers were, that there is such a thing as typographical excellence and tried, within his limitations, to aim at that excellence. After the death of William Parks in Williamsburg in 1750 the typography and presswork of Parker may well have been the best in the colonies. Goddard was therefore fortunate in serving his apprenticeship under such a master. But it must frequently have been a sore trial to get along with Parker, since he was querulous and petulant. In his letters to Franklin he is always complaining about financial problems and the activities of his associates. Yet

Franklin must have respected him, for at the time of setting up the partnership of Franklin and Hall, Parker was called in to appraise the shop as a basis for the financial agreement making possible Franklin's early retirement from the printing business.

John Holt, in 1755 manager of the New Haven shop, was a much different person from Parker. Born in Williamsburg, Virginia, in 1721, he started his career as a merchant and was at first reasonably successful. He married in 1749 Elizabeth Hunter, the sister of William Hunter, printer in Williamsburg and with Franklin joint postmaster-general of the colonies. Probably in the shop of his brother-in-law Holt learned the printing trade. Though he was at one time mayor of Williamsburg, business failures overwhelmed him, and in 1754 he was in New York working for Parker, who soon sent him off to New Haven. Later, in 1762, he rented Parker's New York plant and published the *New-York Gazette, or, Weekly Post-Boy* himself. Holt was active in various anti-British causes, beginning in the mid-1760's with the Sons of Liberty and their attacks on the Stamp Act. He was therefore one of the pre-Revolutionary "radicals," and Parker worried over this a good deal. During the Revolution Holt had to leave New York in front of the British army. For a time he printed in New Haven, then in Kingston, New York, and finally in Poughkeepsie, where he remained from 1778 until his return to New York in November, 1783. Within a few months he died there, leaving his widow to carry on his business. Holt was much interested in the postal system and wrote attacks on its inefficiencies and waste, proposing various reforms. In person he seems to have been affable, perhaps only in contrast to the petulant Parker, though it must be admitted Holt's accounting would have made anybody complain. He suffered many misfortunes, losing his entire printing apparatus more than once to the British. Yet he was always able in some fashion to pull through and keep his business going. His devotion to the revolutionary cause was sincere, and he sacrificed much because of his beliefs. He was no Hugh Gaines, turning from one side to the other as the wind seemed to blow. Sometimes tactless and lacking in finesse, he fought manfully for what he believed.

In July, 1755, William Goddard started his apprenticeship in Parker's New Haven shop. The printing equipment had been originally bought by Franklin from Strahan in London for the use of his nephew James Franklin, Jr., then in Newport. James, whose father had introduced Benjamin to the printing trade in Boston, preferred to stay in Newport with his mother, and so the press was offered to another nephew, Benjamin Mecom, who chose at that point to remain in Antigua. As a result, Franklin at the end of 1754 persuaded Parker to purchase the setup. It was therefore on relatively new and unused type that Goddard started his training. The shop was a busy one. The *Connecticut Gazette* had been begun April 12, 1755, before William started to work in the shop. Through the help of Ezra Stiles the printing for Yale College was done in the shop, and presumably the faculty worried about textual accuracy even if not the appearance of the text on the pages. Much, of this work, of course, was in Latin, and William's early training from his mother and school came in very handy. William probably never had time to associate with Yale College youths of his own age, who then, even more than now, would have scorned contact with a being as low in the social scale as an apprentice. No, he would have been kept busy in the shop being janitor, inking the printing forms with ink balls as the printer made his impressions, delivering the weekly newspaper to the homes in the community, and occasionally being allowed to use his own composing stick. In this shop he saw a post office in operation, though not much of Holt's or Parker's time was taken up by postal work.

In connection with this postal work we have our earliest record of Goddard in this shop. Many years after he had retired from active printing and was living in Rhode Island Goddard reminisced to Isaiah Thomas: "After Defeat of Braddock, July 9, 1755, and the assemblage of an army at Lake St. Sacrament, now Lake George, where, Sept. 30 [Sept. 8], Sr. Wm. Johnson gained a victory over Baron Deskeau & his Regulars & Savages (taking the Baron Prison'r Sir Wm. having only Provincials, under his Command) much Business was done at the New-Haven P. Office and many Posts established to the army &c. &c. under the Direction of Franklin, Parker, &c. At 15 I was sent with a Rider from New-Haven to Middletown & Hartford, thence to N. London, and round by Seaboard to N. H. to estimate the Expense. . . . In 1758, I went to N. York & Woodbridge to assist in the offices there. . . . When I went to New-York in 1758 the American Company of Commedians, under the management of David Douglas, Esq. a Gent. of honour

& Talents (who married the Widow Hallam) performed in a Sail-Loft on Cruger's Dock! Douglas was afterwards King's Printer in Jamaica, a Master in Chancery, a Magistrate, &c patronized by his Countryman Sir Basil Keith. Douglas made a Fortune." Within a few months Parker and Holt had enough confidence in their fifteen-year-old apprentice to send him on this postal surveying trip through the different parts of Connecticut.

Parker's moving of his apprentice to New York in 1758 placed Goddard in a larger printing shop. Here he assisted in seeing through the press (no doubt he regularly used the composing stick now) almanacs and books. Just as New Haven had been the center for postal activity in Connecticut in 1755, New York was the center for the entire colonial postal system under the crown, Parker being comptroller and secretary after 1756. In this shop, under the management of William Weyman, there would have been three or four apprentices and two or three journeymen printers, giving the young neophyte more associates than in New Haven. Goddard's letter reveals that New York had another advantage for him. He developed a love for the theater, a love not too difficult to arouse from someone already appreciative of literary qualities. There is a pleasure in the picture of the eighteen-year-old apprentice sitting or perhaps even standing in the sail-loft watching Douglas perform in a Shakespearean play. By this time Goddard's status in the shop must have been much like that of a journeyman except for pay, because leisure evenings were not the lot of the usual apprentice.

In October, 1761, the apprenticeship ended on Goddard's twenty-first birthday. The full wages of a journeyman printer would now be his after six years of laborious training. His first job in this newly acquired status lasted only a few months because he surely was already planning for his own shop. His employer for these months, Samuel Farley, son of the proprietor of the *Bristol Journal*, had arrived in New York in 1760. Early in 1762 (the first issue of the *American Chronicle* is dated March 20) he felt able to launch a newspaper on his own and secured the services of two journeymen, Charles Crouch (later to publish his own newspaper in Charleston, South Carolina) and William Goddard. On July 8, 1762, the printing shop was almost destroyed by fire; after struggling with two more issues on July 17 and 22, Farley left for Georgia, where he became a lawyer. About this time, and perhaps the fire was the immediate impelling cause, Goddard moved the scene of his activities to Providence, there to start his own printing establishment and his own newspaper.

PROVIDENCE, Rhode Island, in 1762 was far from the metropolis we think of today. Most of the town's 3,500 to 4,000 inhabitants lived only a short distance from what is now Memorial and Market squares over the Providence River. The original settlement plotted out in 1636 by Roger Williams had been on the east side of the river at the bottom of "the Hill." By 1762 homes had been built several blocks north and south along the present Main and Benefit streets. The lovely houses with their Georgian façades we associate so much with the area immediately south of Brown University were mostly to come later, between 1780 and 1820, though one of the most attractive is the Joseph Brown house on South Main Street built as early as 1774. At the same time Goddard was setting up his press and arranging his type the townspeople were welcoming a new addition to their public buildings—the Court-House completed in 1762, now called the Old State House. The first issue of the *Providence Gazette* in its colophon located the new printing shop as "opposite the Court-House." The building of the Court-House marked a definite stage in the race for political and commercial supremacy between Newport and Providence. In the latter seventeenth century Newport had passed Providence in size and importance. The colony government was situated in Newport, and most of the governors had come from this island community. A century later Providence was struggling its way back into the dominant position. Much of the commercial success of Providence in the days before, during, and after the Revolution was based on the mercantile activities of the four Brown brothers, particularly Moses Brown. Political leadership was provided by Stephen Hopkins, who had been governor as early as 1755 and later was to occupy this position several years as well as to sign the Declaration of Independence. Providence as a community had not matured to the point it would by 1800, but the beginnings of that maturity were evident in 1762. Yet this potential for growth did not prevent the town from being raw and crude not only in its appearance but in its attitudes. Gracious living was to come later, though it was not far away. While Goddard was still in Providence, his paper published on April 28, 1764, the act incorporating the College of Rhode Island. Within a few years Providence was able to bulldoze the legislature into moving the institution from Warren to its present location, starting it towards its fame as Brown University. But in 1762 such plans were still only the daydreams of a few. A stroller in the streets would have had his shoes dirtied by the mud under foot and his nostrils filled with the stench of uncollected refuse. The town's hogreeve probably still had a fair amount of business rounding up stray pigs and keeping the alleys free of them. Of course, many of the townspeople were aware that ameliorizing amenities could do much for the beginning-to-be prosperous community. And that is one reason why so many of them, including Stephen Hopkins, encouraged the young printer to set up his press.

William Goddard did Providence's first printing and started her first newspaper, but he was not the first printer to dwell in her confines. That distinction belongs to a seventeenth-century London printer, Gregory Dexter (*ca.* 1610-*ca.* 1700). He printed a couple of Milton's political pamphlets and was associated with the most belligerent of the Puritans, at one time being called up before Laud on account of a Puritan pamphlet he had helped see through the press. In the late 1630's and early 1640's he was especially active as a printer to various New England divines. John Cotton and John Eliot both had tracts appear from his press. In 1643 he printed for Roger Williams *A Key into the Language of America* and began the friendship that was to last so long. The next year Roger Williams continued his quarrel with John Cotton in the famous *Bloudy Tenent*. Probably the printing of this pamphlet, which would not have pleased the members of Long Parliament much more than it did the Reverend John Cotton, caused Dexter to emigrate to Rhode Island in that year. For the rest of his life Dexter was active in the affairs of Providence, being town clerk from 1648 to 1655. In the latter year he was ordained as minister of the First Baptist Church in Providence and more or less retired from other duties thereafter. He never followed the profession of printer in Providence; whether because of disinclination or the lack of opportunity in the struggling colony we cannot tell today. Tradition has it that in 1646 and occasionally thereafter the printers in Cambridge called upon him for expert assistance since he would have known more about all aspects of printing than Stephen Daye or any other person then in the colonies. Isaiah Thomas states that Dexter printed an almanac for Providence in 1644. Though no such almanac has ever come to light, possibly such a one was run off at Cambridge under his direction. An interesting footnote to the career of Gregory Dexter is provided by his daughter Abigail Dexter, who married James Angell, the great-grandfather of the wife of Goddard, and by his granddaughter, Mary Dexter, who married John Angell, grandfather of William's wife.

In Providence and in other parts of Rhode Island there were in the 1760's many relatives of the young printer, particularly on his mother's side of the family. These relatives and friends were numerous enough that in spite of his working there only three years Goddard afterwards always thought of Providence as his home, eventually finding not only a wife there but retirement as well. For example, among these relatives within Providence was his cousin Captain John Updike, who only two years before had given up a seafaring life, married the local Miss Ann Crawford, and settled down to lead a convivial existence at his house on Towne Street and to earn a living as a merchant. While captain of a boat at sea, he flew the flag of the first of the Browns to attain mercantile prominence, Obadiah Brown. The former apprentice had an entree into the drawing rooms of some of the "best" families of Providence. No more would there be the life of the poor apprentice and journeyman in New York.

To get started in his own printing shop required more than energy and willingness to work hard; money was needed. This came from the mother, Sarah Goddard, and she transferred her home from New London to Providence at the same time. Tradition has it that she supplied £300 to finance the new establishment.

This money would have gone for the purchase of several fonts of type and at least one press. For £120 (which Parker called too high a price) Goddard bought these from Thomas Green, who had taken over the Parker shop at New Haven. Even supplies of paper would have to be arranged for, either from England or from one of the colonial mills. The stationery and various legal forms which every print shop sold would have come from England or Holland, the colonial paper not being of good enough quality. Also from England was ordered a supply of books, the usual business sideline of most printers.

Although the son provided the energy and the technical know-how and the mother the necessary capital, something else was needed —encouragement and prospective patronage from the citizens of Providence. Led by Stephen Hopkins, many of the town's stalwarts no doubt assured William that he need not fear on this score. They were aware of the utility, convenience, and prestige that a press would give to the community. Hopkins recognized the value a Providence press would be not only in the town's struggle with Newport but in his own political rivalry with Samuel Ward of the town at the foot of Narragansett Bay.

Possibly in late July and definitely in latter August the new printing establishment was a going operation at its location across the street from the Court-House. Sarah Goddard must have been proud as her son turned out in August a handbill announcing the storming of Morro Castle by the British, a playbill for the local theater before it was banned by a law passed that summer, and a prospectus for a forthcoming newspaper. More from sheer exuberance and pleasure than from necessity the sister Mary Katherine started to spend her time in the shop instead of at the occupations usually considered proper for an eighteenth-century woman of twenty-four, even though that century was generous in its ideas of the proper and fitting for a woman. In a letter, long since lost, to Isaiah Thomas Goddard said he thought these first fugitive printings were in June. More likely not until the end of July did Goddard start getting his printing shop organized, and not until August was he doing any actual printing. The broadside on the fall of Morro Castle can be dated fairly closely since on the twenty-fifth of August the *Newport Mercury* issued a supplement concerning the event of August 14. Probably it was the next day that Goddard got out his handbill, one means of showing the people of Providence that they no longer had to be dependent upon the *Mercury*. On August 25 the Rhode Island Assembly voted a ban on theaters. Within very few days this ban would have been effective, so the playbill for Douglas's company could have been in this same last week of August. When Goddard was in New York four years earlier, he had seen the same company, Hallam's Virginia Comedians, perform in the sail-loft. The manager of this troupe, David Douglas, was, no doubt, in the Parker print shop frequently to arrange the printing of the company's playbills. The two young men must have enjoyed talking together after the business of the day was completed. The printing of the playbills served to the mutual advantage of both men. Douglas's company would then be able to publicize its activities much more effectively; Goddard would have business for his new print shop as well as a bit of free advertising when the readers of the playbill saw his colophon, printed in the shop of William Goddard.

The Rhode Island Historical Society possesses a copy of the new shop's next production. We are therefore no longer conjecturing dates but can say from the printed date that this busy last week of August was culminated on the thirty-first by a prospectus for a newspaper to be called the *Providence Gazette or Country Journal,* whose first appearance was promised for October 20, 1762, Goddard's twenty-second birthday. Several of the characteristics that we associate with Goddard are present in this proclamation, and its tone and language are more appropriate, as is so frequently true of his writings, to a proclamation than a prospectus. Even from the beginning of his career as a newspaperman Goddard was neither humble nor given to hiding his light beneath a bushel.

Printing-Office, Providence, August 31, 1762

To the Publick.

As the Colony of *Rhode-Island* from its first Institution to this present Time, has been remarkable for maintaining the Spirit of true *British* Liberty, by which Means, it has frequently prov'd a Refuge and Asylum for Strangers, who, fond of enjoying all the Privileges and Advantages of their Mother Country, prefer'd this Colony before many others for their *friendly* Indulgence to Strangers of every Denomination of Christians that chose to settle among them, by which judicious Conduct, they are become a flourishing People, and in which the Town of *Providence* (being the first settled Place in the Colony) has no inconsiderable Share; to the Inhabitants of which, I in a more particular Manner address myself, who, at the Request of many Gentlemen, have, at a very considerable Expence, procur'd a complete Assortment of Printing Materials, with which I purpose to carry on the Printing Business in this Town; provided I meet with Encouragement adequate to the Trouble and Expence of the Undertaking: And as it is universally acknowledged a Printer is much wanted in this Place, very considerable Sums being annually sent into other Governments for Printing, to the Impoverishment of this, whereas, if that useful Branch of Business was well establish'd here, it would be an Addition to its flourishing State, and keep its ready Cash circulating at Home, it is not doubted but every Well-wisher to the Town, will contribute towards so laudable an Undertaking, as far as the Execution of it shall merit the Approbation of the Publick: And I take this Method to solicit the Favour of the Inhabitants of this Colony; and from the same generous Disposition they have shewn to young Beginners of other Occupations, I flatter myself I shall find Encouragement answerable to my Expectations. And I beg Leave to assure the Publick, that (as far as I am engaged in their Service) I shall use my utmost Endeavours to serve them with Fidelity and Integrity; and if by my Assiduity and Care, I shall be so happy as to obtain their Esteem, by an impartial Conduct, I shall think my Time well bestow'd. I am determined to avoid entering into the Schemes of any Party, tending either to religious or political Controversy, so far as it might prevent my acting with the strictest Justice.

As every Branch of useful Knowledge, both of a religious and civil Nature, is abundantly diffus'd by Means of the Freedom of the Press; I hope it will induce Gentlemen of Learning and Ingenuity to contribute a few of their leisure Hours in writing some public-spirited Essays, for the Cause of Virtue, displaying it in beautiful Colours, and painting Vice in all its odious Deformity, which will render their Efforts beneficial to the latest Posterity; by which Method they will soon perceive, the Utility of a Printing Press: For I verily believe there is not another Town in *New-England,* of its Extent in Trade and Commerce, that remains vacant of so necessary and useful a Calling. All these Considerations give me great Reason to hope, that not only the Gentlemen of *Providence,* but all the adjacent Towns, will, with a kind and good-natur'd Reception, assist

THE PRINTER.

Gentlemen and Ladies,

As soon as possible after my Affairs are in some Measure settled, and I am establish'd in my Business, I purpose to print a Weekly News-Paper, under the Title of the PROVIDENCE GAZETTE, or COUNTRY JOURNAL, to be publish'd every *Wednesday* Morning, and to contain every Thing remarkable, both *Foreign* and *Domestic*; for which Purpose, I have establish'd an extensive Correspondence, and shall receive not only the *London* Magazines and Prints, but every News-Paper printed upon the Continent of *America,* which can't fail of rendering the *Providence* Gazette, as complete as any Performance of the Kind. The Price will be *only* SEVEN SHILLINGS Lawful Money, per Annum, or equivalent in Currency—and altho' several judicious Men have done worthily towards so useful a Design, in a neighbouring Government, whose

Performances have obtain'd a general Approbation, nevertheless it must be allowed that something of that Nature is very much wanted here, where so many and various Branches of Business are carried on, more especially that in a mercantile Way; I hope no one will imagine I mean to lessen the Esteem justly due to others, or be guilty of Vanity, in attempting to make a public Appearance in that Manner, so necessary at this Juncture, when His Majesty's Arms are engaged in a just and glorious War against two of the most perfidious Nations in *Europe*; and I am persuaded every worthy and public-spirited Gentleman will promote the Circulation of it, as the Design is calculated (in a peculiar Manner) for the Interest of this Town, and all its respective Neighbourhoods. It is intended the Paper shall make its first Appearance on *Wednesday* the Twentieth of *October*, in Case a sufficient Number of Subscribers shall offer.—Subscriptions are taken in by HENRY PAGET, Esq; SAMUEL CHACE, Esq; Postmaster, BENONI PEARCE, Esq; Mr. BENJAMIN WEST, Mr. KNIGHT DEXTER, Mr. EBENEZER THOMPSON, Mr. JOSEPH LAWRENCE, and by the Publick's

> *Devoted Humble Servant,*
> William Goddard.

Among the things that strike us on reading this prospectus, the young printer's first extended published piece of writing, is the clever play on Providence's rivalry with Newport. Newport is never named, but none of the contemporary readers could miss the implications of Providence's "being the first settled Place in the Colony," of the "other Governments," and of the necessity of keeping ready cash at home. Nor would the town's inhabitants have missed the appeal to their local pride when they read, "there is not another Town in *New-England*, of its Extent in Trade and Commerce, that remains vacant of so necessary and useful a Calling." Goddard wanted to impress on his readers that printing was "necessary and useful" and also "laudable." He was, even at this stage of his career, conscious of the social role and importance of a printer in any community. Not for nothing does he within the first clause speak of the "Spirit of true *British* Liberty." The second paragraph opens with the reminder to its readers that, "every Branch of useful Knowledge, both of a religious and civil Nature, is abundantly diffus'd by Means of the Freedom of the Press." For thirty years Goddard supported freedom of the press energetically, vociferously, and fearlessly. Another principle basic to his concept of the press is seen in his statement, "I am determined to avoid entering into the Schemes of any Party, tending either to religious or political Controversy, so far as it might prevent my acting with the strictest Justice." Two words should be particularly noticed, *determined* and *party*. His determination to follow this principle was later to cause him much financial grief. In his later activities we shall see that the word *party* has for Goddard extremely opprobrious connotations; when he uses it, it is not necessary to qualify it by any describing or defining adjective.

Whether Goddard liked it or not, his paper was a mouthpiece of the Providence "party," headed by Stephen Hopkins, in its struggle with the Newport "party," headed by Samuel Ward. Yet in all justice we must admit that Goddard did not hesitate to print correspondence by members of the Ward faction whenever any of its members took the trouble of writing an article for the Providence paper. But the natural interests of Goddard and his potential readers lay in the city at the head of the bay. After all, it was to break the monopoly in Rhode Island of the *Newport Mercury* that the *Providence Gazette* was established. Printing had been done in Newport since 1727, when James Franklin had opened a shop there after he had left Boston following a succession of difficulties with the local authorities, the first of which is narrated for us in Benjamin's *Autobiography*. In 1735 James died, and his widow Ann took over the running of the shop, a practice quite common in the colonies not only for print shops, but for taverns, stores, and almost all kinds of businesses. The "Widow Franklin," as she called herself in her publications, trained her son James as a printer, and in 1748 the firm became Ann and James Franklin. In 1758 they started the *Newport Mercury*, but James suddenly died in 1762, shortly before the first appearance of the *Providence Gazette*, leaving the Widow Franklin to run the newspaper and printing business alone. A few months before her death in latter 1763 she took into partnership Samuel Hall, who continued the business in his name after Ann's death. Curiously, for a short time in 1763 there were two print shops in the colonies named Franklin and Hall, one in Newport and the more famous one in Philadelphia. The *Newport Mercury* was by no means the best-edited newspaper in the colonies. Its appearance was stodgy and its local items under the date-line Newport were matter-of-fact to the point of dulness. None of its anonymous correspondents could match the writing ability of

Stephen Hopkins, who was to contribute frequently to the *Providence Gazette*. From the point of view of a Providence citizen the Newport paper was unsatisfactory; rare was the occasion when an item from Providence appeared. Not much more frequent were advertisements from Providence merchants, even though they had no other outlet. The energetic circulation campaign Goddard put on undoubtedly gave the *Gazette* a larger number of subscribers than the *Mercury*, but the Widow Franklin and later Hall were able to make a reasonable financial success of their venture from their monopoly of the colony's government printing, a monopoly Goddard tried to break but could not.

Goddard was true to his promise in the prospectus and the first number of the *Providence Gazette and Country Journal* (the *or* had become *and*) appeared on October 20, 1762. Before we look at this issue, we might do well to see how much labor was involved in the putting out of a weekly newspaper by a colonial printer. No more authoritative source for this can we find than printers themselves. In 1907 members of a committee of the Providence typographical union had this to say about their 1762 predecessor's paper: "The Gazette was a three-column folio, 8x14 inches, requiring the setting of about 22,000 ems for the first issue. This amount was lessened thereafter by about one-quarter, the standing advertisements filling about one of the pages. Probably four full days of each week were consumed by one printer on the composition and press work for the paper. An average operator would set the entire matter for the Gazette on a linotype in less than four hours. The hand press used in those days could print about 200 papers an hour. The forms were inked by leather balls and the paper was fed into the press twice before both sides were printed." Though Goddard was a skilful craftsman, the equipment of his shop was not much different from that brought over in July, 1638, by the Reverend Jose Glover for the Cambridge shop of Stephen Daye. William must have welcomed the assistance of his sister Mary Katherine.

Most of the first page of the first issue is taken up by an opening address "To the Publick" signed by William Goddard. In this address he spoke of the "utility and advantages" of the printing business in a "mercantile colony" and flattered his readers by saying that their support of the newspaper showed their "publick-spirited-ness." Referring to the Seven Years' War then going on between France and England and involving other countries as well, he assured his readers, "Every Thing that relates to the Honour and Interest of our Country, and the Humiliation of our Enemies, must be peculiarly interesting; and as such, they shall be carefully inserted in this Paper." Also the paper should be "as entertaining and as generally useful as possible." The utility was to be taken care of by an "extensive Correspondence" not only from foreign countries but from all "extensive Settlements on this Continent." Entertainment would rely on extracts from literary works and on essays by public-minded writers, to whom the printer appealed for contributions. The weekly appearance of the paper was to be changed from Wednesday to Saturday (a date rigorously adhered to thereafter). The conclusion was, as in the prospectus, a listing of various people with whom subscriptions could be left.

The bottom quarter of the first page consists of a long article, which is continued onto the next page, entitled "The Planting and Growth of Providence." The historical account ended with a "to be continued," and it was—on January 19, 1765. This unsigned contribution to local history has been identified as from the pen of Stephen Hopkins. The over two-year lapse between instalments seems inexplicable, but Hopkins's interest in the new paper is evident. That such an avowedly local history should have been written in 1762 reveals the pride that the townspeople were taking in the expansion of the once placid village from its original site at the bottom of "the Hill." One result of the appearance of this history was the young editor's receiving, either in 1762 or during the later instalments in early 1765, several letters from Massachusetts (obviously the *Gazette* circulated there) "inquiring how much he received for it, and containing many other remarks insulting to the editor, the author, and the colony." When Goddard told this anecdote in 1817 to his neighbor Judge Samuel Eddy, there must have been many a chuckle over memories of the intense rivalry between Massachusetts and Rhode Island and the former's fear of the commercial ambitions of the port at the head of Narragansett Bay. Newport was not the only city in New England to be alarmed at Providence in the 1760's. No, the neophyte editor did not need to be ashamed of the influence and prestige of his paper as he proudly wrote his colophon at the bottom of page four: "Providence in New

England: Printed by William Goddard, opposite the Court-House; by whom Advertisements are taken in, and all Manner of Printing Work performed with Care and Expedition."

In the second issue, dated Saturday, October 30, the print shop's activities had expanded enough that there was the advertisement: "A variety of Books and Stationery, to be sold cheap by the Printer hereof,—With all sorts of Blanks used in this Colony, neatly printed, —Also New-York Almanacks, for the Year 1763." The supply of books was still small and the book business must not have yet represented much of a challenge to the already established bookshop of Mr. Oliphant, named among those taking in subscriptions in the first issue. Of more immediate importance, both to Goddard and to the community, were the "all sorts of Blanks." The Brown brothers must have visited the new shop frequently to secure printed invoices, indentures for apprentices, bills of sale, mortgages, property liens, rental agreements, and the many forms used in their mercantile operations. The almanacs were another major item of any colonial print shop or bookstore. Not for long would Goddard depend on a supply from Parker's shop in New York. Even though the high tides of the harbors of Providence and New York differ usually only by five minutes, he was aware that his customers wanted almanacs for their own harbor, not for New York nor even Newport.

In this same second issue on page four is an anonymous letter possibly written by Goddard himself. Not only for business reasons but from principle, he would frequently remind his readers of the importance of printing to a community and to its culture. So the signature "A Countryman" could well be a pseudonym for the pen of the young editor as he addressed:

To the Printer of the PROVIDENCE GAZETTE, and COUNTRY JOURNAL:
SIR,
I am one of your Country Subscribers, and although I have no Learning myself, more than what I obtained by my own Industry, without Instruction, I value it in others.—There is generally too much Reflection cast on Country People for being illiterate and aukward; but if the Authors of such Reflections had any Candour, they would make all proper Allowances for narrow Circumstances, the constant Attendance which we and our Children are obliged to give in the Execution of our laborious Callings, the dispersed Manner of our Living, and the Want of Schools. It is as impracticable under these Circumstances to become

learned, or acquainted with the Fashions of the World, which is called
being polite, as a Merchant's Clerk, or a Printer, to become an able
General of an Army, or an expert Seaman; all these Cases requiring
Leisure, Instruction, and Experience. Printing is the greatest Means of
promoting Learning that was ever invented; and I hope that the setting
up of that Business near us, may contribute to our Instruction, and be one
Means of improving the rising Generation, and of wiping away the Odium
cast on us, of being ignorant, rude, and unpolished.
Smithfield,
Oct. 25, 1762.

> *Your Well-wisher,*
> A COUNTRYMAN.

Printing was not just a means of earning a living for Goddard; he
was intensely proud of the cultural role of the printing craft. Four
weeks later, November 27, "A Countryman" from Gloucester talked
on the same theme, this time ending his contribution by a poem whose
rimed couplets and iambic pentameter again laud the wonders of the
printing art. Whether signing his praises of his profession from
Smithfield or Gloucester, Goddard shows the love of his trade which
made him take enough pleasure in its techniques to be a master of
typography.

The business of the shop is well shown by an advertisement
Goddard inserted November 6, 1762. The books he had ordered
from London during the summer had finally arrived, and Mr.
Oliphant had a full-blown rival for the book trade of Providence.
The reading tastes of a colonial community ran to sermons and
theology even in such a secular settlement as this. But, unlike
Boston, Providence read more secular than religious books, even if
the printer thought it expedient to start his list with the latter. We
wonder how sales of Law's *Serious Call to the Unconverted*
compared with those for Ovid's *Art of Love* or with those for that
eighteenth-century tear-jerker subtitled *The Life and Adventures of
a Lap Dog.*

Lately imported from LONDON, and to be sold cheap for ready
Money, by WILLIAM GODDARD, at the Printing-Office near the Court-
House. A Variety of Books, Stationery, &c. &c.—Among which are,
DODDERIDGE's Family Expositor.—and Rise and Progress of Religion
in the Soul.—Jenk's Meditations.—Detham's Astro and Physico The-
ology.—Whole Duty of Man.—Watt's Miscellanies, Sermons, Psalms,
Hymns, and Lyric Poems.—Romaine's Discourses.—Law's Serious Call

to the Unconverted.—Religious Courtship.—Young's Night Thoughts.
—Pomphret's Poems.—The Universal and Female Spectators,— Guard-
ian,—Adventurer,—Tatler, and Rambler.—The celebrated Histories of
Pamela, Clarissa, and Sir Charles Grandison.—Nuptial Dialogues.—
Matrimonial Preceptor.—Conduct of a married Life.—Admonitions
from the Dead.—Seneca's Morals. Adventures of Telemachus.—
History of Charles XII. of Sweden.—Adventures of Roderic Random.
—The Histories of Tom Jones, Joseph Andrews, Fortunate Country
Maid, and Two Orphans.—The Devil on Crutches.—Ovid's Art of
Love.—Pompey the Little; or the Life and Adventures of a Lap Dog.
—Grey's Love Letters.—History of Jemmy and Jenny Jessamy.—
Bayley's Dictionary.—Preceptor.—Salmon's Grammar, and Gazetteer.
—Young Man's Companion.—Hay's Interest Tables.—Complete Jury-
man.—School-Master's Assistant.—Wilson's Epitome.—Mariner's Com-
pass and Kalendar.—Bibles Testaments, Spelling Books, Psalters.—
With a Variety of small Histories and Pamplets, and a few select Plays.
   STATIONARY. Account Books.—Pocket-Books.—Writing Paper
of all Sorts.—Sealing-Wax.—Wafers.—Pencils and Steel Cases.—Ivory
Folders.—Magnets.—Playing Cards.—Small Scales and Weights.—
Scales and Dividers, &c.—Also, a few elegant Pictures, viz. of His Majes-
ty King George III. and his Royal Consort Queen Charlotte: the great
Mr. Pitt, and the immortal General Wolfe, &c.
   BLANKS. Policies of Insurance, Portage Bills, Bills of Lading
and Sale. Letters of Attorney, Administration Bonds, common Bonds,
Deeds, Writs, and Executions; and all Kinds of Blanks used in this
Colony, neatly printed, and sold as cheap as at any Printing-Office in
New-England, or elsewhere; either Wholesale or Retail.

In early December Goddard was able to supply the market for
an almanac "calculated for meridian of Providence," as the title page
of his first one expressed it. For the calculations of the sunrises
and sunsets, the phases of the moon, and the tides he secured the
services of Benjamin West, a self-taught astronomer and mathematician. For the next forty years West, either under his own
name or that of Isaac Bickerstaff, was to be employed in annual
almanacs from Providence to Halifax. So popularly associated
with almanacs was the name of Isaac Bickerstaff that the pseudonym
was continued by various almanac-makers until 1881. It is hard
for us today to realize the role of the almanac in the colonial household. Various almanac wars attest to how important it was to the
printer as a business, Goddard himself getting into more than one
such affair. Frequently the almanacs were printed with blank leaves
alternating with the printed, making possible the keeping of a

household diary. Perhaps we can understand why printers fought over almanacs if we remember that almost the entire population of the colonies was rural and maritime, not necessarily living on the sea, but near enough to be affected by its sights, sounds, and smells.

No matter how profitable the almanac was in its annual season the principal week-by-week chore of the Providence print shop was the publication of the *Gazette.* For Goddard the work involved in this publishing was as much editing as printing. Today staffs of correspondents and editorial writers contribute material to feed into the finished paper we read. Then there was no such person as a professional correspondent or editorial writer. In our sense of the words there were really no news stories or editorials at all. To collect the material for his newspaper, the colonial editor depended upon his own subscriptions to various London papers and those from other colonies. With scissors in hand, he would go through these papers looking for whatever seemed to him worthy of inclusion in his own paper. That is why Goddard emphasizes his "extensive correspondence." Other sources for items for the newspaper were reports brought in by sea captains of vessels just returned from some foreign port. Also, there were the essays commenting on affairs written by anonymous correspondents, including the editor himself. Finally, there was in each issue a date-line Providence, where could be found whatever local news the editor deemed significant, a list of vessels entering and leaving the local harbor for the previous week, and frequently a report of a debate in Parliament as brought in by the latest boat. But if all sources failed because of the indisposition of the weather or of the postrider, then the editor was forced to fall back on his own ingenuity. Such a situation is seen in the issue of January 15, 1763. In the upper left-hand corner under the flag we find: "As the Severity of the Season prevents a regular Intercourse with our Correspondents in the neighbouring Provinces, we imagine the following Story, which is not only entertaining, but moral and edifying, will be pleasing to all our Readers; even to those who may have seen it before." This apology prefaces "The Mercy of Affliction:—An Eastern Story," which covered three-fourths of the first page. The winter storms made the paper temporarily emphasize entertainment instead of either enlightenment or persuasion.

A brief advertisement inserted in the same issue started off one

of those newspaper arguments the eighteenth century was so fond
of. This notice stated: "Very good Encouragement will be given to
any Person who understands Fencing, Dancing, and the Violin, who
will come and set up a School in the Town of Providence." This
was too much for one correspondent, A. L. V., whose righteous
indignation was roused to a fever pitch. The next week Philander
replied to A. L. V., and so it went. A rousing dispute was doubtless
a good prod for lagging circulation, and Goddard must have been
delighted at the abusiveness of his disputants over the virtues and
vices of dancing. Even today we can enjoy the horror of A. L. V.
as he says that the setting up of a dancing school would require the
town to institute a "public Stew or Brothel, . . . so that when Strangers
come here, they may know where to go and be entertained for their
Money." To this correspondent a dancing school "may have the
same Tendency, as if a Man that was over careful of his Wife,
would give another good Encouragement to lodge with her, and
keep her warm in his Absence." Such a school would "excite Idle-
ness, Lewdness, and Debauchery." Goddard made his own comment
by repeating the original advertisement immediately under the
outburst of A Lover of Virtue.

Another advertisement, though not productive of follow-up
letters, still must have provided entertaining gossip for the readers.
Jonathan Staples inserted this notice January 29, 1763: "Whereas
my Wife, *Freelove Staples*, hath eloped from me, and hath refused
to live with me: These are therefore to forbid all Persons from
keeping her, or her Child, thinking to have pay of me, for I will not
pay any Thing for their keeping: And I also forbid all Persons from
trading with, or trusting my Wife *Freelove*, on my Account, as I
will not answer any Debts of her contracting." But Freelove was
not to be denied her pleasures by such a notice. A year and a half
later, May 19, 1764, Jonathan again warned the public about the
activities of Freelove, who "thro' the Advice and Persuasion of
some evil-minded Persons . . . hath been deluded to elope from my
Bed and Board, without any Cause, and to carry off her Child with
her." After this was the usual statement about whatever debts
Freelove might acquire.

At the May, 1763, session of the Rhode Island colonial assembly
a resolution was passed requesting the printers at Newport and
Providence to send in their terms for printing the "Colony's Busi-

ness," and promising "that he will do it for the least, shall have the Business, and if equal, the Printer at Newport shall have the Preferance." Within a few days Goddard must have written his letter to Josias Lyndon, clerk of the assembly. Unfortunately the first page of this letter is missing, but the two pages left tell us a good deal about the financial struggles of the twenty-two-year-old printer.

The Printer at Newport having the Preference, and a great Advantage of me, lays me under an absolute Necessity to lower the Prices of Printing the Acts, &c. otherwise I can have no Pretensions to the Business; at the same Time I must declare that what is now given is much less than would be charged in many other Parts of America.—I have inform'd myself what the Government has heretofore paid for the several Services in printing and if I am employ'd by the Government I engage to print the Acts of Assembly at Thirteen Pounds Nineteen Shillings per Sheet, and for small Proclamations, (which are charg'd £10 at Newport) Seven Pounds Nineteen and Sixpence, and every Thing else in proportion. —The above Prices are as low as the Business will possibly admit of, so as to make the least Advantage; and if the other printer will do it cheaper, I am positive he can't gain a Farthing for his Trouble;—and will only have this Reflection that he has prostituted his Business for the Gratification of his Advocates in that Cause, without those Persons contribute towards the Payment of any Deficiencies; which must be the Case if he performs the work cheaper than for what I have offered.—Permit me also to inform you that without any Solicitation from me, I was apply'd to for my Proposals at what Rate I would print the last Emission of money issued in this Colony; I accordingly deliver'd in my Proposals to the Committee and fully expected to have had the Jobb, as my Price happen'd to be a good Deal less than the Colony had paid for many years before, but my Offer was only made Use of to reduce the Price of the Printer at Newport, and [I] was deprived of the Work, which every reasonable Man must allow I ought in Justice to have had—And I think this Affair of the Money a proper Specimen of my Prices compar'd with what is charg'd and has been charged at N. Port.—I hope you will excuse the Freedom I have taken in sending you this long Epistle; to which I shall only add, that I should be glad of your Friendship, and am (in Haste) respectfully, Sir,   Your very Humble & most
                                                                    Obedient Servant

This matter of printing the government laws after each session of the assembly was very important for every colonial printer, who could usually depend on a fair living if he had no other business than the public printing. Almost invariably the colony capital determines where the printer sets up his press. Until the Revolutionary War few printers managed to keep their heads above water for long without this pecuniary assistance. The colonial assemblies would sometimes guarantee a printer his livelihood if he would locate where the laws could conveniently be printed. An example of this is the £1000 (colony currency—about £175 sterling) offered by the government of South Carolina in May, 1731, to the printer who would locate in Charleston. In the race which followed, three printers arrived as claimants, one subsidized by Franklin, his first attempt at a silent partnership.

Though no £1000 was being offered in Rhode Island, still livelihoods were involved. We should therefore not be surprised at Goddard's trying his best to get this business away from Newport, and we may well doubt the "in Haste" of his closing sentence. He must have worked very carefully over the proposed prices and even the phrases of the letter itself. To find the assembly playing one printer against the other to force down their prices must have irked the very souls of Goddard and his Newport competitors. Only necessity, to use a term from the letter, would have compelled the Providence printer to indulge in price cutting to get his finger into the public pie. In 1762 Providence was not yet prosperous enough to support a printer without the public business; in fact, Boston, New York, and Philadelphia were the only cities in the colonies that did.

Unfortunately Goddard's letter, and doubtless other attempts, was unsuccessful. The public printing remained in Newport until the occupation of that place by the British during the Revolution and the resultant commercial and political decline in favor of Providence. We can see Goddard's failure graphically if we compare the total of £6 12s. 6d. that he received from the assembly during the three years he was in Providence with the £1786 19s. 11½d. that Ann Franklin and Samuel Hall received during the same period. And three pounds out of Goddard's receipts were for one item, the printing in December, 1764, of the pamphlet on the Stamp Act by Governor Stephen Hopkins. The reason for the young printer's having in 1765 to leave Providence for other parts is apparent from this failure. The financial woes of William Goddard were now beginning.

However, by the first part of 1763 the print shop's activities were many and varied. Every Saturday the *Providence Gazette* was seen through the press. An almanac had been published the preceding December, and Goddard was pushing its sales through a vigorous advertising campaign in the columns of his own paper. A complete line of various legal and business forms had been printed and was available to the shop's customers. Broadsides, such as Governor Samuel Ward's proclamation appointing November 18, 1762, as a day of Thanksgiving, were issuing frequently from the shop. (Goddard was paid six shillings for printing one hundred copies of this proclamation.) Also pamphlets were appearing with the imprint: "Providence: Printed by William Goddard."

Perhaps as good a way as any of visualizing the press's activities is to look at the pamphlets put out in one year, 1763, remembering that probably much less than half of the shop's output has survived or been identified by modern scholars. Isaac Backus of Middleborough had a sermon printed in February and Benjamin Lord of Norwich had three released at different times during the year. Joseph Bolles of New London published a pamphlet defending tax support of ministers. The president of the College of New Jersey, Jonathan Dickinson, is represented on the year's list by a discussion of infant baptism, a reprint of the original edition published in Boston in 1746. Apparently Goddard did not mind disturbing the theological tenets of the Rhode Island Baptists. The turbulent financial debate then going on in Rhode Island found "T. R. A Cooper" having a four-page defense of the debtors' position printed on April 6, 1763. This undoubtedly partial listing of a year's pamphlet output of Goddard's press reveals something of the printer's belief in and practice of the principle of freedom of the press. Providence's largest congregation was the Baptist, though the community's traditional policy of religious freedom made for the presence of many other denominations. Both Newport and Providence were dominated by the ship-owning merchants of the two ports. Yet we find the authors on this list include Connecticut Congregationalists, a New Jersey Presbyterian, and a representative of the minority point of view in the currency dispute (at least it was a minority in the Rhode Island Assembly). However, it must not be thought that Goddard printed everything that came into his shop, even when accompanied by a payment for printing. He was carefully following the principles laid down in the prospectus for his newspaper. In spite of his financial problems he had the courage to print this notice in the *Providence Gazette* of February 19, 1763: "The Authors of the Pieces signed PHILAGATHUS and REFORMADO are desired to send for their Copies and Money, as their Performances cannot be inserted in this Paper, consistent, with our own Interest or the PUBLIC GOOD." No doubt the "interest" of the printer influenced strongly this rejection slip, but the "public good" was also important.

Through the newspaper we can see that Providence was now large enough for its citizens to need new and more expanded services. No longer should Boston be depended upon; there were enough people to justify the presence of an increased number of tradesmen. Some local booster, perhaps Stephen Hopkins or one of the Browns, contributed this unsigned advertisement to the *Gazette* of February 19, 1763: "The following Tradesmen are much wanted in the Town of PROVIDENCE, namely, a BRAZIER, a POTTER, a STOCKING-WEAVER, and a CLOCK and WATCH-MAKER.—It is not doubted but each would find ample Encouragement, as there is a large adjacent Country to be supplied with Articles and Work in the Way of those Trades, and none of these Businesses carried on within thirty Miles [the distance to Newport], and that of a POTTER not nearer than BOSTON: Besides the great Sums of Money sent abroad for those Articles, sufficiently demonstrate that each of such Tradesmen would meet with full Employ; and moreover have the Satisfaction of living in a populous and flourishing Sea Port." The circulation of Goddard's newspaper throughout all New England would have brought this notice to the attention of qualified applicants. The printer was making himself indispensable to the community even though in return he was not finding the financial support he had hoped for when he borrowed three hundred pounds from his mother.

The first of Goddard's several moves in Providence occurred in March, 1763. His original location had been "opposite the Court-House" on what is now North Main Street. His move was to the "House of Henry Paget, Esq; near the Great-Bridge." The "great bridge" is now the site of Memorial and Market squares in the center of present-day Providence. On March 12 Goddard advertised books for sale from this new location. Four months later he moved next door to what were probably larger quarters. His colophon of July 9 states that his printing office was "just removed to the Store of Judge JENCKS, near the GREAT BRIDGE, and [the newspaper] published at his Book Shop, just above it, at the Sign of SHAKESPEARE's Head." The business in books, patent medicines, and the like had grown enough to require separate quarters. Sarah and Mary Katherine must have been frequently assisting William in the two departments of his business in these days.

The Shakespeare's Head sign mentioned by Goddard was associated with the *Providence Gazette* for many years. (The house at 21 Meeting Street, now known as "Shakespear's Head," however, was never occupied by Goddard, but by his friend and successor, John Carter.) In 1898 an article speaks of "persons still living" who remembered the sign. It was placed on top of an eight- or ten-foot pole, was of full size, carved out of wood "fancifully painted," and was possibly the work of John Bower. Goddard knew the virtues of advertising. Perhaps he chose this particular sign remembering his first journeyman job on the *American Chronicle*, whose colophon read: "New York; Printed by *Samuel Farley*, at Shakespear's-Head, on the New-dock."

The expanding business caused Goddard to advertise on June 18, 1763, for an apprentice, "about 13 or 14 years of Age, who can read well, and write a tolerable Hand." Six months later he requested a journeyman printer to work at both "Case and Press," as well as another apprentice. There would have been no necessity for Goddard's advertising in any other paper besides his own since the journeymen in all the print shops in the colonies would eventually see the advertisement through the newspaper exchanges of the day.

The respect, both personal and professional, with which Providence viewed the young printer in its midst was made concrete by a resolution passed by the Providence Library Company (founded 1753) on September 5, 1763. "It is voted that Mr. William Goddard Printer in Consideration of his eminent usefulness to this Part of the Colony by introducing and carrying on amongst us the ingenious and noble Business of Printing shall have free Liberty to use the Books belonging to the Library."

A glance at the contents of a typical issue should help the reader visualize the kind of newspaper the *Providence Gazette* and its contemporaries were. One number will do as well as any, and I have picked at random that of November 19, 1763. All the first page and half the second is occupied by London news from the *London Gazette*. The heading on this long article reads: "On Tuesday the 8th Inst. Capt. *Blake*, arrived at *Boston*, in 6 Weeks from *London*, by whom we have the following fresh Intelligence, taken from the *English* News-Papers." On the second page, after the London dispatch, there is a column headed, "From the South-Carolina Gazette, we have the following Advices." After this there are some miscellaneous items under the date-line, "Boston, November 14." Then under "Providence, November 19" there is a statement about the new navigation acts, followed by: "The Western Mails not arriving till 4 o'Clock Saturday Afternoon, obliges us to omit sundry Articles of Intelligence, till our Next; but they afford us nothing very interesting." Below this there is an advertisement for *West's Almanack for 1764*, which had been published the preceding Wednesday. (The frequency of Wednesday as a publishing date makes us suspect that during the first three days of each week the shop was busy with pamphlets, broadsides, etc., but during the last three days the newspaper occupied the attention of the printer and his assistants.) On page three was a poem by the "late celebrated Mr. Thompson, author of the Seasons." The next item was headed, "A most surprising anecdote from Voltaire, of the man with the iron mask." In the second column we find an "Extract from the King of Prussia's Campains," recounting an incident of the 1742 campaign in Silesia. The third column of this page is taken up by various notices and advertisements. First is a notice from the local customs official about certain boat regulations. Then a store is advertised for let. William Brown states his desire to have his stolen horse recovered. Goddard himself advertises requesting his subscribers to pay for their papers. (Eighteenth-century newspapers are filled with similar notices.) A listing follows concerning the past week's activities of the local customs house. Given are inward entries, outward entries, and the vessels cleared for departure. Page four starts with a clipping from the *Pennsylvania Gazette* giving a message of the Assembly to the Governor. The Collector of the Port of New London has a notice. The advertisements, occupying most of the rest of the page, are from John Birkett with a house for sale, from Nicholas Cooke wanting his customers to settle their shipping debts to him, three men wanting to buy ten or twelve horses, the Furnace-Unity Bridge lottery giving notice of a drawing, Nathan Giles seeking to collect some of his past due bills, Smith and Sabin seeking the same thing, and the Estate of Benjamin Hunt trying to find out his creditors. The content of this issue ends by a table of the high tides at Providence for the ensuing week.

The fierce competition for the almanac trade can be recognized by an advertisement on December 31, 1763: "WEST'S NEW-ENGLAND ALMANACK, for 1764, inferior to none in Goodness, and much cheaper than AMES'S ORACLE, may be had of the Printer hereof." A good many Rhode Islanders had not yet been broken of their habit of buying an almanac from Boston; Goddard was appealing to their sense of thrift.

The cultural activities of the community are represented by the printing on April 28, 1764, of the Act of Incorporation of the College of Rhode Island, covering all of page one and most of page two. On May 12, 1764, the town council advertised two children to be bound out. One was a six-year-old girl and the other a five-year-old boy. The interested reader was referred to Ephriam Bowen for additional information. Almost the entire issue of June 23, 1764, is taken up by the publication of the latest Navigation Acts, better known as the Sugar Acts. The community was expanding its cultural opportunities; it was still following certain medieval practices; it was on the threshold of the struggle with England. Even then the community was "not an island entire of itself." Busy with its petty affairs, busy setting up a humane tradition, Providence could not confine its interests to either the petty or the humane but must feel the pinch of the measures taken by Parliament in London against all the colonies.

Of more immediate concern to the printer was his supply of paper. Just about every colonial printer had his troubles getting sufficient newsprint. Many had, like William Bradford in Philadelphia, helped finance a mill upon whose output they would have first call. Goddard was only following this tradition when he contributed his share to the establishment of a paper mill near Providence. On August 4, 1764, the partners advertised: "Ready Money will be given for any Quantity of clean Linen RAGS, and old Sail-Cloth, by JONATHAN OLNEY, JOHN WATERMAN, JONATHAN BALLAU, or the Printer of this Paper." This advertisement preceded the actual operation of the mill, which did not turn out paper until early in 1765. *West's Almanack for 1765,* printed in November, 1764, contained this notice from the four partners about the proposed mill:

As the present embarrassed Situation of the Trade of these Northern Colonies, renders it utterly impossible for us to pay for the large Quantities of Goods that are annually imported from Great-Britain, without reducing ourselves to the State of Slaves and Beggars, it is reasonable to suppose, that every Attempt to lessen the Demand for such Goods, by establishing Manufactories amongst ourselves, for the making those Things which are really beneficial, must meet with the Approbation and Encouragement of all who wish well to this Country.—Amongst many laudable Endeavours in the different Provinces, for the Purpose aforesaid, a spirited Effort is now actually making in the Town of Providence, for carrying on a Paper Manufactory, a spacious Mill being already built, and will be speedily set to work, which, if it can obtain a proper Supply of Linen Rags, old Sail Cloth, and Junk, those being the principal Articles necessary for making that useful Commodity, it's Utility to this Part of the Country will be soon demonstrated by a Saving of some Thousand Dollars, that are annually sunk to us in the Pockets of the European Merchants.

As Wroth has pointed out, New England printers were more dependent upon English and Dutch sources than were the printers of the middle colonies. In writing this appeal for rags, Goddard tried to exploit the nascent feelings of patriotism and local pride. Though he left Providence before he could get much advantage from having his own source of paper, regular advertisements for rags began to appear in the *Providence Gazette* when it was revived in 1766 by Sarah Goddard. A typical appeal is in the issue of August 23, 1766, which includes the prices to be paid: ". . . for Rags finer than Oznabrigs, Two Coppers (3s Old Ten.) per Pound, and Fifteen Shillings, Lawful Money, (20 l. Old Ten.) per Hundred;— and for Rags that are coarser than Oznabrigs, one Copper (18d. Old Ten.) per Pound.—For old Junk, half a Dollar per Hundred. (The above Articles will be taken in Pay for the Providence Gazette, if brought when Payments should be made, in lieu of Cash.)"

Characteristic of the career of William Goddard are his many quarrels. He seemed incapable of being in any place for long without getting into some kind of bitter and tempestuous argument. In assessing the temperament of Goddard, we must not too quickly call him pugnacious and belligerent. His feuds were with competing printers of newspapers and almanacs, with people whose principles and attitudes he distrusted. We must remember also that in the eighteenth century many of the ablest writers carried on literary disputes, which rarely disturbed their personal equilibrium or friendships. Goddard's favorite reading, judging from the number of allusions in his writings, was Pope and Swift, both of whom were active in the literary and political disputes of their day. Though Goddard did not possess the poise to prevent his professional disputes from encroaching on his personal life, still he must have been influenced by the attitudes towards disputation shown by the Queen Anne literary giants.

And so what we have to tell now is merely the first of many arguments for Goddard. It started with the printer's worry that legitimate news was being withheld from his readers. On August 4, 1764, appeared, under the Providence date-line, a letter dated August first from "A Countryman": "As the Secretary of this Colony, in divers Instances, has prov'd himself so totally void of Honor and Integrity, that nothing conducive to the Public Emolument can be expected from him; I therefore send you a Copy of an Act of the General Assembly, pass'd at Newport, Yesterday, which I desire you to insert in your next Paper, that the Public may be duly advised of the Matters therein contain'd." Not surprisingly Henry Ward, the Colony Secretary, objected to being called "totally void of Honor and Integrity" and rushed into print in the *Newport Mercury* for August 13. The following Saturday, the eighteenth, Goddard devoted almost all of page three of his paper to his defense against Ward's charges, this time attaching his name without the disguise of a pseudonym.

The dispute rested here and the two opponents remained silent. Samuel Hall, the printer of the *Newport Mercury*, had kept his name out of this quarrel, but Goddard did not permit him to remain in such Olympian perspective. Some months later when the Providence paper was publishing attacks on the Stamp Act and the Newport paper was printing defenses, Goddard stuck the following alleged advertisement in the *Gazette* of January 19, 1765, as his contribution to the peace of mind of Mr. Hall and his fellow Newporters:

Published last Week, and sold by Mr. S. HALL, at his Printing-Office in NEWPORT, a PIECE entitled,

Modern Eloquence,

or

The Phrase in Fashion:

Being an Essay on genteel Compliment; and contains a Specimen of polite Address, in every Branch, even from calling a Gentleman *Dog*, up to giving the *Lye*, or throwing a *Brick-bat*:—Recommended, in particular, to the Gentlemen and Ladies of the Town of Newport, as a Means to embellish their Conversations, and adorn their Manners against the next General Election.

By Moses Turn-Spit, *Hypercritick.*

No Crab more active in the dirty Dance,
Downward to climb, and backward to advance.
Dunciad.

Pope need not have been too ashamed at the prowess of his disciple in the art of invective. Samuel Hall made no attempt at reply even though the Stamp Act controversy continued for several months.

The struggle of the young printer to make a decent livelihood for himself, his mother, and his sister continued. One of his attempts to help things along was the acquiring of the local postmastership, announced October 6, 1764, in the *Gazette*. Though his father had been postmaster of New London and as an apprentice he had worked in printing shops where a post office was located, this was Goddard's first actual position in the postal system. Long after he had left Providence, he continued to hold the position through the aid of substitutes. Finally, on February 11, 1769, over four years later, it was announced that John Cole had succeeded to the post.

But taking part in disputes with the Newport printer and the colony secretary, being postmaster, and running the newspaper and printing office did not take up all Goddard's time. Unfortunately we know almost nothing today about his social activities during this period. It is therefore a pleasure to find among the deservedly prized possessions of the Rhode Island Historical Society a broadside whose contents suggest the convivial pleasantries of an early autumn evening. The broadside is printed, but in what looks like Goddard's hand there is, "To Miss Sally Kennicutt." Sarah Goddard would have had an active part in the preparations for the social affair for which Goddard printed:

Providence, (Tuesday Morning)
September 25, 1764.

Madam,

As t[he] Close of this Day is de[vo]ted to social Mirth and Gaity, and the Ladies being esteem'd the only *real* Promoters of it,—I take the Libe[rt]y to request YOU to make one at a *Petticoat Frisk*, to be held in the Afternoon, at Mrs. *Goddard*'s, where your Company will greatly brighten the Felicity of the Evening, and be very agreebale to *all*, and in a particular Manner to one, who will think it an Honor to wait on you there, and is, with the utmost Respect,

Your very humble,
and most obedient Servant,
WILLIAM GODDARD.

P. S. The present lowering Sky, it is hoped will be no Discouragement to You,—for You may be assured of a pleasant Afternoon, should the Sun be obscured in Darkness, while the Ladies chearful Presence united, can supply that Want of its hidden Rays.

Not every social evening in Providence would the young bloods of the town be squiring Sally Kennicutts to dances, no matter what happened to Sally's petticoats. The bachelor editor of the local newspaper would have had a good many evenings out on the town. An advertisement in the December 29, 1764, *Gazette* reveals some of the public entertainment available for the citizens of Providence. "Luke Thurston, (Who for many Years past has kept a noted House of Entertainment near the Great Bridge in Providence) . . . begs Leave to signify to all those who have a true Relish for that chearing and delicious Fluid call'd PUNCH, compos'd of genuine Materials, that they may be always gratified by repairing to his Fountain, with such as will stand the Test of repeated Trials, and where a Specimen, however capacious, will, on the FIRST CALL, be exhibited:—And such as prefer the all-animating Juice of the Grape, may, at the same Place, find a Source suitable for the Gratification of the nicest Palates. These admirable Liquors, exhilarating the Spirits and creating a good Appetite, a true Criterion of Health, may be accompanied with many Dishes of high Renown."

For those who preferred drinks other than the "genuine Materials" of Luke's punch, James Tweedy, Junior, advertised his wares on May 11, 1765. At his location "Opposite the Church" he distilled and sold "Anniseed, Cinnamon, Clove, Doctor Stevens's, and Orange Cordials, with many others." He also sold "Choice old Madeira,

Lisbon, Sherry, Teneriffe, Fyal, and Sweet Wines, Nantz Brandy, Rum and Molasses."

During the latter part of 1764 reports reached the colonies of the discussion going on in Parliament and in the British cabinet concerning ways to increase tax revenue. The Stamp Act debate was starting. The pseudonymous letters in the columns of the *Providence Gazette* were increasingly political. Goddard showed his attitude quite early by the full and sympathetic coverage he gave the activities of John Wilkes and his writings in the *North Briton.* One of the most influential of the pamphlets against the Stamp Act was written by Stephen Hopkins and printed by Goddard, who announced its publication December 22, 1764. The title page of this pamphlet has frequently been reproduced because of its graceful appearance. It was a page that Goddard was never to improve upon; indeed it would be hard to do so.

Hopkins's pamphlet, *The Rights of Colonies Examined,* was read by many throughout all the colonies and in England. As would be expected, it aroused an answer, which answer drew forth defenses, attacks, and so on for many months and columns of the *Gazette.* The most prominent of the answers was one entitled *A Letter from a Gentleman at Halifax,* Samuel Hall of Newport being the printer. This placed the two newspapers in opposite camps, even though each editor would probably have preferred to have had both sides represented in his own paper. But those attacking the Stamp Act sent their letters to Goddard, and those defending to the *Newport Mercury.* In part this tendency reflected the attitudes of the two editors, since Goddard made no bones about his own opposition and continued to fight the Stamp Act long after he had left Providence. As late as April 6, 1765, we find him announcing a two-page post-script to be published two days later when "a Piece sent us by the ingenious Author of the Vindication of the Pamphlet, entitled, *The Rights of Colonies examined,* will be laid before the Public." Almost every issue in February and March had had something on Hopkins's publication or on the Stamp Act itself. Undoubtedly many of these comments were written by Stephen Hopkins, then in the prime of his career.

Vigorous as the discussion over the merits of the Stamp Act was, and attractive as the attitude of the *Providence Gazette*'s owner was to most of his readers, Goddard's financial difficulties remained unsolved. Hopkins tried to do his bit for the paper by reviving his history of Providence, one part of which he had written for the first issue of the *Gazette*. This first article was reprinted January 12, 1765. Later, chapters were added to "An Historical Account of the Planting and Growth of Providence" in the issues of January 19, February 2, 9, 16, March 16, and 30. Goddard prefaced the reprinted first chapter by a lengthy appeal to the people of Providence and vicinity for increased support for his paper. He opened this appeal by a statement of the importance of the art of printing, "held in the highest Veneration and Esteem by the most knowing and civiliz'd Nations of the Universe." The British nation has been most especially aware of the benefits derived from printing, "the very Basis and Bulwark of its Constitution." A similar attitude is to be found among the British American subjects, including the colony of Rhode Island. Because their forefathers contributed so much to liberty, religion, and learning, the colony's present inhabitants "of all People under the Sun, ought to manifest their Regard for, and exert themselves to promote the PRINTING BUSINESS amongst them: This they have at present an Opportunity of doing, and it is hoped there will never be Room hereafter to say, that the noble ART of PRINTING failed in this flourishing Part of *New England*, thro' Lack of proper Encouragement, when, at the same Time, it was increasing to the Honor and Advantage of many other Parts of far less Magnitude." Getting down to the particular situation of the *Providence Gazette*, Goddard complained, "The Number of its Benefactors [euphemism for paying subscribers] is inadequate to the inconceivable Expences attending its Publication." Continuing, he stated an ideal for a newspaper which affected him throughout his entire career, "The Ambition of the Publisher to gratify the Public, will always prompt him to aim at keeping pace in the Improvement of his Paper, with the Encouragement it receives, till it shall be found, not only (what it is at present) a Weekly Register or Journal of the most important Intelligence, and other interesting Matters, but a Magazine or Repository of the most valuable Treasures and Curiosities in Literature, selected from the Writings of the most celebrated Authors." After making some explanatory apologies for the interuption to the history of Providence, Goddard concluded his essay, "N. B. The Friends to this Paper, in Town and Country, it is hoped will exert themselves in procuring Subscriptions."

What is most informative of Goddard's intentions is the expressed hope to make his newspaper not only a "Weekly Register or Journal" but a "Magazine or Repository." It has usually been assumed too easily that the only reason why magazines so consistently failed in colonial America was a basic lack of interest in magazines themselves, though it is true that more often than not the so-called magazine of this period was only a monthly version of the weekly newspaper. Therefore the blurring of what we think of as the function of a newspaper with that of a magazine may have had much to do with the inadequate subscription lists for the "magazines" of Bradford, Franklin, and Parker. Today we smile condescendingly at the colonial newspaper's columns filled with letters signed "Pro Bono Publico" and "Philopatriae," but these pseudonymous letters followed logically from Goddard's expressed ideal to combine news and entertainment. In the same issue, January 12, 1765, that carried on page one this statement by the editor, Goddard could with pride say in another context, "As we attribute, in a great Measure, the Approbation this Paper hath gain'd to the interesting Matters sent us by some Ingenious Friends, we therefore beg Leave to present them with our sincere Thanks, and, at the same Time, repeat our Sollicitations for the Continuance of their Favors." And Goddard knew that his readers would comprehend the reasons for his pride.

A last move within Providence was announced March 16, 1765, when it was stated the post office and printing office would be moved on March 19 to a house opposite Nathan Angell's, "near the Sign of the Golden-Eagle." Next week's colophon placed the business "next Door below Knight Dexter's, Esq." Later Goddard was to spend the last years of his life across the street from this location on North Main Street.

Finally in the issue of May 4, 1765, Goddard had to announce the suspension for six months of the *Providence Gazette* with the next issue. As he put it, "His Hopes have vastly exceeded his Success." In spite of the disappearance for the time being of the *Gazette* from the scene the printing shop was to continue its business. Providence was still to have its press, though not its newspaper. The announcement did not say this, but later events make it clear that William left the community shortly after the last issue of May 11, and the shop's operations were continued by his mother

Sarah Goddard and his sister Mary Katherine, by now a skilled printer in her own right.

It must have been with considerable sympathy that Goddard set up the type in his last issue for a notice by his neighbor, Knight Dexter. It, at least, provides an ironic commentary on the whole situation. "KNIGHT DEXTER, returns his Thanks to such of his Customers as have honorably paid him, and should be glad of a Continuance of their Favors.—But as for Those who remain deaf to his friendly Sollicitations, they are just reminded of the near Approach of June Court, which may, by their Neglect, both affect their Breeches Pockets and animal Spirits, between which, 'tis said, there is a very strong Sympathy." The flavor of the language is so much that of Goddard that the writing hand of the newspaperman may be suspected.

THE first person to whom Goddard turned for new employment was quite naturally his old master, James Parker. Parker referred him to John Holt, who was then operating a print shop in New York on his own, though in typical colonial fashion still involved in settling his accounts with his former partner, Parker. Goddard knew his own worth and did not hesitate to demand of Holt, never the best of printers, much more than a job as a journeyman in the shop. At first Holt demurred, but his desire to publish a newspaper made him reconsider. Holt was not sure whether Parker might not want to return to New York from Woodbridge, New Jersey, and personally run his own newspaper. Holt's having a capable newspaperman such as Goddard in his shop would do much to make Parker hesitate in setting up a competing journal. So after a couple of interviews Holt agreed to Goddard's proposals and accepted him as a silent partner in his shop. This agreement was reached probably by the middle of the summer of 1765.

Goddard's interests during the next year and a half kept him frequently on the go between New York and Providence. In Providence the print shop continued its operations under the supervision of Sarah Goddard. The *Gazette* did not appear, but a supply of printed forms had to be maintained. *West's Almanack for 1766* was gotten out in September in time for book-peddlers to carry samples on their first swing around in the fall of 1765. The recorded imprints whose dates can be verified of the second half of this year include a sixty-page theological pamphlet, probably originally a sermon, by Timothy Allen, dated July 1, 1765. On the fifteenth of this same month a broadside offering three dollars reward for the return of a stolen horse was issued for Job Manchester. Another sermon by Timothy Allen, this time running to forty-eight pages, was released with the date September 1, 1765. This, together with the almanac, bore the imprint Sarah and William Goddard instead of just William's name. Business was not booming for the Providence shop; nor was it at a standstill.

The business activities of Goddard may have been limited to Providence and New York, but his political interests were broadening. During most of this period he took not merely an active but a leading role in the fight of the colonies against the Stamp Act. And it was not as a Rhode Islander or a New Yorker that Goddard spoke and wrote in his three publications during the fall and winter of 1765 and 1766, but as "a British-American." We have already seen his activities alongside Stephen Hopkins in the early months of 1765. More than likely during these frantic days of the feud over *The Rights of Colonies Examined* Goddard became an active member of the Providence Sons of Liberty. As late as March 24, 1766, the name of "William Goddard Printer" occurs on a committee to correspond with the Sons of Liberty at Boston and "in the several Colonies on the Continent." Such activities would have found a sympathetic ear in his partner John Holt, one of the most active patriots in New York City.

The first of the three publications was a *Providence Gazette Extraordinary* dated August 24, 1765, and headed, "Vox Populi, Vox Dei." The lead article, whose virulent tone against the hated Stamp Act suggests the pen of either Hopkins or Goddard himself, covers all of page one and ends on the second page with the signature "Colonus." On the second page are resolutions passed at a Providence town meeting on August 13, 1765, attacking the Stamp Act. Extracts are then given from a speech in Parliament by Mr. Barre, who criticized the same act and also praised the spirit of New England. On the third page are accounts of events in New Haven and Boston in the struggle against this law. On page four under a Providence date-line Goddard announced that Augustus Johnston, recently appointed distributor of stamps for Rhode Island Colony, would not undertake his office. (A week later Johnston accepted the inevitable and formally resigned his commission.) The best paragraph of this page-long diatribe, which started with the Johnston resignation, is this: "Able Jockies give it as their Opinion, that the American Horses are of too mettlesome a Breed to stand still under the Operation of Branding, and that whoever should attempt to apply a hot *S* to their Buttocks, would be in no small Danger from their hind Legs: For saith one wittily, *Sure none but Asses will stand still to be branded.* However the said Jockies will not aver that the few Asses here will give much Trouble to the Branding Company." Crude yet effective, heavy-handed yet biting—Goddard's invective almost always featured these qualities. The concluding paragraphs of Goddard's article tell indirectly about his own activities. The paper mill "about a Mile and an Half from this Town" is "just finished" and "in a few Days will be set to work." The *Providence Gazette* "will be resumed as soon as the PAPER-MILL gets to Work; provided the Printer can obtain a proper Number of Subscribers." Further on the same four partners—Olney, Waterman, Ballau (here spelled Belleau), and Goddard—advertised for linen rags. Other printers mentioned who would pay for rags are Timothy Green of New London and Thomas Green in Hartford. These two members of the ubiquitous Green family were seeing to it that they got in their bid for the product of the new mill. The brief colophon at the bottom of the page merely reads, "Printed by S. and W. Goddard."

After seeing this special number of the *Gazette* through the press, Goddard returned to New York and within a month involved himself in his most spectacular blow at the Stamp Act. The name of William Goddard was not associated with this broadside, but now it can be stated without any qualifications that he was completely responsible for the *Constitutional Courant* of September 21, 1765. For our account of this affair we can do no better than use Goddard's own narration of the events as he gave them in a letter to Isaiah Thomas:

During the great alarm and stagnation of business, occasioned by the British stamp-act being passed into a law, to be in operation here, I went from Providence to New-York, and assisted Mr. Holt. He showed me several elegantly written and highly spirited essays, against the unjust tax, which no printer in New-York dared to publish. I volunteered my services, went to Woodbridge, and obtained leave to use the apparatus there at pleasure, where I planned a newspaper with this title.

The

Constitutional   [Join or die.]   Courant.
⎰A snake cut into thirteen parts, with initials in each.   ⎱
⎱emblemating the thirteen colonies, in the centre of the title   ⎰
Containing matters interesting to liberty, but no wise repugnant to loyalty.

Then followed an address from the editor, Andrew Marvel, mentioning the prudent fears of New-York editors, who declined printing the subjoined, awakening performances, lest they and their families should be ruined by the hand of power, &c. observing that I had no family and no such apprehensions, and having competent knowledge of the printing business, I was determined to devote my time and talents to promote the welfare of my devoted country, in opposition to the alarming strides of power, &c., and, intimating if No. 1 was well received, other numbers would follow. The paper was completed ending thus: "Printed by Andrew Marvel, at the sign of the bribe refused, Constitution Hill, North-America." I sent them by a confidential agent to New-York. Thousands were rapidly sold. It excited much alarm in the government. A council was called at the fort, but nothing could be done with the petty Junius, who was, in a great degree, the sole depository of his own secret. When troubles were overpast, by the repeal of the odious law, this paper was noticed in the Annual Register, and Andrew Marvel's address published, the editor of that work observing, that it was the most significant paper that made its appearance during the troubles in North-America. When one of the council at New-York demanded of the hawker Lawrence Sweeney, "where that incendiary paper was published," he could obtain no other reply than "at Peter Hassenclaver's Iron works, may it please your honor." Peter Hassenclaver, a German of wealth, carried on extensive iron works, well known in New-Jersey. Frequently afterwards, daring writings appeared with this imprint— "Printed at Peter Hassenclaver's Iron works."

A reading today of the *Constitutional Courant* makes us wonder why this particular piece of propaganda seemed more inflammatory to its readers, including the British officials in the colonies, than innumerable similar attacks. In many ways the *Providence Gazette Extraordinary* a month before reads better than the *Courant*, but the taunting flag and colophon apparently made up for what the articles themselves seem to lack. In other words, good editing gave the *Courant* its real impact.

As Goddard says in his account, the furor created was immense. The highest praise of all was given by the pirated copies reprinted throughout the colonies. Albert Matthews identifies three different variants of the *Courant*, only one of which would have been printed on the Woodbridge press. It was quickly suspected by the authorities that James Parker was responsible for the single-issue newspaper, but nothing was ever done about it. Why the authorities were so seemingly lax is shown by a remark made in a letter from Cadwallader Colden, Royal Governor of New York, to Benjamin

Franklin, then in London. Colden believed Parker to be the printer, but he went on to say, "The Gentlemen of the Council think it prudent at this time to delay the makeing more particular Enquiry least it should be the occasion of raising the mob, which it is thought proper by all means to avoid." Whether the questioning of Lawrence Sweeney, the hawker of the *Courant* on the streets of New York, was before or after this letter was written, still the Council got nowhere with the carefully instructed Sweeney and neither Parker nor Goddard was ever questioned.

The intensity of Goddard's dislike of the Stamp Act, a feeling shared by most of his fellow colonial printers because of the heavy duties on paper, can be seen in a letter he wrote to Parker three months later, December 13, in which he told the older printer about the events taking place in New York involving the Stamp Act. Governor Colden had been placed in an impasse, and to the sanguine Goddard, "This I hope will cause the Destruction of the Stamps."

The activities of Goddard and the Providence patriots continued during the winter of 1765-1766. Public meetings were held, such as one after which Goddard printed an anonymous pamphlet (attributed to John Aplin), *A Discourse Addressed to the Sons of Liberty, At a solemn Assembly, near Liberty-Tree, in Providence, February 14, 1766.* Many such meetings under similar liberty-trees with similar speeches were held in all the colonies.

Now that the repeal of the Stamp Act was being debated in Parliament, Goddard could turn his attention to his own personal problems. He was much too independent a person ever to feel comfortable as a silent partner, no matter how much responsibility Holt gave him in the production of the *New-York Gazette.* Therefore he put his mind to trying to reactivate his Providence shop. Goddard liked Providence and always preferred to live there in spite of his frequent moves away from it. The *Extraordinary* of August 24, 1765, was more a piece of propaganda than anything else, though remarks were made about reviving the *Providence Gazette.* But in March of the following year he could be more specific. Though news of the repeal of the Stamp Act on March 18 did not reach the colonies until April 26, he did not need to worry for the moment over the unenforced taxes. The operation of the paper mill near Providence assured him of a constant supply of newsprint. All that was needed was a constant supply of customers, and this deficiency Goddard set out to remedy by the *Providence Gazette Extraordinary* and *Supplement* of March 12, 1766.

In spite of the various imprints already issued from the press of Sarah and William Goddard the newspaper had beneath its flag, "Printed and published by William Goddard." Goddard also used his own name as he advertised for "two or three Journeymen Printers, who are willing to be employed at the Westward." Sarah Goddard used hers at the bottom of a notice on the same page requesting "the Assistance of those Gentlemen and Ladies, to whom I have the Honor of being known, . . . in this Colony and other Parts of New-England, towards the Establishment of the Providence Gazette." Though William was making a sincere attempt to revive his business in Providence, he was by no means committing himself.

Most of the space in this number of the *Gazette* is taken up by the usual pseudonymous letters, this time congratulatory in tone and warning the readers that just because they are winning the good fight over the Stamp Act they should not relax their watch over their liberties or the possible encroachments of Parliament. One of the longest of such epistolary essays is signed Colonus, as in the issue of August 24 of the preceding year. The resolutions passed by the Stamp Act Congress are given *in toto*. For our interest the most important item is the "Proposals for reviving the Providence Gazette, &c." which occupied the entirety of page one.

After reminding his readers that he had started the *Gazette* "without engaging such a Number of Subscribers as would defray the weekly Expence thereof," Goddard cites the "present depressed Situation of *North-America*" as a cause for the discontinuance of the newspaper. He says that while he was away from Providence he received a letter from "a Number of Gentlemen who had been his former Readers" asking him to revive the paper. Because of his family connections in Providence, the friendships he has made, and the "fair Usage" of the townspeople, he will now try to reactivate the paper. He agrees to publish a paper every Saturday containing the "public News," "moral Pieces from the best Writers," and occasional "Pieces of Wit and Humour." But, in order to accomplish this goal, he must have in five weeks a minimum of eight hundred subscribers at seven shillings a year each. The final two paragraphs are an appeal for rags for the paper mill. He concludes this appeal by gallantly addressing the "unmarried Ladies," who, "if they will be pleased to distinguish to him such Pieces of the Linen as were Parts of their inner Garments, he will cause it to be wrought into the finest Paper, so that it may be returned to them in Letters, from kind Correspondents who are abroad—And they may rest assured, that Vows recorded on so fair a Foundation, are under the Care of the kind Genius who presides over chaste Wedlock, and can never be broken."

Apparently the letter written by "a Number of Gentlemen" in Providence is the one given on page 57 of *The Partnership*, a pamphlet written and published by Goddard in 1770. Because this letter so well shows the necessity felt by the leaders of the communty, it is worth presenting in full:

Sir,

The particular esteem and friendship which we have for you, makes us regret your absence; but when we consider the loss of you as a printer, we cannot but expostulate with you on that subject.

We have been, and still are of opinion, that this town, regarding it in its situation, and the various lights in which a man of business might view it, would afford a very comfortable prospect to a young man of your occupation, in his settlement among us.

You may be assured, that from the knowledge we have of your expertness in the printing-business, we should prefer you, as our printer, to any other person; exclusive of the other favourable impressions you have made upon us, during the course of your residence here.

We very much deplore the discontinuance of a public paper, in this town, especially at a time when that machine is become necessary for the retention of our rights, by explaining to the people the nature of them, and sounding an alarm when they are in danger.—We make no doubt but a suitable number of good subscribers might be procured, and no press in *America* could more easily be furnished with stock, as the paper-mill is got to work.

In this situation of the town, with respect to the printing-business, we should be much obliged to you for a declaration of your intent, in regard to the reviving your business here, to the end, that if you should altogether decline it (which we hope will not be the case) we might be free to make application to some other printer, which, in such case, we shall do in justice to ourselves.

The foregoing letter is agreeable to the sentiments of all the gentlemen of the town, with whom we have conversed on the subject, although signed only by Sir,

Your most obedient and humble servants,

Daniel Jenckes, John Cole, S. Downer, Nathan Angell, John Updike, Nicholas Brown, Hayward Smith, Ebenezer Thompson, John Jenckes, James Angell, Moses Brown, Job Smith, Jonathan Ballau, Joseph Lawrence, John Nash, James Arnold, John Brown, Joseph Brown, Samuel Nightingale, jun. *Joseph Russel.*

How did Goddard arrive at the figure of eight hundred sub-scribers? In 1766 there were probably not many more than three or four newspapers in all the colonies with this much circulation, and those would have been in Boston, New York, and Philadelphia. This number was not a mere figure of speech to Goddard because he did not revive the paper at the end of five weeks; in fact, when it was finally revived, it was under the actual as well as nominal direction of Sarah Goddard not William. Before this we have pointed out the failure of the Providence shop to get the colony printing. (It took a revolution before Goddard's successor, John Carter, was able to take the public printing away from Newport.) William had calculated his figure on the basis that there would be no government work. The newspaper must carry itself, not just be a prestige item whose losses could be subsidized from other sources. How about the advertising revenue? As today, the space rates were determined by the circulation. If it had eight hundred circulation, the newspaper could justify an increase in its advertising rates, but apparently not before. Publishers of today worry about a "break-even" point in their book sales and circulation. Eight hundred was a break-even point for a colonial newspaper of 1766.

Of additional interest are the remarks about the paper mill. We have Goddard's flat statement that "he has a Part" in it. The business horizon of the young, but no longer fledgling, printer was expanding. Also, there is said about this mill that "Paper of every Sort . . . has been produced from it." Judging from this statement, the ones made the preceding August, and the undated remarks in the joint letter, we can deduce that Rhode Island's first paper mill commenced its operations during the fall of 1765.

By June, 1766, Goddard had given up on the possibility of re-opening the Providence shop and was in Philadelphia looking over the prospects there. Later he described his own situation: "At this time [June, 1766] I had a very complete office in *Providence*, in the colony of *Rhode-Island*, under the superintendence of Mrs. *Sarah Goddard*, my Mother, and was in company with a gentleman

of credit [John Holt] in the city of *New-York*. My inducement
to leave *Providence* was the earnest invitation of Messrs. *Parker*
and *Holt*, who wished to see me employed on a more extensive
theatre [at this point Goddard conveniently forgot his own letter
to Parker requesting aid in securing employment], and offered to
take me into partnership with them, without removing my materials
from *Providence*, or advancing a shilling [this was undoubtedly
true]; but, unfortunately, after I had been a little time in *New-York*,
a dispute arose between my two friends, which gave me great pain,
and made my situation disagreeable, one insisting that I should join
him, in opposition to the other, unless he would submit to particular
terms proposed. I laboured incessantly to prevent an open rupture,
and a news-paper controversy, and happily succeeded, preserving the
good-will of both. I afterwards joined one of them, by consent of
the other, till I could find a more advantageous situation, which I
soon after had a prospect of in *Philadelphia*." It is questionable
that Goddard's labors to "prevent an open rupture" between Parker
and Holt were incessant, but it is true that he did preserve the
friendship of both men. He was Holt's partner and printed the
Constitutional Courant on Parker's Woodbridge press.

The story of William Goddard in Philadelphia is another chapter; however, we must pause a while to see the activities of his
mother and sister in Providence. Even more than William, Sarah
Goddard loved the community where her son had opened the
town's first printing establishment. She was determined to maintain the business not only because of her affection for her neighbors
but because of her tremendous reverence for the "mystick art of
printing," as a poem in the March 16, 1765, *Gazette* had called it.
During the early summer of 1766, when William had given up on
Providence and was sounding out Philadelphia, she was organizing
Sarah Goddard and Company. The "Company" consisted of Mary
Katherine, an active workman in the shop; Samuel Inslee (later to
print Parker's New York paper after the latter's death), brought in
some time during the summer or fall; and a few journeymen and
apprentices. It was not a big shop, but it was busy and succeeded
in bringing out shortly a 204-page volume. Appropriately this
imprint of Sarah Goddard and Company was the *Letters of the
Right Honourable Lady M-y W-y M-e*, announced as "just published" on September 5, 1767. Sarah was paying her respects to

that better-known bluestocking Lady Mary Wortley Montague by means of this first American printing of the *Letters*.

More important to the firm's financial well-being was the revival of the *Providence Gazette* on August 9, 1766. The usual notice "To the Public" on page one apologized for not appearing "at the Time limited in the *Providence Gazette* Extraordinary." The number of subscribers obtained by the March appeal was "inadequate," but Sarah was going ahead anyway. The rest of this notice is adapted from the one which appeared in the first number of the *Gazette* almost four years before.

The next week's issue, August 15, featured a long letter from William, date-lined New York, July 20, 1766. After congratulating his fellow countrymen on the repeal of the Stamp Act, he connected the *Providence Gazette* with this struggle by expressing its devotion to the "Preservation of Liberty." He commented on the attempt to revive the paper five months before. He admitted he had not obtained the minimum eight hundred subscribers, "but though I cannot reasonably expect to make any adequate Advantage of my Printing-Materials, (which cost me near £300, *Sterling*,) where they are, yet I could not be persuaded to take them away; rather choosing, at all Events, to leave them for the Benefit of my Friends, where they are, in the Hands of my Mother, Mrs. *Sarah Goddard*. . . . I have lately sent her as Assistant [probably Samuel Inslee], to enable her to carry on the Business more extensively."

The pleasure and satisfaction Sarah Goddard got from operating the printing establishment comes out not only in such books as that by Lady Montague but in the tradition of entertainment started by William and continued by his mother in the columns of the *Gazette*. One example of entertainment printed August 30 reveals Sarah's appreciation of earthy wit, and the heroic couplets of "The Distressed Maid" provide pleasure to today's readers as well as those of two centuries ago.

> Of all the experience, how vast the amount,
> Since fifteen long winters I fairly can count;
> Was ever poor damsel so sadly betray'd,
> For to live to these years, and still be a maid.
> Ye heroes triumphant, by land or by sea,
> Sworn votries to love, yet unmindful of me;
> You can storm a strong fort, or can form a blockade,

Yet ye stand by like dastards; and see me a maid.
Ye lawyers so just, who with slippery tongue,
Who do what you please, or with right or with wrong;
Can it be or by law or by equity said,
That a charming young girl ought to die an old maid.
Ye learned physicians, whose excellent skill,
Can save, or demolish, can cure, or can kill;
To a poor forlorn damsel contribute your aid,
Who is sick, very sick of remaining a maid.
You fops I invoke not to list to my song,
Who answer no end, and to no sex belong.
Ye echoe's of echoe's and shadows of shades,
For if I had you,—I might still be a maid.

The business of the shop went on apace. On September 20 the *Gazette* requested "a sober, industrious Person, who understands the Business of Papermaking." The paper mill demanded skilled workmen, and the four partners found it necessary to advertise for their services. Another activity of the shop is shown by the issue of October 11. The *Providence Gazette* would accept in lieu of money for its subscriptions "good tann'd Sheep-Skins, fit for Bookbinding." Colonial print shops concerned themselves with the covers of books as well as the contents.

By the end of 1766 William was in Philadelphia preparing himself and securing the necessary printing equipment for his new venture. His mother busied herself supervising the Providence shop and editing the weekly issues of the *Gazette*. Mary Katherine had the sleeves of her dress rolled up and wore a goodly sized apron as she used her own printer's stick in the composition of the paper. The members of the Goddard family were all busy, each in his own sphere.

THE scene of William Goddard's activities now shifts to Philadelphia. Penn's "green country town" was in 1766 the largest city in all the colonies. Though it did not have Boston's fishing industry, it did have a much larger trade with Britain, the West Indies, and the other colonies than did the older settlement. Its population, approximately 30,000, had surpassed Boston's for several years. Not only was its trade vigorous, but its commercial basis was variegated, auguring well for the future. In spite of British restriction iron was smelted in the vicinity and many of the local citizens had financial interests in the small iron furnaces scattered between the Delaware and Susquehanna rivers. Another active force in Philadelphia's prosperity was, and is, the richness of the farm lands of Lancaster County and the Cumberland Valley, only a few years before opened up for settlement. Contributing to this agricultural well-being were the farming abilities of the Pennsylvania German settlers. In the Palatine their forebears had learned how to rotate crops and how to conserve the soil while reaping the benefits of each harvest. The products of these hard-working German farmers were going into or through Philadelphia, just as during the winter of 1777-1778 the soldiers of Washington's army watched the bulging wagons of food pass by their Valley Forge encampment on the way to the British army in Philadelphia.

Inevitably an expanding, prosperous community suffered many growing pains. Quarrels were sometimes bitter over the location of street lamps, the marketplace, and its "shambles." There were acrimonious debates on the subject of what should happen to the overhead arch where Arch Street today reaches Front Street. All these and many more subjects of local interest could be expected to fill the columns of a newspaper and provide the necessary fuels for the heat of an extensive circulation. But Philadelphia was more than an economic center; it was also a political center. As yet it had not become the capital of the colonies, even figuratively, but it was very much the political capital of the province of Pennsylvania. And this colony's politics eventually thoroughly enmeshed Goddard, causing both his success and his failure.

The distinguishing feature of Pennsylvania's political life in the 1760's was the existence of two parties, proprietary and antiproprietary. The colony was still under the proprietary control of the descendants of William Penn. The irritations produced by this control were many, and matters were not helped by the seeming arrogance of certain members of the Penn family. Some of the dispute originates in the inevitable pattern of the ins forming one party and the outs forming another. Whatever the causes, the presence of the two parties, unorganized though they were, was obvious to all observers. The struggle between the two was most intense in the provincial assembly, which was frequently chafing under the reins of the governor's veto power over its actions. Within the assembly the proprietary forces were led by such men as James Wilson and John Dickinson. The antiproprietary party found its leadership in Joseph Galloway, Thomas Wharton, and Benjamin Franklin. Franklin was in England during most of the 1760's and could participate only through his correspondence with various members of the assembly. Franklin's son, William, was very sympathetic to Galloway and Wharton in spite of his position as royal governor of New Jersey and having, as a result, to be secretive in his efforts in their behalf. Possibly William Franklin had dreams of becoming governor of Pennsylvania were it made into a royal colony.

We have already seen the vigor and intensity with which Goddard had participated in the Stamp Act struggle of 1765. This same struggle had, of course, gone on in all the colonies. In Philadelphia, as in the other colonial capitals, the newspapers had been active in their opposition to the potential duties, many of which directly affected the livelihood of the colonial printer. Among those who had expressed themselves in favor of the Stamp Act was Joseph Galloway. Under the pseudonym of Americanus he had in Bradford's *Pennsylvania Journal* of August 29, 1765, defended the legal right (Galloway was one of the most prominent members of the Philadelphia bar) of Parliament to tax the colonists. Who Americanus was did not long remain a secret, and many vituperations were cast at the writer's head. Typical of these was a broadside issued, probably from the press of William Bradford, in early 1766. This broadside, called "A Receipt to Make a Speech," is stated with not very subtle irony to be by J—— G——, Esquire, patently Joseph Galloway to any Philadelphia reader. The alleged author of the "receipt" goes on to give his formula for making a speech sound pretentious and say nothing. The satire is obvious enough to be almost abusive. Whether Bradford printed this on order or for himself is not important since his dislike of Galloway is apparent either way. Though Hall and Sellers were not as vocal in their opposition to Galloway, still Galloway and Wharton found it more and more difficult to insert articles into Franklin's old newspaper.

David Hall, in a letter to William Strahan on June 12, 1767, dated the beginning of Galloway's dissatisfaction back to late September, 1764. At that time Galloway had told Hall he wanted to insert a yet-unwritten article, and John Dickinson, who was contesting Galloway's seat in the Pennsylvania Assembly, came to Hall about the article. The election was only a few days off; in fact, it was to occur just one day after the next appearance of the *Gazette*. If Dickinson was to reply to Galloway before the election, he would have to do it in the same issue in which Galloway's article would appear. Therefore he requested permission to see Galloway's article before publication, so that he could make whatever rejoinder seemed appropriate. This Hall agreed to. Later when Galloway brought in his article, Hall told him of the conversation with Dickinson. Galloway refused to allow his opponent to see the article. "Then I [Hall] told him, I did not think I could print it; upon which he grew very angry, told me, I was a Partial Printer, that I had used him very ill, and that he would complain to Mr Franklin." (Franklin was still a partner in 1764.) Goddard was later to give accounts of the reactions of Galloway when frustrated that sound very much like Hall's narrative.

As part of this picture we cannot ignore the absence of Benjamin Franklin; in fact, his absence affected the circumstances of Goddard in Philadelphia more than his possible presence. Franklin had been the colony of Pennsylvania representative, in effect representative of the provincial assembly, in England since 1757. Except for a less than two-year period in the early 1760's he had been away from the colonies for almost ten years and was not to return until 1775. During his absence he received regularly the Philadelphia newspapers and many letters from his friends and family. However, Franklin had somewhat lost contact with what was going on in the colonies at this time, and his reputation had been severely tarnished for many colonists by his actions after the Stamp Act was passed by Parliament and before its repeal. As representative of Pennsylvania he had fought against the act's passage. Once Parliament passed the act, Franklin seemingly had no idea of the intensity of the colonial opposition and committed the *faux pas* of securing the position of customs collector for several of his friends, most of whom were compelled to resign their offices under considerable public pressure and permanent embarrassment to their prestige. So badly was Franklin regarded as a result that William Franklin and Joseph Galloway thought it necessary to rehabilitate his reputation. They were much annoyed in this attempt to find the columns of the two Philadelphia newspapers almost closed to them. And so they welcomed the opportunity when an experienced printer and newspaper publisher came into town to look over the situation.

When Goddard printed the first number of the *Providence Gazette*, he was establishing his business in a community which had had no printing shop previously, let alone a newspaper. He had the citizens of Providence behind him even though they were reluctant to part with their seven shillings for annual subscriptions. Philadelphia was quite different. Two newspapers had for many years shared the public's trade. Though the Franklin and Hall shop was the more active of the two, being the largest in all the colonies, Bradford had managed to get along. Franklin had retired from active participation in 1748 but had continued to draw out generous returns from his partnership. In early 1766 it was announced in the *Pennsylvania Gazette* that the old partnership of Franklin and Hall had expired and was to be replaced by the firm of Hall and Sellers. Sitting in Holt's printing shop, Goddard must have welcomed this news when he read it. Franklin had been a good, even imaginative printer and was always a fierce competitor for any business. David Hall, though competent, lacked Franklin's imagination and keen business sense. Bradford could be called adequate as a printer and not much more. One of his chief contributions to the printing business was a dogged persistence, which gave him some of the official printing from Pennsylvania and New Jersey, though the Franklin and Hall shop had the lion's share. And so all in all it must have looked like a very good opportunity for a skilled experienced printer to exploit.

In March, 1766, Goddard had tried to revive the *Providence Gazette*. By June this attempt seemed to have failed, and Goddard paid his first visit to Philadelphia. He had read the Franklin and Hall announcement, but also he had procured a letter of introduction to Governor Franklin, probably from Parker though Goddard does not name him. Goddard sought out the governor in Philadelphia, gave him the letter, and indicated his availability as a printer. The younger Franklin "semed transported with the information" and immediately sent the printer on to Joseph Galloway, who received him "with great joy." Afterwards (in *The Partnership*, the 1770 pamphlet in which Goddard reveals so much about his first years in Philadelphia), Goddard, with some bitterness, described his reception by Galloway in these terms: "He acquainted me that he had long determined to have a press that would *'faithfully serve the public,'* that all the printers of the public papers here were villains and scoundrels, entirely under the dominion of a party, who monopolized the press, greatly to the prejudice of the province, and to the injury of his character, &c. He said he was extremely pleased that I came so opportunely, . . . and [he] would secure me the government's printing business, which, he assured me, was always at his command, . . . and many other great and important advantages, besides cash whenever it was necessary, if I would admit him as a partner." No wonder the young printer thought his future lay in Philadelphia not Providence.

Shortly after this interview Goddard returned to Providence to make the necessary arrangements with his mother and sister for the running of the print shop and paper mill there. Some elzevir type was sent from Providence to Philadelphia and orders were sent to England for type to replace this. Most of the type for the new shop was ordered from William Strahan in London by Galloway.

The second issue of the revived *Providence Gazette* had a letter from Goddard dated New York, July 20, 1766. This letter, referred to in Chapter IV, contained this remark, somewhat cryptic to the Providence readers, as a postscript: "In my present Situation, I have much greater Prospects of increasing my Fortune, than I have ever had before." Doubtless most of those who read this "N.B." thought that the young Goddard was suffering from a case of sour grapes and was talking big to cover up his own failures. Yet even the most skeptical observer, had he known both the Providence situation and the Philadelphia prospects, could not have thought the case overstated.

In his shuttling back and forth between Providence and New York Goddard may have missed seeing some articles in the *Pennsylvania Journal,* which would have forecast for him not such pleasant prospects. It is, of course, impossible to say now whether Goddard knew Galloway's attitudes towards the Stamp Act and whether Galloway knew about Goddard's activities concerning the same act. Several things fall into place if we assume mutual ignorance; however, the ease with which each man could have found out about the other's past makes us hesitate in making such an assumption. Viewing the situation from the character of the two men, we are tempted to conclude that the shrewd, cautious Galloway may have had the benefit of this knowledge but not the impulsive Goddard. Perhaps Galloway's awareness may help explain why he set such importance in having financial control over Goddard. No matter what the extent of each one's knowledge, their mutual roles would have seemed appropriate, even if expediency was primary and not just secondary. Anyway, William Bradford was still rankled by the Americanus article of August, 1765, though it had appeared in his own paper—possibly this fact intensified the irritation. Finally, Bradford through some means, perhaps through his postmastership of Philadelphia, got his hands on a copy of a letter from Galloway to Benjamin Franklin, dated September 20, 1765. In this letter Galloway stated with apparent pride that he was Americanus and denounced the disorders against the Stamp Act. His expressed hope in September, 1765, that the colonists would submit to the law (repealed March 18, 1766) must have made many a Philadelphian smile at the haughty lawyer when they read the letter in Bradford's *Journal* of September 11, 1766. The original Americanus article was also reprinted in this same issue so that no reader could possibly miss the point. Galloway's election as speaker of the Pennsylvania Assembly less than a month later must have greatly irked the opponents of the Stamp Act.

The next week's issue, September 18, of the *Pennsylvania Journal* returned to the attack with an unsigned two-page essay in a supplement. Three individuals were named as collaborators in a conspiracy to foist the Stamp Act upon the colonists. These three were Joseph Galloway; John Hughes, a friend of Franklin's who had been named Stamp Act Collector for Philadelphia; and Benjamin Franklin, who "is generally believed to have had a principal hand in promoting the Stamp Act." This theme was played upon again for the opening two and a half pages of the September 25 *Journal*. So vigorous was the campaign against Galloway and Franklin (Hughes was regarded as a mere chattel in their hands) that a proper metaphor to describe this preparation for the arrival of Goddard in Philadelphia would not be the stage was set but rather the trap door was poised open for its victim.

In November Goddard came to Philadelphia to open up his printing business. Prospects seemed glowing for the twenty-six-year-old printer. Though on a modest scale, the Providence shop was functioning adequately, the *Providence Gazette* was appearing regularly, and the Providence paper mill was beginning to be a source of regular profits. In Philadelphia Goddard was assured by Galloway that his election as Speaker of the Assembly meant the public printing was under his control and would be delegated to the new shop. The factor which had led to his failure in Providence was to be remedied in Philadelphia. Everything seemed auspicious.

Among the first things to be settled was the partnership agreement. Galloway introduced Goddard to his close friend Thomas Wharton saying that the Quaker merchant would become a third partner and lend his prestige, influence, and money to the business. Wharton greeted Goddard in true Quaker fashion, "Friend Goddard, I bid thee welcome." A discussion ensued about the actual articles of agreement, which were signed the first of December. At first Galloway and Wharton demanded a third each of the profits for their shares as a return for financing the new shop, but finally permitted Goddard to retain half the profits because neither financier wanted his connection known publicly. The agreement, preserved for us in *The Partnership*, provided that the expenses and proceeds of the new shop were to be divided into four parts, Goddard receiving two. It was explicitly stated that the printer was to manage the shop "without making any charge for his trouble, experience or knowledge." (No wonder Goddard later commented,

"Thus I purchased the Assembly's printing work.") The agreement was for fifteen years, beginning January 1, 1767. During this time the partners were to make "reason and justice the standard and rule of their conduct towards each other." William Goddard was "to keep a free press." The agreement concluded "that in case *Benjamin Franklin,* Esq; on his return to *Pennsylvania,* should incline to become a partner in the business aforesaid, that he shall be admitted as such, and in that case that the shares . . . shall be as follows, to wit, Two ninths thereof shall belong to *Joseph Galloway,* two ninths thereof to *Thomas Wharton,* two ninths thereof to *Benjamin Franklin,* Esq; and three ninths thereof to *William Goddard.*" Even though Galloway and Wharton seemed most interested in securing a newspaper in whose columns they could regularly contribute, they were taking no chances on missing any possible profits or losing the economic control of the business. Goddard himself was verbally assured that he was not to worry about money and not to stint himself in securing good and sufficient equipment. Because the shop was to be in the name of William Goddard, all the charges resulting from this generous credit were in one name. And this was true even when Galloway himself wrote to Strahan in London and ordered a supply of type to be sent to Goddard.

The first dispute among the three partners was over what was then called entrance money, the down payment necessary to make effective an annual subscription for a newspaper. Goddard proposed that one half the annual charge of ten shillings be required. Galloway and Wharton objected and forced the printer to yield with the result that no entrance money was required for the soon-to-be-published newspaper. Because of this the more subscriptions came in for the paper the more the paper began to go into debt.

During all this time William Franklin had been busy behind the scenes doing his bit to help get the business started. In particular he made the arrangements for the location of the shop. The governor told about his own activities in a letter to his father, dated November 13, 1766. After describing the refusals of Hall to print any of the articles given to him, he continued:

The Consequence is that your Friends (who would have set up a Press above a year ago, but that they did not know but you might chuse to be concern'd in the Printing Business on your Return) have at length engaged one Goddard, who served his Apprenticeship with Mr. Parker, to set up a Printing Office in Philadelphia & publish a Newspaper. Mr. Galloway, & Mr. Thos. Wharton, for his encouragement, have entered into Partnership with him & have agreed to advance what Money may be necessary. But as their Motive for doing this is not merely for the Sake of Profit, but principally to have a Press henceforth as open & safe to them, as Hall's & Bradford's are to the other Party, they have put it into their Agreement as I understand, that when you return you shall have it in your Power to be concern'd, if you chuse it, in the Place of one of them. The young Man has brought several good Founts of Letters with him, but his Press he was obliged to leave with his Mother, who carries on the Business at Providence. They therefore desired me to ask my Mother to lend them the old Press which Parker used here, & they would either buy it of you, or pay you what you thought reasonable for the Hire. My Mother told me she had no objection to my letting them have it, but she did not chuse to do it of herself, lest Mr. Hall might be displeased with her for it. At the same Time she said that she should be glad that the Printer would take the old House in which it was, as it stood empty & had not brought in any Rent for a great while. I accordingly let them have the Press, & they have agreed with my Mother to take your old House in Market Street. There is a new Mahogany Press there, which they seem Desirous to purchase if you incline to part with it, but I suppose they will write to you on the subject. What I have done is for the best, & I hope it will prove agreeable to you. There is, indeed, really a Necessity for their having a Press of their own, while their publick Affairs continue in their present critical situation, for it is with great Difficulty they can get Hall or Bradford to consent to print any Thing for them, & when they do some of the Proprietary Party are sure to have it communicated to them before it is published. Hugh Roberts, and many more of your old Friends, have determined to encourage the new Printer all in their Power, & to go about the several Wards to get subscriptions to the News-paper. The Members of Assembly will do the same in their respective Counties, & let him have all the Publick Work. So that I am in hopes that by the Time you return they will lay the Foundation of a very valuable Business, worth your while to be concerned in, if you should think it proper or convenient. But I am likewise in hopes that when you do return you will have something far better worth your Acceptance than that can possibly be made. However, as all Things in this Life are uncertain, it may not perhaps be amiss for you to have it in your Power to engage in this Affair.

I am, Honoured Sir,
Your dutiful Son
Wm. Franklin

By December 23, 1766, Goddard was ready to announce the forthcoming appearance of the *Pennsylvania Chronicle and Universal*

Advertiser in advertisements in both the *Pennsylvania Gazette* and *Journal.* Sarah Goddard must have been proud when she reprinted this notice in the *Providence Gazette* of January 24, 1767. The advertisement was immediately run off by Goddard as a broadside, the back of which he used as a type specimen sheet. The announcement, "Proposals," said that the first number was to "be given gratis" as an inducement for subscribers. Three principles were to guide the new paper: secrecy, freedom, and impartiality. (The last must have semed like utter hypocrisy to David Hall and William Bradford.) Goddard tried his best to put himself on good relations with his competitors in Philadelphia by stating his paper would give "the freshest Accounts of Such Occurrences as shall happen between Thursday and Monday." Both the *Gazette* and the *Journal* appeared on Thursdays, and Goddard was trying to imply that the Monday appearance of the *Chronicle* would merely supplement, not supplant, the two existing papers. The subscription and advertising rates were to be those already prevailing in Philadelphia.

From the extensive credit at his use and his own lofty ideas Goddard planned the setup of the *Chronicle* on the largest scale yet attempted by any newspaper printed in the colonies. The page was a large folio with four columns instead of the customary three. This scale of printing cost him an additional £200 a year for paper but fitted into his grandiose schemes. Modeling his plans upon the *London Chronicle*, Goddard tried to make his *Chronicle* the paper of his dreams. His goal was a paper that its readers would want to preserve in bound annual volumes in their libraries. Like a learned quarterly of today the pages were numbered consecutively from issue to issue. When a year was elapsed, the numbers could then be bound with an index to the whole. Each issue was to be dated for a full week, i.e., July 1 to July 8 instead of merely July 8. (Subsequent references give only the second of these two dates.) Goddard approached his goals near enough that the *Chronicle* was undoubtedly the best newspaper Philadelphia and perhaps the colonies had ever had.

The editorial plans were not the only ones to be made; the business of the newspaper must be set going. The publisher had promised that Philadelphia subscribers would have the paper delivered to their doorstep. Carriers therefore had to be hired. The postal system being what it was, Goddard had to employ his own riders for points outside Philadelphia. The bill of one of these riders, John Borrows, shows how much this cost Goddard. Borrows wanted £95, Pennsylvania currency, for carrying the *Chronicle* the sixty miles to New Brunswick, New Jersey, from January 27, 1767, to June 27, 1770, and the thirty miles to Trenton from June 27, 1770, to November 20, 1774. (That the *Chronicle* had ceased publication nine months before November seems not to have bothered Borrows, though it is quite possible he could not read what some one else had written for him.) The securing of subscriptions had also to be tended to, since the members of the Pennsylvania Assembly referred to by William Franklin were not as energetic as the governor thought they would be. The editor carefully organized part-time subscription agents. An advertisement in the August 17, 1767, *Chronicle* reveals how extensive this system was. All thirteen of the colonies are represented; the West Indies and Canada have agents; and even in London a coffee house would take in subscriptions. A summary tabulation of the numbers of these agents shows both the extent and thoroughness of this organization:

Canada	2	(Halifax and Quebec)
New England	11	
New York	6	
New Jersey	17	
Pennsylvania	18	
Delaware	4	
Maryland	8	
Va., S.C., N.C., Ga.	5	
West Indies	5	
London	1	
Total	77	

Probably the entire network of agents was not in operation by the date of the opening issue, but there was enough activity for the *Chronicle* to start with seven hundred subscribers and soon pass the thousand mark in circulation. Goddard was not only a good newspaper editor but a good circulation manager.

After all this fanfare the first number of the *Pennsylvania Chronicle* appeared January 26, 1767. The clean-cut appearance of its pages made the competing *Gazette* and *Journal* seem particularly sloppy in their editing. The notice "To the Public" was brief but quite confident in its tone. The actor David Douglas, who that same evening appeared at the New Theatre in Southwark in *Mourning Bride* and *High Life Below Stairs*, must have given his heartiest congratulations late that night when the actor and the printer adjourned to an oyster bar for mutual toasts and felicitations. Indeed the affairs of the shop were going forward so well that by the second issue Goddard was advertising for both a journeyman printer and an apprentice.

But not everybody was so pleased at the paper's immediate success, and particularly unhappy was David Hall. The day after the *Chronicle* first appeared Hall wrote bitterly to Franklin in London. Hall pointed out that the new printing office occupied quarters owned by Franklin and even used a press belonging to him. To add fuel to Hall's fire, the subscription agents had freely used the name of William Franklin in their appeals. Hall also smelled the hands of Galloway and Wharton. (Common gossip in Philadelphia was surprisingly accurate.) He said that some people reported Benjamin Franklin to be "a Partner in the House; but this, I will never allow my self to believe, having still, as I always had, the highest Opinion of your Honour, and know, that you will never forget that Clause of our Agreement, by which, tho' you are not absolutely prohibited from being any farther concerned in the Printing Business in this Place, yet so much is plainly implied." For a couple of paragraphs more Hall continued to attack the behavior of Governor Franklin.

Franklin, by this time informed by the letter from his son and another from Galloway about what was going on, replied on April 14 to Hall. He defended himself from the charges at some length:

> You are right in believing that I am not a Partner in Mr Goddard's Printing-House. It was set on foot without my Knowledge or Participation, and the first Notice I had of it was by reading the Advertisement in your Paper. I had indeed by the same Conveyance a Letter offering me a Share in it, which I declin'd accepting before my Return, not only because I did not well know the Person, but because I did not care to be again concerned in Business, unless on settling my Affairs when I got Home it should appear necessary for the Support of my Family. Indeed I had not the least Idea of any Agreement between you and I, either express'd or imply'd, as you say, in any of its Articles, by which I was "prohibited from being any further concern'd in the Printing Business in Philadelphia, after the Expiration of our Partnership." I have not

a Copy of our Articles with me here; but I am confident that if you examine them you will find this a Mistake. I could not possibly foresee 18 years beforehand, that I should at the End of that Term be so rich as to live without Business. And if this did not happen, it would be obliging myself to the hard Alternative of *Starving* or *Banishment*, since Threescore is rather too late an Age to think of going 'Prentice to learn a new Trade, and I have no other! This I say, not to justify my engaging with Mr Goddard, for I have not done it. And I hope I shall have no Occasion to do it. I know there must be a very great Sum due to me from our Customers, and I hope much more of it will be recovered by you for me than you seem to apprehend. When that is got in, I suppose I can use it in such a Manner, as that with my Office and the few Rents I have, my Circumstances will be sufficiently affluent, especially as I am not inclin'd to much Expence. In this Case I have no purpose of being again concern'd in Printing. But I may lose my Office, I may receive much less of my Debts than I hope for, I may find myself going behind-hand, and I am sure you would take no Pleasure in seeing me ruin'd, or oblig'd at my time of Life to quit my Country, Friends & Connections, to get my Bread in a strange Place, especially as my not following my Business could not hinder others from interfering with you. I am in short, so far from conceiving it possible that I should make such an Agreement tho' forgotten, that, on the contrary I believe such an Agreement was never made by any Man in his Senses.

Though this reply did not make Hall content, he had to accept it with as much grace as he could muster.

The perturbations of Hall are found in his correspondence during this year with William Strahan, under whom he had served his apprenticeship and by whom he had been recommended to Franklin. On January 31, five days after the *Chronicle* had first appeared, Hall told Strahan he would appreciate "your being punctual in sending the News Papers by every Opportunity, and getting your acquaintances at Bristol, Liverpool &c in England; and likewise . . . Dublin, Belfast, Cork, London Derry &c. If you have any Correspondence in these places, will be more wanted now than ever." Two months later, March 31, Hall repeated this request for additional foreign correspondence, adding a request for exclusives, "And I must repeat my Request, that you will write no Political Letters, or Letters of News, to any One but my self." Franklin's former partner was really worried about the new competition, which he realized was no mere flash in the pan. On April 30 Hall again complained to Strahan, this time stressing the nefarious activities of Governor

Franklin and his friends. "I must be crushed in order to make Way for another, who, they think, will be more condescending, and will implicitly obey their Commands; all under the Pretence of *preserving the Liberty of the Press.*" Goddard's "Proposals" obviously had a very hollow ring in the ears of his fellow Philadelphia printers.

On May 26 Hall, feeling not quite so "crushed" because he had picked up that portion of the public printing at the disposal of Governor Penn, not the assembly, wrote to his old master about one who within a few years figures prominently in Goddard's career in Philadelphia. ". . . Town [Benjamin Towne] had been down to Maryland, to see if there was any Opening for him there, on the Decease of Green the Printer in that Province, but that he had returned without Success. I also informed you, that he was gone to work with Goddard on great Wages [apparently Goddard paid his journeymen the highest wages in Philadelphia], as he said, but that his going to him was no Disappointment to me, as I never had any real Occasion for him, all the Time he worked with me, and if it had not been to serve him, I would not have employed him at all; and that I understood since he went away, that he had been with Mr Galloway, on his Return from Maryland, before I saw him." Though this is getting ahead of our story, the interview between Towne and Galloway does substantiate the charges later made by Goddard against Towne.

Oblivious to the petulant worries of David Hall, Goddard was busy with the multifarious activities of his shop and his newspaper, whose circulation was steadily climbing to its position as largest in all the colonies. Though polemics and controversy were the life-blood of this large circulation, Goddard did not forget that he was entertaining his readers as well as instructing them. For example, in the February 9 issue under the Philadelphia date-line he printed this item: "About a Fortnight ago, the Wife of an old Gentleman of this City, who is now upwards of 84 Years of Age, took her Flight from this World to the World of Spirits, and her Husband affectionately followed her to the Grave, on Crutches;—since which, he has had the Resolution to take into his Arms, by Marriage, a young vigorous Nymph of Twenty-five, who kindly consented to supply the Place of the deceased Matron. May they enjoy all *possible* nuptial Felicities!"

But such light pieces could not prevent the *Chronicle* from doing its work for the antiproprietary party. Among the goals of this group had been the rehabilitation of the reputation of the long-absent Franklin. This Goddard set out to do by reprinting various articles originally inserted in London newspapers by Franklin under different pseudonyms. The public was to be shown that, even though it had been unaware, the colony's representative had been busy promoting its affairs.

Accordingly, in the third number of the *Chronicle*, February 9, an essay signed "A Lover of Justice" set out to defend Franklin against the charges made several months earlier in Bradford's *Journal*. This article ended by a note from the editor saying that later issues of the *Chronicle* would reprint articles Franklin had written. A week later the first of these articles was featured on page one and prefaced by this sentence: "Agreeable to our Promise, we now lay before our Readers three of the Pieces wrote and published by Dr. *Franklin*, in Defence of *North-America*, and in Answer to the Writers who stiled themselves TOM HINT and VINDEX PATRIAE, extracted from several *English* News-Papers sent us by a Correspondent." This campaign to restore the damaged reputation of the doctor continued at intervals until June 9, 1769, by which time twenty-four different Franklin items had been published. There is, of course, no way of determining the effectiveness of this campaign since succeeding events restored Franklin's prestige among his fellow countrymen before his return to Philadelphia in May, 1775. However, the *Chronicle* campaign must have contributed something to the popularity enjoyed by Dr. Franklin when he again was in the colonies.

William Bradford was not the kind of man to whine about Goddard's success behind his back. Instead he boldly went into the attack in the columns of his *Journal*, and for several weeks Philadelphians had a real newspaper battle in their midst. While the battle was going on, Goddard in the *Chronicle* of April 13 traced its origin back to the defense of Franklin by "A Lover of Justice" on February 9. Various replies to this article were printed during the next few weeks in the *Journal* and the *Gazette*, but as yet nobody had to use dashes for the names he was calling his intended victims. However, dashes were soon to be the order of the day. A premonition of the language and events to come is seen in the March 9

Chronicle. As a good reporter, Goddard was becoming aware of the gossip going on though he still seemed unaware how the struggles of 1765 provided the real background for his own difficulties and Bradford's bitterness. Aware and yet unaware, Goddard with typical vehemence wrote: "As some *few* Persons, in this City, have taken the Liberty to asperse and vilify the Printer of this Paper, a Stranger to them, behind his Back, and have had the *great Resolution* to *whisper* a Threat that he should be *roughly handled*, for the Freedom of his Publications, that is, for daring to maintain the *Liberty of the Press*, he thinks proper just to *hint* to those *heroic Calumniators*, that such Behaviour only becomes *Assassins*;—and as to *Gentlemen*, who *may* conceive a Dislike to some of the Pieces in his Paper, he has no Doubt but *they* will judge with Candour of the Printer, and always pursue a more honourable Conduct."

This article was in the *Chronicle* on Monday, and Bradford made his reply on the following Thursday, March 12. In this article Galloway, "with a *Stamp* on his *left* shoulder," was connected with Americanus and Goddard must have had some thoughtful moments when he looked up the back issues of the *Journal* and discovered the significance of Americanus. The satire in the remark by the pseudonymous writer, Thomas Jackson, V.S., that the "Printer of the CHRONICLE . . . *keeps* a *free* and *impartial Press*" must have bitten in deeply as he conned the connotations of the word *keeps*. Cornered, Goddard could do nothing but defend himself in his next issue.

Galloway and Wharton were watching their newly established printer closely and compelled him to print in the March 23 *Chronicle* a lengthy attack on the various writers being featured in the *Journal*. This attack, signed Lex Talionis (the Biblical eye for an eye and tooth for a tooth), really blew things wide open. A copy of this issue in the Yale University Library has in Goddard's hand this note at the bottom of the page, "The Piece signed *Lex Talionis* was inserted in this Paper very much against the Printer's Inclination—to avoid Persecution from imperious tyrannical Party-men. W.G." Though this note was probably written years later, we discern the editor's contemporaneous discomfort in the apologetic sentences he wrote to preface Lex Talionis: "It is hoped the Publication of the following Piece will not be thought a Deviation from the original Design of the *Chronicle*, when the Occasion which has been given

for it, by a late Performance in another Paper, is considered.—
Besides, the Reader may be assured, that the Author of *this* Piece
has complied with the Printer's reasonable Demand, of making himself known to him, a Demand he shall always think necessary to
make in Writings of this Nature; and that if any Persons shall think
themselves aggrieved, the Publisher will not hesitate, on the same
Terms, to do them all the Justice that can be expected from a Press
established on Principles of *Secrecy, Freedom,* and *Impartiality,* even
tho' they should be the *very Persons* who have insidiously endeavoured to injure him (a feeble Effort!) by the grossest Misrepresentations." In contrast to the editor's tone Lex Talionis did not hesitate
to call Thomas Jackson a vile scoundrel and his opponents "Grub
Street Writing Gentlemen."

What hurt the young printer most among the reactions to this
piece was a letter he received over a month later from his mother,
still in Providence. In the first paragraph she warned her son:

It is with aching heart and trembling hand I attempt to write, but
hardly able, for the great concern and anxious fears the sight of your late
Chronicles gave me, to find you involved deeper and deeper in an unhappy
uncomfortable situation. In your calm hours of reflection, you must see the
impropriety of publishing such pieces as *Lex Talionis,* let the authors be
ever so great and dignified, for every one who takes delight in publicly
or privately taking away any person's *good name,* or striving to render
him ridiculous, are in the gall of bitterness, and in the bonds of iniquity,
whatever their pretences may be for it. The authors of such pieces
cannot be your friends, and I conjure you to let all such performances be
dropped from your otherwise credible paper. My spirit is moved within
me, dreading the direful effects that have too often sprung from such
insignificant trifling wrangles in the beginning. Oh my son, my only
son, "hearken to wisdom before it is too late—doth she not stand in the
streets, and in the high places? to you O men I call, and my voice is to
the sons of men—and also at the door of our hearts"—and its effects
would be righteousness and peace, if not opposed by our ungovernable
wills. I heartily wish it was within the reach of my faint efforts to convey
to you what threescore and almost ten years experience has taught me,
of the mere nothingness of all you are disputing about, and the infinite
importance and value of what you thereby neglect and disregard—a jewel
of inestimable value.—I know corrupt nature and our own wicked hearts
will prompt us to think—must I then bear such injurious treatment from
any person on earth!—Must I give up myself to be vilified and abused
by these men!—But remember, we are not under the OLD LAW OF RETALI-
ATION, an eye for an eye, &c. for ever blessed be our gracious Redeemer,

who has abrogated it, and substituted a much more glorious one in its place, no less than the law of universal love; and why should you, or any one else, try to revive what was disannulled above seventeen hundred years past? If such writers were but possest with the spirit of universal love, instead of revenge and resentment for affronts, they would pity and pray for their fellow-sinners, considering we all daily use our greatest benefactor with more ingratitude than one frail creature can another.

But the writers in the *Journal*, now abetted by the *Gazette*, did not wait a month to reply. The *Journal* of April 2 had an article, signed Philo Libertatis, attacking the "Delaware-crossing gentleman," i.e., Joseph Galloway. This was on Thursday, and on the following Saturday the dispute erupted into physical violence. William Bradford not only ran a printing business, but he also owned Philadelphia's most prominent tavern, the London Coffee House at the corner of Front and Market streets. Because of its location so near the docks the coffee house had become the center for information concerning boat sailings and other marine intelligence. (As a result the *Journal* featured more marine advertisements than any other Philadelphia paper.) It was therefore necessary for Goddard to visit the London Coffee House regularly to scan the postings by ship captains and brokers. On this Saturday he made his usual trip; and, as though expecting trouble, he carried a printer's cross, one of the tools of his trade. Within the tavern he soon found himself being attacked by Mr. Hicks, one of the writers of the articles in the *Journal*, and several of his friends. But let Goddard himself describe the incident, as he did in the *Chronicle* of April 13:

I was immediately surrounded by a number of persons unknown to me, with Mr. *Hicks* at their head, who became *grossly abusive*, and treated me with *great insolence*. He repeated the designs he had formed to *break my bones*, and that he had prepared a *suitable weapon* for his purpose. This, with many other insults I received from Mr. *Hicks* and his confederates, all which I bore with as much temper as I possibly could, on such an occasion. After Mr. *Hicks* had spit his venom to his satisfaction, against the author of *Lex Talionis*, and received the plaudit of his associates, who in their triumph treated me with language too indecent to retort, he went to another part of the house—I walk'd up towards the fire-side, and understanding that my letters were misrepresented, I expressed a wish, that those gentlemen of character, virtue and moderation, who with disgust had seen the infamous treatment I had met with, would hear those letters which were then the subject of conversation. Upon this, a person of Mr. *Hick's* party, unknown to me, came up, and order'd me about my business; I told him, I had as much business there as himself, and refused to be turn'd out of doors.—Without further ceremony he struck me, and having my *cross* in my hand, I essay'd to defend myself, not knowing how many I should have to encounter; but before I could get disengaged from my cloak, my assailant was entirely hid from me, and I found myself in the hands of *those men* that had before encompassed me with *malignity in their countenances,* who long struggled to obtain that instrument I would freely have resigned to one I knew; and, with Mr. *W. Bradford's* assistance, who *humanely* and *disinterestedly* lugg'd me by the hair, I was forced out of his doors in the most cruel manner, before my friends were sufficiently apprised of my critical situation, to afford me that relief which their inclination would have led them to have given me; while he who first assaulted me, was suffer'd to remain unmolested; so that six or seven men have the *merit* of forcing a single man out of the doors of a public house, and of gaining, as a trophy, to their *immortal honour,* a weapon that the *Gentlemen of the Faculty* would not call by any other name than a TOOTH-DRAWER.

The quarrel continued in the following Thursday's *Gazette* and *Journal.* Goddard's account of the London Coffee House incident was reprinted and followed by a brief note from William Hicks denouncing Goddard as an "infamous Rascal." The *Chronicle* of April 20 featured a new defense. This time Goddard boasted of the "solid satisfaction" he had in "gaining a very large Addition to my List of Subscribers." He also stated that though only three months old the *Chronicle* had the second largest circulation in the colonies. The *Gazette* and the *Journal* of the twenty-third had a letter signed Z attacking Goddard's "poison of scandal." The next *Chronicle* had in it a letter from Lex Talionis attempting to clear Goddard personally of any blame for what the pseudonymous author had written. Ten days later William Hicks wound up the quarrel by an article covering all the first page and running over into the second of the *Gazette* of May 7. Most of this article was taken up by an exchange of letters between Governor Franklin and Hicks, each giving different versions of a conversation between the two men. Hicks wanted to know the name of the author of Lex Talionis, and the governor refused to give it and denied having promised such information. The quarrel burned itself out at this point for want of any new fuel.

Though this particular dispute had died down, the feelings of the Philadelphia printers were still raw, and it took little to start them shouting for each other's blood. The *Gazette* and *Journal* of May 21 featured a letter signed W.Z. attacking the previous *Chronicle* for "asserting that the young Woman that was found drowned in the River Christiana, had, for some time, been under a melancholy Turn of Mind. The Delusion she was under was the very opposite Extreme." Goddard defended himself against the accusation of inaccurate reporting in his next issue of the twenty-fifth. W.Z. returned to the attack on the twenty-eighth. The last word was from Goddard on the first of June. It must be admitted that the conclusion of his article was well-nigh unanswerable and very effective. He quoted the famous passage in *Tristram Shandy* (one of his favorite books) in which Uncle Toby addresses a fly as he throws it out the window, "This World surely is wide enough to hold both thee and me." For almost three months the Philadelphia printers found their world wide enough.

The extensive circulation Goddard boasted of is evinced in several ways. An advertisement in his *Chronicle* could and did secure replies from all through the colonies. The following letter must have given the printer considerable satisfaction, coming as it did from his birthplace:

New London April 8th 1767

To Mr Thomas Wharton
Merchant in Philadelphia

Sir, In Mr Goddard's paper No 9 [March 23] I see that their is a Fire Engine Advertiz'd for Sale by Daniel Ellis Esqr and I want one of that kind very much. Should be very much Oblig'd to you to Ingage it for me on the lowest Termes you can (if it be a good One). In two or three days Capt Wm Harris will sail for your Place in a Small Sloop with Fifty or Sixty hogsheads of Molasses wich shall ship to you for to Dispose of for my Accountt & would have you ship me the Engine by his Return. Should be glad you'l write by the Return of the Post if I may depend on the Engine on accountt that I must git one made in Boston if this should be Disposed of before the letter comes to hand. Please to favour me with the Price Current of West India Goods & you'l oblige Sir Your humble Servant

Nathaniel Shaw Junior.

The increased business of the shop is also indicated by the additional employees hired by Goddard. On February 2 he advertised for both a journeyman and an apprentice. On April 27 a carrier of the newspaper to "the lower Part of this City" was demanded. Again, on May 4 the expanding business made it necessary to try to secure another journeyman, and the July 20 issue carried an advertisement for an apprentice. This last notice is interesting because it reveals quite a bit of what was expected of a printing apprentice in those days. "WANTED immediately, as an APPRENTICE to the PRINTING BUSINESS, an honest sprightly Lad, about 14 or 15 Years old, who can read well, and write a tolerable Hand, and understands something of Grammar."

Several of the journeymen who worked for Goddard later became printers on their own account. Typical of these is Isaac Collins, who in 1770 left the Philadelphia shop and moved to Burlington, New Jersey, where he took over the printing establishment formerly operated by James Parker, who had died a few months previously. Collins became immediately printer to the colony of New Jersey and later, then in Trenton, was printer to the state. Another future New Jersey printer in Goddard's shop was Shepard Kollock, whom Douglas McMurtrie calls a nephew of Goddard. Kollock may have completed his apprenticeship under Goddard, but of that we cannot be sure. After serving in the Revolutionary army, Kollock started New Jersey's second newspaper, the *New Jersey Journal*, at Chatham. In and out of Goddard's employment during all the seven years of his Philadelphia sojourn was Benjamin Mecom, the constant worry of his uncle Benjamin Franklin. William Franklin, probably in 1768, wrote to his father and well described the difficulties Goddard had with this flamboyant printer: "Cousin Ben Mecom is starving at Philadelphia and would have been, I suppose, in jail [for debt] by this time if it had not been for the assistance my mother and I have afforded him and his family. Goddard would have given 35 shillings a week [probably a high wage for a journeyman printer in the 1760's] to him if he would have worked as other journeymen do, but he insisted on coming and going just as he pleased, on which Goddard and he quarreled and parted." In 1769 Franklin reported, "There was nothing [for Mecom] to do but go back to journey work for William Goddard."

The shop's activities included not only the regular printing of the *Pennsylvania Chronicle* each Monday but numerous blanks, handbills, and pamphlets as well. On August 3, 1767, Goddard announced that he had finished the printing of the laws passed at the last session of the colony assembly. One of the promises made to him by Galloway was being fulfilled. Later Goddard, thinking his shop had not enough equipment, insisted that he had tried to turn this particular printing job over to Hall and Sellers but took it on at the insistence of Galloway. We suspect Goddard did not persist very long in his demurral.

The same issue that announced the completion of the printing of the colony's laws carried an advertisement amusing to us of the twentieth century even if the eigtheenth century took it for granted: "WANTED, A woman, to take the Care and Management of a Tradesman's House, who is a Bachelor. There are four or five Men and Boys to wash, mend and make for; the whole House-work she must do herself, and have no Children. Any such Person, being genteel and well recommended, may have good Wages, and live very happy. It is in a remarkable healthy large Country Town, one Day's Ride from Philadelphia. Inquire of the Printer hereof [the usual formula for a blind ad]. N.B. The Person will be wanted in a Month or five Weeks."

On August 17 Goddard printed a notice which he must have been proud to write and append "The Printer." He said: "The CHRONICLE . . . circulates in all the *English* Colonies on the *Continent*, the *West-Indies*, and the principal Cities in *Great-Britain* and *Ireland*—That it is honoured with the Subscriptions of most of the Gentlemen in *America* of superior Stations in Government, as well as of the first Distinction among the Learned; and that it has been favoured with many Pieces Religious, Moral, Philosophical, Instructive and Entertaining, by its learned and ingenious Correspondents, of whom, without just Imputation of Arrogance, it may boast of having a greater Number than any other Paper in *America*. . . . The quick Circulation of the Paper through all Parts of this Province, and the neighbouring Colonies, where it is as generally received as any Paper on the Continent, renders it an advantageous Vehicle for ADVERTISEMENTS."

Goddard's boasting of his large circulation irked his fellow Philadelphia printers, and Bradford was not slow to rise to the bait. The *Pennsylvania Journal* of August 27 contained a letter to the printer making fun of Goddard for calling the *Chronicle* an "infant bark," as he did in his first paragraph of the seventeenth. The article can only be described as mildly uncomplimentary, but Goddard could not let well enough alone and published lengthy replies on September 7 and 14, in which Pope is quoted three times and *Tristram Shandy* is again called upon for a last word. One slap at Bradford on the seventh must have found its mark and provided amusement for other colonial printers: "Bad Work in Printing, by the Typographers in America, is called Bradfordian." Having given Goddard's hair a vigorous pull the preceding April, Bradford did not think it necessary to stir up more of a tempest, and the matter was dropped. Thomas Bradford, the son of William, must have felt particularly chagrined when in a letter of June 3, 1768, he received a suggestion from Benjamin Rush in Edinburgh, "I think you had better alter the form of your newspaper in imitation of Goddard's." In spite of Goddard's always carrying a chip on his shoulder, he did know how to edit a good newspaper.

During September, 1767, the proprietor, John Penn, and the provincial assembly argued over Goddard's being selected to print the assembly laws. Penn demanded in a letter written on September 25 the "Right of Nominating or at least of sharing in the Nomination" of the printer. The next day the assembly, about to adjourn, met to consider the governor's letter. In typical legislative fashion a committee was appointed which reported that it did not have time to make a proper search of the "Precedents in Support of the Right of the House to appoint the Printer of the Laws and Proceedings of Assembly." It was recommended that the affair be held over until the next session of the assembly, when a more thorough search could be made, a recommendation that was accepted. Then in the next session neither the assembly nor the governor saw fit to raise the issue again, and John Penn lost his point by default. During the next three years Goddard received £223 8s. for the four times he printed the assembly's laws.

Not only was the print shop a busy place, but its proprietor found it possible to profit from a sideline in imitation of Franklin. We cannot date when Goddard started to sell paper to printers in other colonies, but we do know that paper from Hagey's mill in Philadelphia was being sold, with the printer acting as jobber, to Jamaica, Carolina, Newport, Providence, and New York. Among the reasons for Goddard's frequent trips through the colonies during the next three or four years may have been his attempts to take advantage of Philadelphia's being a primary center for the manufacture of paper.

On Wednesday, December 2, 1767, Goddard issued a special

number of the *Chronicle*, which he headed: "Having received a Series of Papers, intitled, '*Letters from a Farmer*,' &c. with several other Pieces from our Correspondents, all which we are importuned to publish as speedily as possible; and as we find there will not be Room in our *Monday*'s *Chronicle*, to insert the Whole—from a Desire to oblige, we are induced to give this Half-Sheet [two pages instead of the customary four], containing such of the Pieces as we could get ready, beginning with the *Farmer*'s first Letter, being, as he observes, on a Subject of the utmost Importance to the Welfare of our common Country." Immediately there follows Letter I, entitled "For the PENNSYLVANIA CHRONICLE. Letters from a FARMER in *Pennsylvania* to the Inhabitants of the *British* Colonies." Thus appeared the first number of the famous *Letters from a Pennsylvania Farmer* by John Dickinson. Why Dickinson sent the letters to Goddard we do not know, though the *Chronicle* circulation may have been sufficient reason. Later, in *The Partnership*, Goddard reported that at the time he had never even seen the author. Dickinson would have been familiar with the Philadelphia gossip about Galloway's and Wharton's connection with the *Chronicle*, but that was not enough to deter him from sending his manuscript to Goddard. The letters, twelve in all, were published one in each issue until the fifteenth of February. Hall and Sellers showed their realization of the importance of the series by rushing the first one into print the day after Goddard issued it. Bradford was slower, but he caught up a week later by printing both the first and second letters. Thereafter regularly on Mondays Goddard printed a letter which the *Gazette* and *Journal* clipped out and published on Thursday. Nor were the two older Philadelphia papers unique in doing this. All but three colonial newspapers printed Dickinson's defense of the colonial cause. No wonder Goddard wanted to hurry into print an edition of all the letters; even his mother urged it: "Your friend judge C[has?]e, and I think it would be a good scheme in you to print the *Farmer*'s Letters in a pamphlet, and that soon, as they appear to be the completest pieces ever wrote on the subject in *America*. They are universally admired here." No doubt Goddard would have printed this pamphlet but for the vigorous opposition of Galloway and Wharton. In *The Partnership* the publisher described their reaction in these words: "They were angry, they fretted, they *swore* and *affirmed*, that they [the letters] were too inflammatory for this latitude. . . . Mr. *Galloway* exclaimed, with a countenance expressive of the deepest envy, that they were '*damned ridiculous! Meer stuff! fustian! altogether stupid and inconsistent!— only a compilation by Dickinson and Thomson!*'" In an unsuccessful attempt to counterbalance the effect of Dickinson's letters Galloway and several of his friends inserted articles into the *Chronicle* signed by such pseudonyms as A Countryman, A Miller, Frank Meanwell, Jack White Oak, A Barbadian, A Country Farmer, and Son of Liberty (this list was compiled by Goddard himself). As Goddard frankly put it, the attitude of Galloway and Wharton "deprived me of a job that would have produced a handsome sum, which fell into other hands."

The disagreement among the partners over John Dickinson's letters, though it did not come to the attention of the public, was the first important break in the relations between Goddard and the two prominent Philadelphians. The story of this disagreement is practically the story of the remainder of Goddard's stay in Philadelphia. As early as June 22, 1767, the young printer had proposed in a letter to Galloway and Wharton that the partnership be discontinued after the two men had severely berated their junior partner the evening before. This was patched up by the offer of £500 to Goddard to set up a bookstore. Though the offer was never fulfilled, it did serve its purpose in keeping the partnership alive, because a certain amount of gullibility was part of Goddard's character. The affairs of the three partners continued in this state for several months. The circulation of the *Chronicle* kept expanding, particularly so while Dickinson's *Letters* were running in it, and Goddard's time and attention were fully occupied by the busy shop.

Goddard was trying to make his business financially secure. In the January 11, 1768, issue he announced that the *Chronicle* would be reduced from its expensive folio size to a more manageable quarto in an effort to save £200 a year on his paper bill. He justified the reduction of size in terms of its increased convenience to the readers. The quarto-sized paper began to be used the first of February, when the *Chronicle* ran to eight pages instead of the previously customary four. Another business problem was the collection of bills, especially from the many subscribers who had been receiving a newspaper each week for the past year. Though Goddard makes no point of how successful he was as a bill-collector, it is doubtful he took in most of his ten shillings. For example, at the Historical Society of Pennsylvania is preserved a receipt to Jasper Yates for a year's subscription to the *Chronicle*. In spite of the subscription's ending with the January 25, 1768, number, the actual payment of the ten shillings was not made until July 4, 1768, by which time no doubt Jasper Yates had received another six months' supply of Goddard's paper. Such late payment and even no payment at all were common practices.

In May, 1768, Galloway and Wharton entertained the printer one evening. They proposed to him that he should sell out his Providence shop and have his mother and sister move to Philadelphia. They promised to "take a genteel house" for the family and "advance a sum sufficient to set up her [Sarah Goddard] in a store of books and stationery." Money was also to be allowed to the mother "for her superintendence of family affairs." Goddard's feeling about the community of Providence is illustrated by one of the arguments he used against the proposition—that he wanted a place where he could retire should his Philadelphia attempt prove unsuccessful. The two senior partners managed to persuade the always sanguine Goddard of the sincerity of their offer and the benefits that would accrue to him. He wrote to his mother, who replied that she would prefer to remain in Providence, "for my life is almost at a close, and I can hardly think of removing so near the period of my days into a strange part of the world, to launch into a new set of acquaintance, and leave all my former ones, the companions of my youth, and the supporters of my old age, as well as my daughter, who seems by nature designed to take care of her mother in sickness, when wanted, which is not so properly the sphere of sons, and cannot be expected of them." Nothing daunted, William then traveled up to Providence and succeeded in doing in person what he had failed to do by letter. He relinquished his postmastership of Providence and sold the print shop and the *Providence Gazette* to John Carter, Mrs. Goddard's partner since September, 1767, for $550.00.

Shortly after his return from Providence, Goddard, his nerves apparently very much on edge, got into another quarrel with William Bradford of the *Pennsylvania Journal*. Goddard started the fracas with an article in the August 22 *Chronicle* berating Bradford by name in his capacity as local postmaster for keeping other newspapers from the hands of the tempestuous printer until their news items had to be used a week later. There is no need here to go through all the details of the charges, countercharges, and new countercharges which went on in all three Philadelphia papers for almost every issue in September. By persistence Goddard got in the last word on September 26, when he accused one of his attackers, John Stanly, of being a convicted forger from Virginia. Seemingly there was enough truth in this particular charge by Goddard that the other papers let the matter rest there.

In November Goddard got out his hatchet again over an article which had appeared in the Annapolis *Maryland Gazette* attacking him. One sentence of Goddard's defense is interesting to us because of what it tells about the *Chronicle*'s circulation: "I came to *Philadelphia* expressly to support the liberty of the press, and this I have maintained invariably to the satisfaction of the most numerous subscribers that any paper has on this continent." In 1770 we learn, in another connection, that the *Chronicle* had 2500 subscribers. Though the circulation in 1770 was greater than in 1768, it contrasts with the average circulation of a pre-Revolutionary colonial newspaper—500. Goddard may have bungled his finances and his personal relationships, but he knew how to run a good newspaper in an age when circulation was not to be helped by either the pathos and calculated masochism of contemporary comics or the jejune sensationalism of sex crime reporting. The colonial reader got his entertainment from a poem by Prior or Pope in the Poet's Corner and an essay by John Wilkes or Samuel Johnson on the front page. It must be admitted that added entertainment came from reading about Goddard's acrimonious disputes, enough that following each affray there was an immediate increase in circulation.

During this same month, November, 1768, Sarah and Mary Katherine arrived in Philadelphia from Providence. The *Providence Gazette* of November 5 gave Mrs. Goddard's farewell to the people of Providence, and a week later John Carter announced his assumption of the business. Goddard went to his partners for the fulfilment of the promise of a house but was disappointed again and had to secure living quarters for the family himself. Though Goddard regarded what he secured as no more than suitable, his partners disagreed with him. Fortunately *The Partnership* has preserved for us a conversation between William and Wharton. Even though the accuracy of the transcription is open to possible doubt, the dialogue is entertaining and revealing.

Wharton. William Goddard, we do not approve of thy proceedings.
Goddard. Why Mr. *Wharton?*
Wharton. Thee has taken a house very unsuitable to thee. How came thee to do it, without first consulting *Joseph Galloway* and myself?
Goddard. It is a very convenient house, Sir, and a good neighbourhood. I like it very much Sir.
Wharton. That is not what I mean—I tell thee *William,* we disapprove of the proceedings.
Goddard. This Mr. *Wharton* you might have prevented, by an attention to your *solemn* promise.
Wharton. I tell thee Friend *Goddard, thee has* done wrong—and *thee shall* suffer for it. A house in an alley would answer thy purpose well enough.
Goddard. Mr. *Wharton,* if you have no respect for my friends, I will show them that I have; and as we did not come out of an *alley,* we will not be driven into one by Mr. *Wharton.* [We must remember that Goddard always regarded himself as a patrician.]
Wharton. Very well, young man! *thee shall* smart for this.
He retires, comes again, and renews the dialogue.
Wharton. I have something more to say to thee.
Goddard. Very well, Mr. *Wharton,* I shall attend to you.
Wharton. Friend *Goddard,* I have been told *thee has* removed a press into thy mother's house, which is a proceeding I very much dislike.
Goddard. I did this to oblige my mother, Sir, who requested me to let her have a press for the printing blanks and small work, while I conducted the large.
Wharton. William Goddard, thee has sinister views.
Goddard. Mr. *Wharton* I have no views but such as are upright, and my intention, and that of my friends, is only to serve the company.
Wharton. I am confident *thee intends* to set up a press *independent* of us—therefore, without multiplying words, I order thee *William Goddard,* to bring that press immediately back. *Thee shall* do it, or we'll take measures that shall be unwelcome to thee.
Goddard. I shall advise with my mother, and if it is her mind that I comply with your request, I will gratify you—and on no other terms.
Wharton. See that *thee* do'st it.

To appease the wrathful Wharton, Sarah Goddard returned the press to the shop. By this time she was a woman in her seventies and doubtless would have preferred the quieter pace of her own household to the inevitable noise and confusion of her son's establishment. Her difficulties in adjusting to life in Philadelphia are shown in a letter she wrote to her sisters in New England: "I have been much indisposed this winter yet through the goodness of God I am in a better State of Health then I have been for Sometime when I first came to this City the Air and Climate did not Seem to Agree with me if I Stay I hope it will become more Natural. . . . Katey is now under preparation for the Small Pox and Expect her to be inoculated Some day this week."

Interesting though it would be, rarely can we follow in any detail the process by which a printing job in those days was negotiated, seen through the press, and finally paid for. Fortunately we can more or less do so for some printing Goddard did for the Library Company of Philadelphia in 1769. On March 13 the Library Company voted to absorb another subscription library, the Union Library Company. This absorption created the task of recataloguing and relabeling the newly acquired stock. On June 13 at a meeting of the directors of the Library Company a seven-man committee was appointed. The seven men quickly chose a two-man subcommittee "to agree with some Person to print six thousand Labels to be fix'd in the Books, and Ten thousand Notes for the Use of the Library." On July 10 agreement for this printing job with William Goddard was reported. By October 30 the committee could report that the labels were all printed and part of the notes completed. On April 9, 1770, "The Committee for procuring Notes for the Use of the Library, report that they have compleated that Business." Finally, on May 21, 1770, the secretary recorded: "William Goddard having produced his Account for printing Labels, Notes &c: amount'g to £20.3.6 from which having deducted £10 for a Share in the Library, which he agreed to take, an Order was Drawn on the Treasurer for the remainder, being £10.3.6 & the Secretary is ordered to make out a Certificate & deliver it to said Goddard." Three types of labels were printed, different only in the ornamentation, for the Library Company. The job for printing six hundred catalogues did not go to Goddard but went to Joseph Cruikshank, from whose bill another ten pounds was deducted for a library membership. As Goddard received his certificate of membership from the secretary, he might well have remembered the action of the Providence Library Company, which in 1763 had voted him a free membership with no printing obligations attached.

But ten pounds from the Library Company was not enough to

remove Goddard's financial troubles. During 1768 Goddard had printed bills for the *Chronicle* and sent them to his subscribers. In *The Partnership* Goddard states that he was compelled to bill his customers because his partners had failed to provide him with any ready cash. Apparently Galloway and Wharton intended to keep Goddard in debt, allowing him only enough money to maintain the paper, so that the printer would remain under their thumb. One of the journeymen in the shop, Benjamin Towne, was a representative, according to Goddard's accusation, of the two older men. This charge is partially substantiated by the remarks made by David Hall in his previously quoted comments on Towne. Benjamin Towne, whose name will occur frequently in this chapter, had a variegated career as a printer. He was never known for the strength of his principles, nor was he clever enough to take advantage of his own unscrupulousness. After leaving Goddard in 1770, he practically disappears from sight for four years, probably working as a journey-man. In 1774 he started under his own name a printing establish-ment in Philadelphia. At the outbreak of the war he was printing a tri-weekly paper, the *Pennsylvania Evening Post*, the city's first evening paper. When the Americans controlled Philadelphia, he was pro-American; when the British were in control, Towne was among the most vociferous of the anti-Americans. The British not remaining in Philadelphia, Towne found himself *persona non grata* to both sides. John Witherspoon took advantage of the situation and forced the shilly-shally printer to print "The humble Con-fession, Declaration, Recantation, and Apology of Benjamin Towne, Printer, in Philadelphia." At one place in the ludicrous "Confes-sion" Towne is made to say, "But I unfortunately became an under-strapper to the *famous* Galloway in his *infamous* squabble with Goddard, and did in that service contract such a habit of meanness in thinking, and scurrility in writing, that nothing *exalted* . . . could ever be expected from me." A sentence towards the end gives at least a physical description of Towne: "I hope the public will con-sider that I have been a timorous man, or if you will a coward from my youth, so that I cannot fight—my belly is so big that I cannot run—and I am so great a lover of eating and drinking that I cannot starve." Thanks to Towne's ability to change sides rapidly, the *Pennsylvania Evening Post* was the only paper in Philadelphia to maintain continuous publication during the war. In 1783 the paper was made into a daily, the first daily newspaper in America, but it lasted only another year before disappearing. Towne died in poverty in 1793 in Philadelphia.

In December, 1768, Goddard had to make a trip to Connecticut and Rhode Island to wind up his affairs there, particularly to collect "considerable debts." Sarah on the seventeenth of December deeded to her son her remaining interest in the property of her late husband, Dr. Giles Goddard, in return for which William agreed to allow her support from his Philadelphia shop. Also a debt of William to the mother of £109 resulting from the Providence printing establishment was to be wiped out. Most of Goddard's business on this trip was therefore in New London, where he wanted to sell various items of property belonging to the estate of his father. Before leaving, William placed the shop "under the management of Mr. *Towne*, subject to the superior direction of Mrs. *Goddard.*" So many of the annual subscriptions fell due in January that Goddard wanted to make sure the payments would not fall into the hands of Galloway and Wharton. Also there was a commitment to print the votes and proceedings of another session of the colony assembly. So that the work would not be all under the supervision of the not too competent Towne and because he did not have a sufficient number of figures in his type-cases, Goddard hired Dunlap to print a portion of the proceedings. The sojourn in New England lasted almost three months. Goddard could neither collect much from John Carter, just starting for himself, nor sell the principal piece of property in New London. (The colonies were in an economic depression in the latter 1760's after the Treaty of Paris in 1763 ending the Seven Years' War.) On his return the printer found that, though Dunlap had finished his portion of the government printing, Towne was still not through. Goddard had to pay a £25 penalty for a late printing, but he hurried the task through to completion.

On March 7, just after his return, Goddard spent the evening with Galloway and Wharton. They complained about many things in the operation of the shop, including the failure of Towne to be in complete charge during Goddard's absence. Finally they demanded that the young printer either buy out their shares or sell out his own altogether, and he must make up his mind in three days. In no financial position to think of buying and with a low stock of paper on hand, Goddard tried to delay matters by a letter the next day. In this letter he offered to buy out Galloway and Wharton if they would accept a three-year bond for everything they had put into the business, though he would not take as a partner a "representative" of Galloway and Wharton. After a few weeks of squabbling the upshot was that Goddard found himself unable to keep Galloway and Wharton from selling their shares in the business to Towne. Since there could be no pretense of Towne's having any money, he nominally assumed a debt for £526 to the two retiring partners, payment to be taken out of income from assembly printing. The new articles of partnership were signed on May 19, 1769.

William had been trying hard to avoid the financial trap set by Galloway and Wharton with the resulting partnership with Towne, whom he despised. On May 11 he was in Bristol, New Jersey (at Mr. Haight's), and tried to borrow one hundred pounds from John Smith, a prosperous Quaker of Burlington. Smith had been a subscriber to the *Chronicle* from the very first issue. Not only was Smith a subscriber but he was one of Goddard's most frequent literary contributors. Under the pseudonym of Atticus, he wrote seventy non-political essays starting with the *Chronicle*'s second issue in February, 1767, and continuing until August, 1770. Over three weeks before the first appearance of the *Chronicle* Goddard had written to Smith thanking him for his subscription and requesting the Burlingtonian to write articles for the paper. (Possibly Goddard had learned of Smith's literary proclivities during his association with James Parker.) Though the two men had not met by 1769, on August 11, 1768, Goddard had replied to a request from Smith saying that he would collect certain tombstone inscriptions "both in this & the other Provinces." Writing from Bristol on May 11, 1769, Goddard said that in return for the hundred pounds he would "undertake to reprint the Numbers of Atticus, in a handsome Volume, for the good of Mankind for which they were designed; & will make you a Present of as many as you may want for yourself & Friends." Apparently Smith turned Goddard down, for the following day, May 12, the printer again wrote to Smith, apologizing for disturbing him so soon after the death of a child. A week later Goddard signed the agreement with Towne, though Towne's name does not appear on the colophon of the paper until November 20.

During most of the second half of 1769 Goddard was again in

New England. So worried was he about the affairs of the shop and the malevolence of Towne under the direction of Galloway and Wharton, who had not as yet given any written release to Goddard for the former partnership, that on July 16 he signed an agreement formally turning over the management of the shop during his absence to one of the journeymen, Theophilus Cossart. In September Goddard was back in Philadelphia with an unnamed friend, who wanted to buy Towne out. Towne offered to accept £500 for his share but demanded that the assembly business go with him. This demand effectually put an end to the offer, and Goddard and his friend returned to New England. During the rest of the year he remained there trying to wind up his affairs in New London and Providence. He may have collected from John Carter at this time since he speaks of returning to Philadelphia with six hundred dollars in his possession.

It must have been during this trip and with some of the six hundred dollars that Goddard arranged for the purchase and manufacture of what is thought to be the first printing press made in America. The *Boston News-Letter* of September 7, 1769, printed the first notice of it: "We are informed that Mr. Isaac Doolittle, Clock & Watch-Maker, of New Haven, has lately compleated a Mahogany Printing-Press on the most approved Construction, which, by some good Judges in the Printing Way, is allowed to be the neatest ever made in America and equal, if not superior, to any imported from Great-Britain: This Press, we are told, is for Mr Goddard, of Philadelphia, Printer." In the preface, dated February 12, 1770, to Volume III of the *Chronicle* the printer placed an N.B. "An elegant Mahogany Press, made by an ingenious Watchmaker, at *New-Haven*, is just received from thence." In spite of all the difficulties the business of the shop and the circulation of the *Chronicle* were continuing to increase.

No doubt one of the chores Goddard had to attend to in New England was the winding up of his affairs as postmaster of Providence. It was probably in connection with a debt he had contracted to the postal system that on December 15, 1769, he and his sister signed a bond to Benjamin Franklin, who as chief administrator of the colonial postal system had had to make good on Goddard's debt. The bond, the standard one of the period, provides that if the sum of sixty pounds is not paid within six months then one hundred and twenty pounds shall be collected. At Franklin's death this bond was willed to his son-in-law, Richard Bache, though apparently never collected.

Early in January, 1770, Goddard was in New York, visiting friends there on his way south. He picked up a letter from his mother written on December 23. She condoled him for his various troubles but assured him the *Chronicle* was daily getting new subscribers and once everything was cleared up would be able to support them. The very next day a friend wrote him the news of his mother's death on the fifth and begged him to return as soon as possible. Mary Katherine was particularly anxious for his return because Towne was threatening to take away office records and start his own newspaper.

Mrs. Sarah Goddard died on Friday and was buried the following Sunday, the seventh, in Christ's Church Burial Ground at 5th and Arch streets. There is no doubt of the esteem she was held in by many people. The most complete account of her life and personality appeared in the January 22, 1770, *New-York Gazette*, reprinted in the February 10th *Providence Gazette*, as an anonymous letter "To the Printer." The writer, saying he was "no relation to the family, nor very intimately acquainted" (possibly either John Holt or James Parker) gives a brief summary of her family and her life. The eulogistic article concludes: "Her uncommon attainments in literature, were the least valuable parts of her character. Her conduct through all the changing trying scenes of life, was not only unblameable, but even exemplary—a sincere piety, an unaffected humility, an easy agreeable chearfulness and affability, an entertaining, sensible and edifying conversation, and a prudent attention to all the duties of domestic life, endeared her to all her acquaintance, especially in the relations of wife, parent, friend and neighbour. The death of such a person is a public loss, an irreparable one to her children!" Such a lengthy obituary was unusual in colonial newspapers.

The death of the mother, though it relieved some of the more immediate financial problems, by no means made life easy for William. An illustration of his difficulties is this anecdote in *The Partnership*:

On the death of my mother, he [Joseph Galloway] paid my sister a visit; and after condoling with her for the great loss she had sustained, for which he expressed the utmost concern, . . . he pulls a paper from his pocket, containing an estimate of the value of my business, and by a *false view* of it, endeavoured to prevail on my sister to sell it for a trifle; for says he, "your brother will not, he cannot return here—you have no friends here—you would live much happier in *New-England*—and may make something for yourself by a sale of this interest. You shall be paid annually a certain sum to be agreed on." My sister saw his baseness, and that he was a man who could smile with a dagger in his hand, told him that she knew the business was very valuable, and that she should listen to no such proposals. To this she generously added, that although by the sudden death of my mother, one half of the interest became hers, by law, yet she would give it all up to me, as it was designed for me. Mr. *Galloway* represented it a *losing business*, and was so *kind* as to wish to take it off my hands, to carry it on himself, to prevent my being a further *sufferer*. I have it not in my power, on this occasion, to make him a *suitable* return for his *benevolence*; it must therefore, like his other *virtue*, be its own reward.—After all this *kindness* and *generosity*, this *jewel of a man*, finding my sister deaf to his council, came no more to shew his *friendship* and *regard*—but set his *tools* and *emissaries* to work, to blast my reputation, and ruin my interest in this province.

The preface to Volume III of the *Chronicle*, already quoted from, confirms the sister's assumption of Sarah Goddard's financial interest in the print shop.

Though the affairs of the shop became more and more involved as Towne tried his best to ruin Goddard (and perhaps it was to escape these very involvements), the ever-hopeful printer during the early part of 1770 tried to expand his business to other towns. In a letter to Isaiah Thomas, written April 22, 1811, just after Thomas had published his *History of Printing*, Goddard recalls: "W.G. [William Goddard] contemplated the Establishm't of a Press at Al[exandria] in the Beginning of 1770—but the Death of his invaluable Parent, Sarah Goddard, uniting with other misfortunes, checked his promising Plan in the Bud. W.G. also made preparation for opening a Printing House in Norfolk—but his Plan was defeated by untoward Events."

The kind of trouble Goddard was having with Towne at this time is well shown by an incident narrated in *The Partnership*:

My enemies had made themselves acquainted with this affair [a debt owed by Goddard], no doubt by means of my mother's and my own private letters, which were intercepted and broken open, so that all my private affairs became known to those who were endeavouring to destroy my fairest hopes in life, and gave them an opportunity to wound me, before I could put myself in a posture of defence. Two letters, one from, and the other to, my mother, were accidentally found in Mr. *Towne*'s apartment, broken open, where he had concealed them for months, in a repository of his own.—This was judged an excellent opportunity to destroy me. The plan was fixed at once, and Mr. *Towne* was to be the *traitor*. He therefore neglects finishing the *Chronicle*, in order to bring me to the office; and the late publication he could, as he had often done, impute to me; and if I came to finish it, as he expected, he could bring the sheriff upon me, and the point would be settled; and he could take possession of the office, in behalf of his masters, and fix their standard there. About 3 o'clock, Monday afternoon, finding Mr. *Towne* absent, and the *Chronicle* not published, I went into the office, and soon put it in a way of publication. In the mean time, Mr. *Towne* comes to the door, which was fastened, in order to keep out the people, who were continually coming for the paper. Finding me there he goes to the *German* church, where the sheriff was attending a funeral. He there hung over the pew door, in which the sheriff sat, till the solemn service was ended, then followed him to the edge of the grave, and after the corpse was deposited, this *perfidious man* whispered the sheriff in the ear—*"Don't you want to see Mr.* Goddard? *I will, if you please, take you to him*![”] The sheriff said he wanted to speak with me, on some business, and went with him to the office. Mr. *Towne* suddenly bursts open the door and says—*"There he is, Mr.* Redman![”] While this gentleman was going toward the fire, Mr. *Towne* snatches up the form that I had been preparing, and which I had just left, (to wait on a gentleman of my acquaintance, at my dwelling-house) and ran off with it, and, as I understand, put it in the possession of the JUNTO, who lay on their arms all that night. My people thinking that Mr. *Towne* acted by legal authority did not oppose him.—The sheriff soon went home. My sister waited on him, to know wherefore he took away my materials. He behaved with the humanity and politeness of a christian and a gentleman, assured my sister he had no hand in it, and laid open the treachery of my partner, declaring, if he knew where to find him, he would recover the form, if possible. He seemed to entertain a proper idea of this unjustifiable proceeding. My sister then asked him, whether he had any demands upon me; he said he had nothing but a bill of cost, which had occurred (by means of Mr. *Towne*, and his patrons) in my absence.—This was immediately discharged— And as my sister was administratix to my mother's estate, she thought proper to advertise the city of Mr. *Towne*'s conduct. This alarmed the *fugitive* so much, that he came to my sister, and said—*"For God's sake, suppress the advertisement, and I will bring back the form.—It has played the devil with me."*—This was done, and the paper was published.

A second theft of the forms was made by Towne, and Goddard had to go to his partner's rooms to get them back. Finally during the spring Towne absented himself from the shop altogether. Lawsuits were threatened, and Goddard had to raise bail for himself. At the end of May Goddard learned that the individual whose absence in Europe had prevented his winding up the affairs in New London had returned, so he made a quick trip northwards and finally settled the sale of the property.

Not too long after Goddard's return to Philadelphia Towne erupted into print, and the whole business soon came to be the gossip of the city. Towne was attempting, by means of an advertisement in the *Pennsylvania Journal* of July 12, 1770, to have as many as possible of the subscribers pay their money to him:

Whereas a partnership was some time ago entered into between WILLIAM GODDARD and BENJAMIN TOWNE, which, on experiment, is found to be inconvenient, I, the said BENJAMIN TOWNE, do therefore for legal as well as expedient considerations, decline the connection and desire that no person in future will rely on my credit as a partner in their contracts and dealings with the said William Goddard.

And whereas a person is appointed, on behalf of the principal creditors of the press to receive so much of the subscription money due from the inhabitants of the city and districts for the Chronicle as will discharge his debt, the said Benjamin Towne therefore can only desire the subscribers for the said paper, in other places, to pay their subscription money to him (at Mrs. Marsh's in Second street, near Christ Church) as he has been a considerable sufferer by the partnership, and only wishes to have the company's debts paid.

July 12.   BENJAMIN TOWNE.

The *Chronicle* of the following Monday, July 16, said nothing in reply to this notice, but Towne's name was dropped from the colophon, which read, "Philadelphia: Printed by William Goddard, at Market-Street, next Door to the Post-Office." But Goddard, not one to be silent for long, had his say in an article in the *Journal* of the nineteenth. The article, much too long to quote here, took up in detail the "absolute falsehoods" of Towne's notice and attacked, though not by name, the "two party men" behind Towne. The first sentence will suffice to give the flavor of the article, whose tone is surprisingly mild for the usually vituperative Goddard: "It has been my great misfortune to be concerned in business, for some time past, with a very unworthy man, under the name of *Benjamin Towne,* formerly a journeyman in my office, a person very little known here, till he was drawn from obscurity to be made a scape goat of his superiors, to bear off their iniquity."

A week later Towne returned to the attack in the *Journal* of the twenty-sixth by announcing that an answer to Goddard would shortly be published. This answer was printed on July 31 as a two-page broadside, entitled "To the PUBLIC, and particularly the kind Customers of the PENNSYLVANIA CHRONICLE, &c." Goddard was described in typical eighteenth-century fashion: "The *hot temper* and *choleric disposition* [not far from the truth] of my *unhappy* partner, *William Goddard*, incapacitates him from reasoning, with *coolness* and *decency*." The tirade continues for most of the two folio pages.

The day after Towne's broadside was printed Goddard had one of his own in the hands of the much entertained Philadelphia readers. Goddard showed that he was no mean hand at invective by writing this opening sentence: "THE JUNTO, after several *private* Meetings and Adjournments at the *Theatre of Scandal*, in Fourth-Street, during *two long Weeks* past, and a prodigious *Waste* of Paper, and much *Inkshed*, have *at last* sent forth one *Benjamin Towne* with a STINK-POT in his Hand, full charged with fulsome Panegyrics on their own *dear selves*, and the most infamous Falshoods and Misrepresentations that ever disgraced Humanity, calculated for the inhuman Purpose of poisoning the Minds of the Public, to the Prejudice of my Character." Actually Goddard's handbill was more of an "Advertisement," as he entitled it, than anything else. What he was advertising was the forthcoming appearance of a pamphlet defending himself from the accusations made the day before. Considering that he had only just thought of writing this, the contents Goddard gives for his defense constitute a surprisingly accurate statement of what was eventually published. He says: "I have now only, on this Occasion, to beg the Favour of the Public candidly to suspend their Judgment respecting my Conduct, till I can lay a complete State of my Case before them, which I am now preparing for the Press, under the Title of 'An historical Account of the Rise and Progress of the PENNSYLVANIA CHRONICLE, &c. wherein the Conduct of *Joseph Galloway*, Esq; and Mr. *Thomas Wharton*, SENIOR, my late Partners, is fairly stated, and properly exposed; including their Attempts to prostitute and enslave my Press, to the Exclusion of the *Farmer's Letters*, which *they* judged too *inflamma-*

tory for this Latitude, and the Admission of such Pieces only as abused *their* Enemies, and served their own ambitious *Party Purposes* —and in which *Benjamin Towne*, the present *Favourite, I. H-t*, alias *Jack Traveller*, and some other under Characters will appear in their native Colours.'—This Work will contain the Articles of Co-partnership between *Galloway, Wharton* and *Goddard*, a *remarkable* Dialogue between the two latter, and some curious Anecdotes, &c. &c." No longer was there vague talk about "two party men" or the "duumvirate," as Goddard had phrased it on July 23 in the *Chronicle*; Galloway and Wharton were now named. Tongues in Philadelphia must have wagged furiously.

On August 3 in both the *Gazette* and *Journal* Towne printed a last reply before disappearing from the scene. In this article he denied that anyone besides himself had written his broadside of July 31. What probably worried Goddard more was his request for subscription money from *Chronicle* readers, though the number of those obedient to Towne's request was apparently very small. Goddard printed a notice in the *Chronicle* of September 3 assuring subscribers and advertisers that all the firm's books were in his possession. He dated his partnership with Galloway and Wharton as lasting until May 19, 1769. The Towne connection lasted from that date until February, 1770, when "Mr. Towne . . . eloped from his business." Inevitably Towne came in for some more abuse.

An event which may or may not have anything to do with what has just been narrated is the announcement in the *Chronicle* of August 20 of the moving of the print shop from its location on Market Street near Front to Arch Street, "about mid Way between Front and Second Streets, on the North-Side, (a few Doors below Messrs. Benezet and Bartow's Store)." The colophon on the last page of each issue hereafter reads: "Philadelphia: Printed by William Goddard, in *Arch-Street*, between *Front* and *Second Streets*."

The only reply of Galloway and Wharton to their names being broadcast was, in true merchant fashion, their sending Goddard a bill for £38 17s. 6d. This was one from William Strahan in London for various English magazines and the *London Chronicle*. Goddard's account in *The Partnership* is this: "I sent a lad to Mr. *Galloway*, with a written message, that *I should be glad to converse with him on business*. He said he would not—he had *no business with me*, I then sent to know, as he had '*no business with me*,' why he sent in an account against me. He said he had paid the money in *England*, and would be repaid. I gave myself no further trouble about the matter, and am determined never to pay a farthing of it, until Messrs. *Galloway* and *Wharton* step forth and discharge their debts, when I shall willingly pay one half of that account." On August 21, 1772, Strahan complained in a letter to Franklin that he had not been paid by Galloway (thereby refuting Galloway's remark to Goddard) for his debt and others for types, in all amounting to £172 15*s*. 2*d*. He had already written to Philadelphia about this on December 6, 1770, and again on August 7, 1771. Finally in this letter he asked Franklin to help him collect. "It is hard I should suffer by the Madness and Ingratitude of Goddard whom I never had the least Concern with. It was Mr. Galloway's Order that I obeyed; and to him I look for my Reimbursement." Possibly Strahan was able to collect in the 1780's when Galloway was a resident Loyalist in London and a pensioner of the Crown. Galloway then lost most of the arrogance Goddard and others of his colonial contemporaries complained so much of.

During latter August and early September Goddard was busy writing his announced publication as Philadelphians eagerly awaited the promised scandal against two of the city's most prominent and wealthy burghers. Finally on September 17 the *Chronicle* advertised: "Just published, and to be sold at the printing-office, in Arch-Street, between Front and Second Streets, THE PARTNERSHIP: OR THE HISTORY of the Rise and Progress of the Pennsylvania Chronicle, &c. wherein the Conduct of JOSEPH GALLOWAY, Esq; Speaker of the Honourable House of Representatives of the Province of Pennsylvania, Mr. THOMAS WHARTON, sen. and *their Man* BENJAMIN TOWNE, my late Partners, with my own, is properly delineated, and their Calumnies against me fully refuted. . . . Number II of this History is in the Press, and will be published as speedily as possible." The second part or "Number" was released on September 28, Goddard wanting to get it out before the Pennsylvania Assembly elections on the first of October. The announcement in the October 1 *Chronicle* for this second part says that a second edition is "now in the Press." This second edition was apparently published October 8, a date given at the end of an advertisement in some of the extant copies of the pamphlet. By October 29 the printer of the *Chronicle* could advertise that some of the third "edition" were available in the print shop. No wonder in the copy of *The Partnership* that late in life Goddard sent to Isaiah Thomas (now in the possession of the American Antiquarian Society) he wrote: "Several Editions of this Work were published, & produced, by a rapid Sale, many Hundred Dollars." It may well have been the acquiring of these dollars that prompted the printer to flirt with the idea of establishing a branch in Norfolk. Altogether several thousand copies of his seventy-three page pamphlet must have been printed.

On Election Day, October 1, Goddard saw the *Chronicle* through the press, announcing there that his readers could find him at the polls, and then went to do what he could against the election of Galloway to the assembly. In this issue he said the "freeholders and freemen" will only vote for "Men of real Merit," obviously not including Galloway. The article continued: "Alarmed at this noble Resolution, AMERICANUS, we hear, in a Panic, mounted his Galloway [that Galloway was the name of a breed of horses provided this pun], and fled to Bucks, in order to get into the Assembly, even, to use his own Words, if he should 'come in at the *back Door.*'" The election verified this prophecy, Galloway being elected from his country residence in Bucks County, not from Philadelphia as he had been before. Though there are no copies extant, apparently an anonymous broadside defending Galloway against Goddard's attack was circulated just before the election. The *Chronicle* of October 8 greeted the newly elected member from Bucks County with this welcome:

On Thursday the —*famous* AMERICANUS, who, on Monday last, was *properly distinguished* by the virtuous and discerning Freeholders of this City and County, arrived in Town, on his *much-jaded* Galloway, from Bucks (whither he had precipitately fled, as mentioned in our last) with the *great* and *important* News, that he had by a *masterly Stroke* in *Politics* obtained a Seat in the Assembly as a Representative for that County—so now that great '*Friend to Liberty*' still '*soars* ALOOF *on the Wings of Fame and Fortune,*' (as his Apology [an apparent reference to the broadside with Galloway's defense] expresses it) regardless of those who should *presume* to assert that he (a Non-resident) *smuggled* himself into the House at the '*back Door,*' contrary to the Tenor of the Bill he once drew up in order to deprive a Non-resident Member for another County of a Seat in the Assembly.

Affairs of the *Chronicle*'s belligerent editor continued along after this outburst at a reasonably even keel. To show his opposition to

British actions and to whatever Joseph Galloway favored, Goddard dropped from the flag of his paper on January 28, 1771, the cut of the royal arms. As we know, Galloway was a supporter of Lord North's policies and an opponent of colonial political attitudes.

In his advertisement for *The Partnership* on October 29, 1770, Goddard had stated, "The Narrative of Mr. Galloway's Election for Bucks County is received, and will be laid before the Public in due Season." This promise was fulfilled by a notice in the *Chronicle* for July 29, 1771, announcing that Goddard had just published and was selling for fourpence each a pamphlet entitled, "A TRUE AND FAITHFUL NARRATIVE OF THE MODES AND MEASURES pursued at the *Anniversary Election*, for *Representatives*, of the *Freemen* of the Province of *Pennsylvania*, held at *Newtown*, in and for the County of *Bucks* on *Monday* the first Day of *October*, *Anno Domini* 1770"—all this written by a "Bucks County Man." The style in which the pamphlet is written makes us think Goddard the author. This conclusion is indirectly supported by his including a copy of this along with *The Partnership* and *The Prowess of the Whig Club*, both of which have his name printed on them as author, in a parcel sent many years later to Isaiah Thomas. On all three is written in Goddard's handwriting, "return." Fortunately for us Thomas never did, and we can still look at Goddard's own copies of these three pamphlets in the library of the American Antiquarian Society in Worcester, Massachusetts.

The *Narrative* has on the title page a quotation from Goddard's favorite Tacitus, which he freely translated, "Men that are above all fear, soon grow above all shame." The text, covering five octavo pages, opens: "I have for some time past observed the turnings, windings and twistings of a certain self-important person, to wriggle himself into power and authority, without having any abilities, either natural or acquired, to secure to himself that awe and reverence he would proudly and vainly arrogate to himself." The alleged means whereby Galloway got himself elected from Bucks County after realizing that the Philadelphia voters were in no mood to return him to the assembly were to have William Yardley present himself as a candidate only to announce his withdrawal the morning of the election. In the resulting confusion Galloway's name was presented. Before the afternoon was over, Galloway was declared elected, thanks to the obsequious help of the Bucks County sheriff.

(Any reader interested in the manner of conducting a colonial election will find this pamphlet fascinating reading, irrespective of the merits of Goddard's accusations.)

The "Bucks County Man" was doing his bit towards the forthcoming annual assembly election on October 1. Galloway feared the animus of his former partner enough that sometime during the middle of September, 1771, Goddard found himself in the Philadelphia jail as a debtor. The affairs of the three-way partnership had never been wound up. Since all bills had been in the name of William Goddard and since he refused to pay them unless Galloway and Wharton paid their share, it was not difficult to incarcerate the recalcitrant printer. But being in jail did not silence Goddard. Signing himself "A Friend to Liberty," he published in the *Chronicle* of September 23 an article over a column long attacking Galloway by name and recommended "to the particular attention of AMERICANUS's present constituents in the county of Bucks." A Friend to Liberty started by showing how even the worst of men have some pangs of conscience over their misdeeds. What then must be the feelings of one who has tried to destroy the liberty of his country? Contrasted with this are the feelings of a patriot. Just as Cato serving his country contrasts with Caesar seeking the ruin of Rome, so "Who would not rather be a FRANKLIN, gloriously defending the liberties and the honour of his distressed country, before a BRITISH SENATE, than the first Minister of State [Galloway as Speaker of the Pennsylvania Assembly] endeavouring to enslave and ruin his countrymen?—And who would not rather be a DICKINSON, in a private station, armed with truth, supported by the immutable laws of nature, the common inheritance of man, and leaning on the pillars of the BRITISH CONSTITUTION, nobly exerting his great talents for the preservation of the invaded rights of his country, than a GALLOWAY, asserting the cause of slavery, reviling *American* honour, treacherously undermining the capital pillars of the Constitution of his NATIVE COUNTRY, and slandering one of her ablest Advocates?"

Goddard did not have to wait long for a reply to his article. That same afternoon an unnamed member (Galloway?) read the *Chronicle*'s comments to the Pennsylvania Assembly. A committee was appointed to prepare a resolution "shewing the sentiments of the House." On the next day, the twenty-fourth, the committee brought in a resolution to which the assembly quickly agreed: "The House taking into Consideration the Publication in the *Pennsylvania Chronicle*, Number 245, signed *A Friend to Liberty*, with another Piece, dated *German-Town, September* 20, 1771, published by *William Goddard*, Printer, who is now confined in the common Gaol of the City and County of *Philadelphia* under divers Executions for Debts. *Resolved*, That the Charges and Reflections contained in the said Publications against the Honourable *Joseph Galloway*, the Speaker, are false, scandalous and malicious, a daring Insult to, and a Breach of the Privileges of this House. *Ordered*, That the foregoing Resolve be published in the *Pennsylvania* Gazette and Journal, and that the Clerk of this House immediately furnish the Printers with a Copy of the same." (Fortunately for Goddard colonial legislatures had not discovered the punitive measures exercised by their twentieth-century counterparts' committees.)

On the twenty-sixth the *Gazette* and the *Journal* published the assembly's resolution, but Bradford now came to the support of Goddard and inserted a vigorous attack on Galloway and the assembly immediately after the resolution. Bradford in no uncertain terms indicated his position: "For my Part, I not only consider it [the resolution] disgraceful but, dangerous, as it may be a Precedent hereafter to intimidate the Press, and infringe the Liberties of the Subject.—And I am sorry to find the Representatives of a free People indulging *Rancour* and *Malice*, under a Mask of preserving *Dignity* and *Honour*."

Emboldened by this support and showing no fear of the "privileges" of the Pennsylvania Assembly, Goddard busied himself in the Philadelphia jail preparing copy for the September 30 *Chronicle*. With Mary Katherine in charge of the shop he did not need to worry about the paper's meeting its printing schedule. Issued just the day before the election, the newspaper had more than two pages devoted to an attack on Galloway and an appeal to the voters of Bucks County not to re-elect their present representative. The names of the members of the assembly who had voted against the resolution passed on the twenty-fourth were printed; Andrew Marvel, made famous in the *Constitutional Courant* of 1765, had a letter; A Freeman and A Freeholder both expressed their horror of Joseph Galloway; and generous extracts were given from the original Americanus article of 1765 along with the comments on it as given

in *The Partnership*'s "Postscript." Compared to this persistent flow
of invective, the article of the week before which had aroused the ire
of the assembly was as gentle as a newborn lamb. Though Galloway won the election, he must have felt uncomfortable whenever he
thought of his former partner's truculence and fearlessness. Probably this was the issue of the *Chronicle* Franklin was referring to
when he wrote to his son William on January 30, 1772, from
London: "I cast my eye over Goddard's Piece against our friend
Mr. Galloway, and then lit my Fire with it. I think such feeble,
malicious Attacks cannot hurt him." Obviously not everybody in
Philadelphia agreed with Franklin.

In the *Chronicle* of October 14 Goddard could finally announce
his release: "The Printer of this Paper, impressed by the most lively
Sentiments of Gratitude, takes a sincere Pleasure, on this Occasion,
of returning his warmest Acknowledgments to a Number of respectable Citizens, who, on the first Notice of the relentless Severity of
Messrs. *Galloway* and *Wharton*, his former Partners in the Printing
Business, generously united and made him a Loan of Money sufficient to extricate him from the Iron Hand of Oppression. He
now enjoys the Sweets of Liberty, and is enabled, by the Generosity
of some Friends, to continue in Business, in which his utmost Endeavours shall ever be [ex]erted to give all possible Satisfaction
to the Public, and shew himself not altogether unworthy of the
Favours he has received."

To show that the three or four weeks in jail had not soothed
his spirit or intimidated him, Goddard published in this same issue
another attack on Galloway. The article was signed by A Friend to
Liberty *"not 'confined in the Common Gaol, under divers Executions
for Debts.'"* A week later Goddard clipped another attack on Galloway from his friend John Holt's *New-York Journal*. The Philadelphian was not hiding his hatred under a bushel.

April, 1772, was a busy month for William Goddard. First, he
changed the location of his printing establishment. This time he
moved from Arch Street to Front Street "nearly opposite the London
Coffee House." On better terms with the Bradfords now that he
was in bitter opposition to Galloway, Goddard doubtless found it
much more convenient to be just across the street from Philadelphia's
chief center for gossip among seamen and merchants and tradesmen
of the town.

A more important event in this month was another eruption of the Goddard-Galloway feud. It started innocently enough for Goddard with announcements in the *Journal* and *Gazette* for April 16. In the *Journal* Galloway was offering £50 reward, and in the *Gazette* Governor John Penn £100—both for information leading to the capture of the writer of a mysterious letter. On the fourth of the month Joseph Sellers, a blacksmith living on the road from Philadelphia to Chester, was given a letter by some strangers, which he was requested to send to Joseph Galloway. As Galloway expressed it in his £50 reward notice, whoever had written the letter was "accustomed to use stops or points in his writing." Apparently many people in those days were not. What Galloway received was this:

To Mr. JOSEPH GALLOWAY, Esqr.
I stand in need of 50 pounds & Desier you would, not fail to let me have it against the 10. of this month, by leaving it close behind the 5 mile stone between Philadelphia & Darby and I shall pay you in a year with intrest. Sir—I shall pay you to a day—
N.B. If you dont leave it you shall sorely repent it in a few; days and wish you had left it; you shall be sure of it again
from a Chester Countryman.

The version of this letter printed in the *Gazette* adds at the end, "April ye 2. 1772." The 5 Mile Stone was, of course, the stone marking five miles on the country road then winding its way leisurely over wooded hills but now the busy Chester Avenue in southwest Philadelphia.

The feud having been given such reams of publicity, it is not surprising that suspicion should fall on Goddard. Therefore on Saturday, April 18, he was haled into court before Chief Justice Allen and then released on bail. But let Goddard continue with the story as given in the following Monday's *Chronicle*, as he employed his choicest invective and poured on the abuse.

This was at the Instigation of Mr. *Galloway*, MY OLD INVETERATE ENEMY, grounded *solely* on the Evidence of one WILLIAM EVITT, [Printer!]* who deposed, *not that I wrote the Letter*, but *that he heard me say I wrote it*, after the Publication of the Proclamation, &c. This *Evitt* is the most wretched, drunken, contemptible Sot that can any where be found, and the Matter deposed of the *most improbable* Kind. I

---

* Brackets in original.

certainly am not Fool enough to confess a detestable Fact of that Sort
to him, if I had been guilty of it—yet such Stress has been laid on the
incredible Evidence of that worthless besotted Wretch, that I have been
taken into Custody, &c. on the Strength of it. . . . I really cannot but
pity Mr. *Galloway,* my *great* and *capital Enemy,* that he should be
reduced to such contemptible Shifts for Revenge and Mischief against
me, as to run pimping and sneaking up a dirty Alley to the House of such
a Wretch as *Evitt,* to SOLICIT Evidence against me, and there to dance
Attendance until *Evitt's* drunken Fit could be far enough over for him
to awake, and be capable of talking.

To this article, signed "Monday Morning 5 o'clock," Goddard appended this N.B.: "An ingenious Gentleman of distinguished Honour
and Probity, whom Mr. *Galloway* had *slandered,* having told him,
as became a Man of Spirit, that if he, (*Galloway*) was in a firm State
of Health, he would instantly give him the Discipline due to such
an infamous Scoundrel, Mr. *Galloway,* with his *usual Intrepidity,*
swore the Peace against him—and thus honoured him with a Share
of his Malice, in Company with *W. Goddard.*"

A week later the *Chronicle* contained another specimen of
Goddard's invective against Galloway. Nothing new had happened,
so the printer was forced to repeat himself a good deal in his
article, this time dated at eight o'clock Monday Morning. He did
include this emphatic statement of his innocence: "I do declare IN
THE MOST SOLEMN MANNER, and with THE SAME SINCERITY as if I
was sworn on the HOLY EVANGELISTS, *That I am not the
Author, Writer or Sender of the Incendiary Letter, said to have been
received by* Joseph Galloway, *Esq; and contained in the Governor's
Proclamation—and further, that I was not* DIRECTLY *or* INDIRECTLY
*concerned in Writing or sending the said Letter, or privy thereto in
any* RESPECT *whatsoever, or had any* KNOWLEDGE *thereof, until it
was publicly reported thro' the Town, and published in the several
News-Papers.*" This article was immediately followed by one of
the "characters" the eighteenth century was so fond of, probably
written by Goddard himself. It was entitled "A SHORT CHARACTER
of a SLANDERER." Appropriately it ended with the familiar
quatrain from Shakespeare beginning, "Who steals my purse steals
trash."

No further news was available until the *Chronicle* of May 11.
This time Goddard headed his article, "FRESH NEWS from the 5
Mile [figure of stone] Stone." To this title he appended a footnote:

"Curiosity having lately led several People to the 5 Mile Stone, on Purpose to look at it, it may not be thought amiss to give a View of it here, which may gratify those who have similar Desires, without Danger or Expence." The fresh news was that another letter had been received from the blackmailer.

On Friday morning last, between 7 and 8 o'Clock, as ISAAC PEARSON, Esq; one of the Representatives of *Chester County*, was coming to this City, from his Seat at *Darby*, in Company with a young Gentleman of the Name of HILL, he observed a Letter on the Edge of the Road, lying with the Seal upwards, about half a mile from Mr. *Galloway*'s *Monument, the ever memorable 5 Mile Stone*, and near the same Distance from the *Lower-Ferry* on *Schuylkill*. Mr. HILL dismounted from his Horse, took it up, and found it was directed in this Manner—"*To Mr. George Gray These*," to whom it was immediately after delivered, with an Account of the singular Manner of meeting with it. Mr. *Gray*, upon opening it, discovered two sealed Letters inclosed, one directed "*To Jos Galloway These*," and the other "*To Jos Sellars These*," with a positive Injunction for their immediate Delivery, in the following Terms, without a Signature:

"*Mr. Gray*
    take the within Letters Directly to where directed or you may expect"

Mr. *Gray* sent Advice to Mr. *Sellers*, who is his Neighbour, that he had a Letter for him, written, as he thought, by Mr. *Galloway's 5 Mile Stone Correspondent*. Mr. Sellers being curious to know its Contents, waited on Mr. *Gray* without Delay, and received his Letter, which contained the following Words:

"*Mr. Sellars*
    If you watch or help to watch for Galloway any other Time as you did before you shall repent it very shortly so I would have you be still—"

Mr. *Galloway* having retired to *Bucks County*, a few Days since, to recover his *Spirits* (which are said to be *much exhausted* by his late *fatiguing Manoeuvres, Midnight Councils* and *Watchings*) Mr. *Gray* hath not yet had an Opportunity to execute his *whole Commission*, by the Delivery of his Letter, being commendably unwilling to *awaken* the Fears of his Family, during his Absence; so that the Contents of Mr. *Galloway*'s Letter remain as yet a profound Secret—But whenever he receives it, and thinks proper to lay it before the Public, he shall be welcome to a Place in his *beloved Chronicle*, IN PERPETUAM REI MEMORIAM—and the Printer assures his OLD NEVER-TO-BE-FORGOTTEN PARTNER, that he considers an Injury offered HIM as CRIMINAL as if it was done against an HONEST MAN.

Alternating entertainment with news items, Goddard in the May
25 *Chronicle* had the 5 Mile Stone, pictured in his May 11 issue,
give its comments on the affair. The resulting essay is a fair sample
of the printer at his satiric best.

On June 1 Goddard published the text of the letter sent to
Galloway almost a month before, but by now a third letter had been
added, dated May 23. All threatened vague reprisals if the £50
was not soon forthcoming. At the conclusion of the article Goddard inserted an alleged advertisement written in the newspaper
jargon of the day: "WANTED immediately—A *fresh* Evidence,
who can tell a tolerably *plausible* LIE, and swear to it afterwards,
agreeable to Directions, *Ev-tt* being now considered a mere *Marplot*.
—Such a *useful Person* may meet with a lucrative *Jobb*, and receive *great Encouragement*, by applying at the Sign of AMERICANUS
—in Despair. N. B. The Person must be able to read Writing, and
must learn to distinguish a Semicolon from a Comma."

For Goddard the finale of the affair of the 5 Mile Stone was
his trial on the charges brought against him by Galloway. On
Tuesday, July 7, Goddard spent the day at the Mayor's court, then
meeting in the State House (now called Independence Hall). His
case was not called up, nor was it the next day, when the grand
jury was dismissed in the evening. On Thursday morning the discharge of the case was moved and granted by the presiding justice.
According to Goddard's account, Evitt, who forfeited a bond for
his appearance, left Philadelphia on the fifth, "and the next Day was
seen *staggering* up the *Lancaster* Road, about thirteen Miles from
this City." That the whole business had worried Goddard more
than he would admit is shown by the rather petulant tone he uses in
summing up: "And thus hath ended a Prosecution that hath given
me much Trouble and Vexation, brought my Business and Character
into Danger, and threatened my total Ruin, and which would have
been the Event, if the manifest Asperity and Rancour of the Charge,
and the contemptible Deficiency of the Evidence, had not induced
a Number of worthy Men of Character and Influence to appear for
me in the Crisis of my Distress, and for which 'Heaven will reward
them.'" From then on the affair dropped out of the newspapers,
and apparently no further effort was made to find the unknown
letter-writer.

The end of September, 1772, found Goddard once more trying to defeat Galloway's re-election. He issued a broadside reprinting an article from Holt's *New-York Journal* of October 8, 1771, which had attacked the Speaker of the Assembly and wondered how the people of Pennsylvania could ever be duped into electing such a man. On September 26, in the last issue of the *Chronicle* before the election, Goddard had a two-column article prefaced by a cartoon. The caption on the cartoon of two horses is detailed enough to give a good idea of the contents: "AMERICANUS, *heavy laden*, with the 5 *Mile Stone* on his Back, trampling on the Goddess LIBERTY, the *Bill of Rights*, and *Pennsylvania Charter*, on his Way to *Bucks County Election*, (accompanied by the *Buckram Marquis* of *New Barrataria* [Wharton was at this time much involved in a land development scheme in the Wyoming Valley, for which the name New Barrataria was proposed],) begging Relief from his *Burthern*." Goddard concluded the article by swearing that Galloway could never expect the printer to give up the campaign: "If the Rage and Wildness of Party should, after all, sanctify his Villainies, and again give him a Seat in the Senate, let him represent what County he will, or sit on what Seat he may, I shall (unawed by any of his *resolving Brethren*) take the Liberty to hold his Picture, taken from Nature, up to View, shewing him as he is—an Enemy to his Country, a Disgrace to *Pennsylvania*, and a 'Blot and a Stain to *America*'—and while I live I shall exert my utmost Abilities to detect and expose him in every Attempt to injure the Cause of Liberty and his Country, to expose his Ignorance, and to shew the Weakness of his Head, and the Wickedness of his Heart; not doubting but I shall find a Support amongst the *disinterestedly Good, the Friends of Liberty and our excellent Constitution*." A third prong in his attack on Galloway was another broadside issued on October 1, Election Day itself. This was a letter presumably written by a not too literate chimney sweep offering to exchange places for a year with Galloway. It was headed, "To the printer of the Penselvaney Kronical mr. Godard."

The results of all this electioneering on Goddard's part were announced in the October 3 *Chronicle*. Galloway won his seat, though still from Bucks County. But the more surprising thing is that Goddard was almost elected to the assembly. He felt obligated to thank publicly those who had given their "*spontaneous* Suffrages" in his behalf. That Goddard came close to election is attested by a letter Franklin wrote to Abel James on December 2, 1772, from London: "I do not at this Distance understand the Politics of your last Election, why so many of the Members declin'd the Service, and why yourself and Mr. Fox were omitted (which I much regret) while Goddard was voted for by so great a Number."

During 1773 Goddard's energies were a good deal taken up by his starting the *Maryland Journal*, a story to be told in a later chapter, and his sister Mary Katherine probably edited as many of the *Chronicles* as did William. Therefore the assembly elections of 1773 lacked the fervor of former years. Goddard undertook no campaign of harassment before the electors went to the polls and only noticed the annual event by this brief comment on October 18: "The noted Joseph Galloway, is, to the Disgrace of Pennsylvania, again elected Speaker of the Assembly! Perjury, Subornation, and the basest Treachery, we may see, thro' blind Party Rage, are sometimes no Disqualifications to a Place of Trust. Those who patronize such Crimes, we may suppose, as Junius observes, feel for their own."

During latter 1773 the colonists were agog over the East India Company and tea. Familiar to everybody are the various incidents climaxed by the Boston Tea Party. In Philadelphia Thomas Wharton was appointed one of the agents of the Company to handle the tea. Goddard greeted this announcement in the October 23 *Maryland Journal* by attacking his former partner viciously. On the twenty-fifth he was able to state that everybody in Philadelphia who had been appointed agents for the despised tea had resigned his commission, including Thomas Wharton. The bitterness of three years before was enough behind for Goddard to rub only a little salt into the wounded pride of his former partner: "The Printer of this Paper thinks it incumbent on him to mention, on this Occasion, that Mr. *Thomas Wharton*, senior, *prudently* took the HINTS that have been given him, and hath actually made a *decent Renunciation* of his *dangerous* and *disgraceful* Office of *Tea Commissioner*; so that he is now—'*despised something less than he used to be.*'—And, at the same Time, the Printer assures his *old Partner*, that he is pleased to see this Dawn of Virtue in his Conduct, and hopes he will not, for the Sake of rendering this single virtuous Act the more *conspicuous*, let it stand *alone*. Whenever any Thing meritorious in his future Life appears, the OLD COMPANY

PRESS shall be heavy laden with Panegyric—for *this* CHRONICLE, like those of *old*, is designed to record the Deeds of *good Princes*, as well as those that are *bad*."

The remainder of Goddard's Philadelphia story can now be briefly told. Less and less of his attention was devoted to the *Chronicle* during the winter months of 1773 and 1774. Not that this means that the paper was allowed to come out irregularly or be slovenly in its appearance. Mary Katherine proved her mettle as a printer and a newspaperwoman. From her brother she had learned both things well. Quite likely Goddard during the summer and fall of 1773, while he was getting his Baltimore shop into functioning order, had in mind the running of the two shops concurrently. For six months the Philadelphia and Baltimore newspapers overlapped, but by February 8, 1774, Goddard called it quits for the *Chronicle* for reasons to be given in the next chapter. In his farewell statement thanking his subscribers and friends Goddard expressed his gratitude for their patronage and support "amidst the *Rage* and *Wildness* of *Party*, the *Insolence* of *Office*, the *gigantic Strides* of *arbitrary Power*, and the more dangerous *Plots* and *Manoeuvres* of *secret Conspirators*." Goddard's seven years in Philadelphia had given him much to remember, and Philadelphians had had their best-edited newspaper before the Revolution.

IN 1773 things were not going well for the British postal system in the colonies. During the latter part of the year Hugh Finlay, the system's surveyor for Canada as well as the colonies, was sent out into the field to discover at first hand what was happening. Typical of his findings is this excerpt from his journal, dated October 28, 1773:

He [Thomas Vernon, deputy postmaster for Newport] says that there are two Post Offices in New Port, the King's and Mumfords [Ben Mumford, postrider between Newport and Saybrook; Peter Mumford, postrider between Boston and Newport], and that the revenue of the last is the greatest. It is the same in Boston, both Mumford and the rider of the upper Stages (Hyde) receive much postage for which they do not account. It is common for people who expect letters by Post finding none at the Post office to say *"well there must be letters, we'll find them at Mumfords."* It is next to impossible to put a stop to this practice in the present universal opposition to every thing connected with Great Britain. Were any Deputy Post Master to do his duty, and make a stir in such matter, he would draw on himself the odium of his neighbours and be mark'd as the friend of Slavery and oppression and a declar'd enemy to America.

To comprehend Finlay's comments, we must go back to February 17, 1692, when William and Mary made a grant to Thomas Neale, a court favorite. This grant gave Neale the privilege of conducting in the colonies a postal system from which he would receive all the revenues in return for six shillings a year. Neale's only interest was in these potential revenues; so on April 4 he delegated the actual running of the system to Andrew Hamilton, a former governor of the Jerseys, Neale never even seeing the shores of America. By May, 1697, Hamilton reported a deficit of £2,360 for the operations under the postal monopoly. Neale died in 1699 and his interests under the original grant were assigned to Hamilton and an Englishman named West, as creditors of the estate. Finally, in 1707 the crown purchased the rights of West and Mrs. Hamilton (Hamilton had died in 1703) for a reported £1,664 and took the system under its own wing. Not until 1711 did Parliament pass the Act of the Ninth of Queen Anne, which regularized the postal system for the home country and the colonies and provided an explicit legal basis for future operations. John Hamilton, the son of Andrew, was appointed Postmaster General for America, and headquarters for the far-flung colonial system were installed at New York.

In 1773 the deputy postmaster general, the person in charge of the system, was Benjamin Franklin. He had been in England most of the time since 1757 and was not to return to Philadelphia until May 5, 1775. Under Franklin's direction the service had been improved a great deal, and the increased efficiency had made the colonial postal system into a source of revenue for the crown. But the developing ill-feeling between the colonials and the home government was reflected in the operations of the post office.

The chief complainers in 1773 against the vagaries of postal operations were the newspapermen. Their obvious dependence on mail made them hypersensitive to defects in the system. Usually wherever there was a newspaper, the editor acted as local postmaster. This was fine for the particular editor who secured the appointment, but woe betide his competitors. Those competitors frequently found their mail arriving late; also they were compelled to pay heavy charges for the carriage of their papers. Therefore many printers, as we have seen, organized their own system of independent riders to deliver newspapers.

Typical of the newspapermen who felt themselves sufferers from postal inequities was William Goddard. During his years in Philadelphia the local postmaster was William Bradford. Commencing with the very first issue of the *Chronicle*, Goddard had instituted a system of riders. The bill already referred to in the previous chapter from John Borrows charges Goddard for the "carriage of your Newspaper from Philadelphia to New Brunswick . . . and . . . from Philadelphia to Trenton." This close acquaintance with delivery problems no doubt was an impelling force behind Goddard's campaign in early 1774 against the official postal system. But, as we have seen, Goddard's difficulties with Bradford as postmaster were not his first contacts with the colonial post office. His father, Giles

Goddard, had been village postmaster of New London as well as its doctor. As a printer's apprentice, Goddard had worked under James Parker, at that time comptroller of the postal system under Franklin. While still with Parker, the young apprentice had made in latter 1755 a postal surveying trip through Connecticut. And from 1764 to 1769 he had been the local postmaster of Providence, even though during most of this time his mother and his sister had done the actual postal work.

During the six months that Goddard was simultaneously publishing the *Maryland Journal* in Baltimore and the *Pennsylvania Chronicle* in Philadelphia the postal riders between the two cities became very much his concern. In the *Journal* of November 20, 1773, a notice reads: "A POST-RIDER will be speedily established, by the Printer of this Paper to set out from hence every Thursday Afternoon, for Philadelphia, and to return hither the Tuesday Evening following." After three months of publication for the new paper there was already enough difficulty in sending and receiving mail for the publisher to be willing to pay for a regular rider out of his own pocket. A week later, November 27, two notices appeared in the *Journal*, one relative to the *Chronicle* and the other to the new Baltimore paper: "The PENNSYLVANIA CHRONICLE . . . will, by the Establishment of a new Northern Post, be able to visit its old Friends in this Province, from whom it hath, for some Time, been cut off by an arb[itrary] Decree of a malicious Postrider, late a Hostl[er in t]he Service of one of the D. Postmasters Gene[ral]." The second notice, less vituperative in its tone, says: "The MARYLAND JOURNAL, &c. will, positively be published, regularly, every Thursday Morning, as soon as the new Philadelphia Post is established, which it is expected will be the Case in about a Fortnight. Then our Customers will have the earliest Intelligence from the Northward, before they could possibly obtain it by any other Mode of Conveyance." Goddard was able to fulfil his promise, as a heading in the December 9 *Journal* reveals: "Advices received by the newly established *Northern Post*, who arrived here on *Tuesday last*." The advantages to a newspaper of having its own riders are clearly shown by the December 30 issue, where we read: "Yesterday evening, Mr. Butler, one of the post riders, lately established by the Printer of this Paper, arrived here, express, from New-York, with the following interesting intelligence, having left the same at Philadelphia, where it was printed and distributed as a Christmas-Box to the Public—and we have, for some time, delayed publishing *this paper*, in hopes of being able to close the old year with eclat, which we have now the pleasure of doing by the publication of the unexampled, spirited, and noble conduct of our brave countrymen, who disdain to wear the CHAIN—and who are unalterably determined to be FREE." Directly after this notice is a long account of the Boston Tea Party of December 16. Two weeks' time between Boston and Baltimore was not bad for colonial days.

So far everything we have described was done solely as a business measure in connection with getting news and delivering newspapers. But doing all this work and observing the colonial difficulties with England made Goddard think beyond his immediate problems to those of the entire thirteen colonies. On December 16, 1773, he suggested what was in his mind in a letter to John Lamb of New York: "Mr. Wm Stenson . . . will communicate to you a Sketch of a Plan I am forming to give a firm Opposition to a certain unconstitutional Act of Parliment now operating in the Colonies."

By February, 1774, Goddard's plan had matured enough for him to act. He first closed his Philadelphia paper and had his sister, Mary Katherine, transfer to Baltimore, so that she could manage the shop and newspaper while he was absent, just as she had been running the *Pennsylvania Chronicle* during William's frequent and prolonged trips to Baltimore in 1773. The last issue of the *Chronicle* was dated February 8, 1774, and a farewell statement hinted at the great things to come:

Urged by very important Reasons, which will hereafter, and in due Season, be fully and clearly stated to the Public, I have come to the Resolution of *suspending* the Publication of the PENNSYLVANIA CHRONICLE &c. (which hath now completed it's *seventh Year*) until a Matter I have engaged in, of a very interesting Nature to the common Liberties of all *America*, as well as to myself, as the Printer of a Public Paper, is brought *nearer* to a Conclusion. . . . Sensible that my Designs are just and laudable, I am determined to persevere, until a Question that will necessarily arise, of the last Importance to this Country, receives a constitutional Decision, in an American Court of Justice. . . .

N.B. The new *constitutional* Post, which under Favour of the Public, hath been lately established between this City and *Baltimore*, will be continued in the most regular, and punctual Manner.

Nine days later, February 17, Mary Katherine Goddard officially took over the management of the *Maryland Journal*, not to relinquish it for almost ten years. The first sentence of her announcement of the new management implies that her brother had already started on his trip northward: "An Affair in a very high Degree interesting to the common liberties of all AMERICA, as well as to the Printer of this Paper, having made it necessary for him to repair, for a few Weeks to an Eastern Colony, I esteem it my indispensable Duty to acquaint the Public. . . ."

Goddard started north with his plan well formulated in his mind. The very phrase, "constitutional post," used in the *Chronicle*'s farewell remarks became the name for his projected establishment. He had an already existing system of postriders between Baltimore and Philadelphia. Possibly John Borrows continued in Goddard's employ until November, 1774, to ride between Philadelphia and Trenton; at least the bill already referred to would so indicate. If this is true, Goddard already had the nucleus of his proposed postal system and could base his arguments on facts, not on fantasy or whim. His plan was, of course, to set up a completely new postal system independent of the British.

Though we have no record of his visit, probably his first stop was Philadelphia. In this community Goddard possessed about as many enemies as friends. Unfortunately in his newspaper wars in the city he had fought against, even though the choice was not his, the persons who would have been of most help to him in his present situation. Typical of these was William Bradford, who later participated in Goddard's "constitutional" scheme but would have demanded at this time more assurance than what his erstwhile competitor could give on his own. Nor would Goddard's Philadelphia reception have been helped by the various debts he had left lying around. Moreover, the particular group in the city that the Baltimore printer was appealing to for support included his former partner Joseph Galloway. In most of the colonial communities, especially in New England, the local committee of correspondence and the town meeting were indistinguishable. When the request from Boston's committee to set up other committees came to Philadelphia, the Pennsylvania Assembly under the speakership of Galloway made the Philadelphia committee one of the prerogatives of its speaker. The resulting committee of correspondence, never to become noted for its vigor, was therefore chairmaned by Galloway and had for its members his friends. In the colonies above Pennsylvania, by contrast, many of the members of the local committees had been Sons of Liberty in the 1760's and had known about Goddard's anti-Stamp Act activities in 1765. Goddard planned to go from one committee to another and make the members his backers for the new postal system. To get their help required that he secure letters of introduction from one committee to others; in spite of the handicaps he did manage to secure at least one such letter from the Philadelphia committee, whether from the group as a whole or only from an individual member we cannot now say.

In New York it was another story. Goddard had several friends there among those pressing the cause of the colonies, and they were in control of the local committee of correspondence. Chief among these was John Holt, publisher of the *New-York Journal.* There was also John Lamb, who seems to have taken the thirty-three-year-old printer in tow. It was to him Goddard had written the preceding December. No doubt there were enough others familiar with Goddard's having published the anti-Stamp Act *Constitutional Courant* in September, 1765, that his prestige as a vigorous supporter of the colonial cause was high in the inner councils of the New York Committee of Correspondence. So it was with little difficulty that he acquired letters of introduction dated February 28, most important of which was the one to Boston. The members of the New York committee were favorably impressed by the plan but wanted the support and agreement of other communities. Leaving New York on the twenty-eighth Goddard continued his travels, bolstered by this support and encouragement.

During his New York stay Holt and Lamb must have talked for some time with Goddard concerning the best tactics to use in his campaign. The crucial importance of Boston would have been apparent to them, and so our traveler made only short stops on his way to the Hub City. After New York his first visit would have been New Haven. Apprenticeship memories did not long detain him as he pushed his way on to New London, the scene of his birth and the first fifteen years of his life. No doubt Goddard told some people of his proposal as he had in New Haven, but he did not wait for the calling of a town meeting to formulate public opinion. From New London the sanguine printer moved up the Thames River to Norwich, a brief day's ride away. Again his stay must have been little more than a night or two before plunging on to Providence.

As editor of the *Providence Gazette* in the early 1760's, Goddard had participated in the struggles between Providence and Newport. Many people in both places knew the name of William Goddard, especially in Providence, where he had both friends and relatives. In these towns Goddard stopped long enough to make a more thorough canvass of the sentiments of the local committees of correspondence and other citizens. We do not know the exact dates of his stay in Providence, but the Congregational minister of Newport, Ezra Stiles, later President of Yale, was an indefatigible diary keeper, and for March 11 he entered: "The Sons of Liberty at Philadelphia [the phrasing of this remark suggests that Goddard's Philadelphia letter may not have been from the local committee of correspondence at all but from persons active against the 1765 Stamp Act] and N. York have sent Mr. Goddard to sollicit us in N. England to unite in opposing the parliamentary Post Office in America, and in setting up Provincial Post Riders." This meeting attended by Ezra Stiles was later reported in a London newspaper of April 14, which was clipped by Purdie and Dixon and placed in their *Virginia Gazette* of June 9 under a London date-line. "*Extract of a Letter from* Newport, *in* Rhode Island, *March* 12, 1774. 'By an Express from Philadelphia, and New York, last Night, we are informed that a Resolution has been come to, at—— [probably New York], to take the Post Office out of the Hands of Government, and to appoint Regulations themselves; and I think it is probable they will soon take the Custom-house into their own Possession, and ship home the Commissioners.' " Purdie and Dixon added in brackets after the clipping an expression of their sentiments: "So let it be."

Like the New York Sons of Liberty, those in Providence and Newport looked with strong favor on the plans. The Newport Committee of Correspondence gave Goddard a letter of introduction dated March 10 to its Boston counterpart to add to the ones he already had. In fact, Goddard probably attended a meeting of the Newport committee before one in Providence. Providence, not too hurried, gave only verbal promises for the moment but assured the roving printer that a letter would soon follow his arrival in Boston, a promise that was fulfilled.

On Monday, March 14, William Goddard swung his weary legs off his horse in Boston. Perhaps that very night he turned his letters over to William Cooper, clerk of the town meeting of Boston and secretary of the local committee of correspondence under the direction of Samuel Adams. Goddard's plan seemed perfect to Adams, and there was no doubt much enthusiastic discussion concerning its merits and methods to get it into operation during Monday evening and Tuesday morning and afternoon. So enthusiastic was Boston's reception of Goddard that he must have pinched himself at times to see if it was all true.

On Tuesday (probably at seven in the evening, the customary time) a town meeting was held in the Selectmen's Chamber. The secretary's minutes for the meeting show only one topic of discussion that night.

Mr. Goddard of Philadelphia, who is come this way on the design of establishing Post Riders, independent of those established by Act of Parliament, attended, this Evening by invitation,—
Letters from the Committees of Correspondence at New York and Newport in Rhode Island on the subject of Provincial Post Riders, were laid before the Committee and read—
Upon a Motion made. Voted, that
    Joseph Greenleaff Esq
    Dr. Benjamin Church
    Dr. Thomas Young
be a Committee to prepare a piece for the Spy in order to shew the utility of the proposal for Provincial Post Riders—
Voted, that this Meeting be Adjourned to next Thursday Evening. 7. O Clock.

Somehow it seems appropriate that the only action taken at this first evening's meeting was the selection of a committee to prepare something for the press. We suspect that the members must not have spent too long discussing the possible merits of the proposal, but instead agreed on that quite soon (though no resolution was placed in the minutes) and passed on to the more engrossing subject of how to bring the public around to their conviction. By this time the Boston patriots had well developed techniques of persuasion, and we can perceive the experienced direction of Sam Adams and others during the ten days of Goddard's stay in Boston as they worked out the appropriate tactics for the campaign. First, a committee to write articles for newspapers. Next, on Thursday, March

17, another meeting was held in the Selectmen's Chamber. Goddard was present, and the proposed postal system was again the sole item on the agenda for the evening. A committee was selected to confer with the local merchants (some of whom are named in the minutes, nothing being left to chance). And at the meeting on Tuesday, March 22, "a number of the principal Merchants of the Town attended by desire in order for a conference respecting the practicability of the Scheme for Colony Post Riders."

But other things were happening between the seventeenth and the twenty-second to forward the "Scheme for Colony Post Riders." By the nineteenth the Boston town clerk, William Cooper, must have received from the Providence Committee of Correspondence the promised letter, dated the seventeenth. This said that the committee had received letters from New York and Newport relative to the proposal. "We are full in Opinion that the Parliment of Great Brittain have no Right to impose that Regulation on us for the Purpose of Rasing a Revenue in America without our Consent." The letter goes on to assure the Boston committee that Providence will back up whatever plans the Boston town meeting makes. The signatures of seven Providence citizens then follow.

Within two days the committee appointed on the fifteenth had a news item in Isaiah Thomas's *Massachusetts Spy*.

Last Monday [March 14] arrived in this Town, Mr. WILLIAM GODDARD, Printer in Philadelphia and Baltimore—The Cause of that Gentleman's tour is interesting to all the Colonies, and we are happy to find that all through which he has come are so thoroughly engaged in it. Every Colony to the Southward of us, manifest their readiness to come into the measure, provided we adopt it, and we are informed there is not the shadow of a doubt of its being as warmly patronized here as any where. How cheerfully will every well wisher to his Country lay hold of an opportunity to risque the channel of public and private intelligence out of the hands of a power openly inimical to its Rights and Liberties. Several Meetings have already been held on the interesting subject, and on the Morrow Evening it is hoped to be concluded so far that Mr. Goddard may proceed Eastward, with a moral certainty of carrying his point throughout the Colonies.

Thomas also printed as from a New York to a Boston gentleman the letter Goddard had brought from New York.

Another press outlet for the Boston Committee of Correspondence was the *Boston Gazette*, published by the ardent patriots, Benjamin

Edes and John Gill. Its March 21 issue reprinted the news item from the *Spy* of the seventeenth and followed this by a letter written "To —— —— ——, Esq" and signed Hortensius, in which various objections to Goddard's proposal were refuted. In the last paragraph of the letter, added after the name of Hortensius as a kind of postscript, is this statement: "We are informed the Patriotic Doctor Franklin is severely threatened with the loss of that Place [deputy postmaster general] under the British Minister." The writers of this paragraph realized that the affection for and the prestige of Franklin could be one of their biggest obstacles, whereas a Franklin removed from his position could be used to their advantage. Therefore they concluded the letter: "Many of the Patrons of this new Scheme were much concerned lest it should appear ungrateful to Doctor Franklin, especially at a Period when he has given such signal Proof of faithfulness to his Trust, in obtaining and sending over the treasonable Letters of Hutchinson, Oliver, &c. But perhaps the new Post-Office may be beneficial and more agreeable to the Doctor than ever was the old one." Not until April 25 could the *Boston Gazette* confirm the rumor of Franklin's dismissal, which had taken place January 30.

The *Massachusetts Gazette* in its account on the twenty-fourth summarized the progress so far (progress perhaps more wished for than actual): "That a considerable Fund is already raised for the Support of the new Posts at Philadelphia and Baltimore.—That in Virginia, Maryland and Pennsylvania, they will certainly establish such Riders. That at New-York the Citizens there are determined to open Subscription Books for the like Purposes, as soon as the Town of Boston has given a Sanction to this Capital Plan.—That at New-London, Norwich, Rhode-Island and Providence, they appear heartily in the Plan, but only wait for Boston." This news item was read by the royal governor of Massachusetts, Thomas Hutchinson, and worried him. He clipped it out and mailed it to Lord Dartmouth in England.

The meeting of the Boston Committee of Correspondence on March 22 attended by "a Number of the principal Merchants" mentioned earlier featured the appointment of a committee on the subject. Five persons were appointed and "Mr. Adams the Chairman, and Mr. Goddard were desired to attend the Committee." Probably for this group Goddard prepared a subscription form. An undated copy of this in his handwriting is in the Boston Committee of Correspondence papers in the New York Public Library.

With considerable pride Goddard sat down the day after this meeting and wrote an exuberant letter to John Lamb in New York. He was bubbling with enthusiasm, confidence, and plans as he told his hopes for the future. For the citizens of Boston "I have not Terms to convey to you the Sentiments I entertain of their Magnanimity, Wisdom, Patriotism & Urbanity." The Boston committee was to meet that evening to answer the letters from New York, Newport, and Providence and to write new ones for various towns to the north, "whither I shall proceed with all Dispatch, determined to *do Business*, & nothing will damp my Ardor but an Idea that I cannot suffer myself to entertain that my Countrymen will abate of theirs." He hoped New York would start the ball rolling, so that the city would have "the Glory of originating one of the greatest Plans that, as they say, was ever engaged in since the Settlement of this Country." Articles should be written for the New York papers and for Bradford's *Pennsylvania Journal*. Cards and handbills "under a Variety of Signatures" should be scattered. Near the end of the letter he says, "I have had the Pleasure of drinking the Health of the Committee of Correspondence at N.Y. Mr. Lamb, & other Friends of Liberty in your City, in Company with the first Characters here."

At the town meeting on Thursday the twenty-fourth, held again in the Selectmen's Chamber, the final plans were made for Goddard's trip north. In the name of the committee appointed the preceding Tuesday a letter, probably written by Sam Adams, was presented for the northern towns and entered into the minutes. This letter, dated March 24, 1774, and addressed to Marblehead, Newbury Port, Portsmouth, and Salem, well shows the arguments used by Goddard in support of his proposals.

Gentlemen

The Bearer of this Mr Wm Goddard has brot us Letters from our worthy Brethren the Committees of Correspondence of New York Newport and Providence, recommending to our Consideration the Expediency of making an Effort to constitute & support a Post throughout America in the room of that which is now establishd by an Act of the British Parliament. When we consider the Importance of a Post, by which not only private Letters of Friendship and Commerce but *publick*

Intelligence is conveyd from Colony to Colony, it seems at once proper & necessary that such an one should be established as shall be under the Direction of the Colonies; more especially when we further consider that the British Administration & their Agents have taken every Step in their Power to prevent an Union of the Colonies which is so necessary for our making a successful opposition to their arbitrary Designs, and which depends upon a free Communication of the Circumstances and Sentiments of each to the others, and their mutual Councils. Besides, the present Post Office is founded on an Act of the British Parliament and raises a revenue from us without our Consent, in which View it is equally as obnoxious as any other revenue Act, and in the time of the Stamp Act as well as since it has been pleaded as a Precedent against us. And though we have appeard to acquiesce in it, because the office was thought to be of publick Utility, yet, if it is now made use of for the purpose of stopping the Channels of publick Intelligence and so in Effect of aiding the measures of Tyranny, as Mr Goddard informs us it is, the necessity of substituting another office in its Stead must be obvious. The Practicability of doing this throughout the Continent is to be considerd. We by no means despair of it. But as it depends upon joynt Wisdom & Firmness our Brethren of New York are sollicitous to know the Sentiments of the New England Colonies. It is therefore our earnest Request that you would take this matter so interesting to America into your consideration, & favor us by the return of Mr Goddard with your own Sentiments, and as far as you shall be able to collect them, the Sentiments of the Gentlemen of your Town & more particularly the Merchants and Traders. And we further request that you would, if you judge it proper, communicate your Sentiments in a Letter by Mr Goddard to the Committees of Correspondence of New York & Philadelphia &c. It is our present opinion that when a plan is laid for the effectual Establishment and Regulation of a Post throughout the Colonies upon a constitutional Footing, the Inhabitants of this Town will heartily joyn in carrying it into Execution. We refer you for further particulars to Mr Goddard, who seems to be deeply engagd in this attempt, not only with a View of serving himself as a Printer, but equally from the more generous motive of serving the Common Cause of America. We wish Success to the Design and are with cordial Esteem,

Gentlemen,

Your Friends
& fellow Countrymen

At this same meeting a reply to the New York committee was recorded in the minutes. Then the Boston meeting voted that "Mr. John Pitts be a Committee for the purpose of presenting a Subscription Paper for the supporting a Constitutional Post Office in the Colonies, to the Gentlemen of the Town for their signing." No stones were being left unturned by the energetic Boston Committee of Correspondence.

The next day the happy Goddard left Boston for his well-planned trip. Before leaving, he called on Sam Adams, who gave him a personal letter to Elbridge Gerry to help push things along for the printer when he was in Marblehead. Nor did Adams let the matter rest while Goddard was beating the bushes in the provinces. On March 29 letters were sent to the Newport and Providence Committees of Correspondence in reply to theirs. On the thirty-first Adams wrote to James Warren in Plymouth about the new proposals. Not for nothing did Sam Adams win the reputation of being one of the most effective agitators for the revolutionary cause.

Goddard followed carefully the route planned for him in Boston. His first stop was probably Marblehead, where he called on Gerry and other members of the local committee. On the evening of the twenty-eighth he was in Salem and presented his Boston credentials to the committee of correspondence in that community. The next day a meeting, doubtless attended by Goddard, to discuss the proposal was held, but no action is recorded as being taken. Apparently Goddard's plan was to present his letters in each town, talk more or less privately with some of the individual committee members, and then proceed on his way without waiting for a formal reply in the expectation of picking this up on his return journey to Boston.

On the thirty-first one of Franklin's friends, Tuthill Hubbart, wrote to him in London about all the goings-on. Hubbart said that Goddard had originated the new postal plan. In a more personal note he added, "indeed some says that you are threatned with being displaced from the Office and they shall have it in their Power to reinstate You and make it equally proffitable to You."

Of more serious importance to Goddard was a letter written April 5 by John Foxcroft, who had assumed Franklin's postal responsibilities, to his superior in London, Anthony Todd. Under the British laws the activities of the Baltimore printer were illegal, and the appropriate authorities were looking into the punitive possibilities. Foxcroft was in consultation with the New York colony attorney-general and Mr. Jones, a lawyer in the city of New York, both of whom saw difficulties in the way of a succcessful prosecution of any case; "however they are both of opinion that it will be best to commence a prosecution against Goddard as soon as sufficient proof can be had against him, to have the Matter determined, whether he can be held to bail or not? 'if he can not, our Jurisdiction is so circumscribed that a prosecution will have no effect and the Law be entirely evaded." The paragraph describing Goddard to Todd deserves quoting not just for its derogatory picture but for the supercilious attitude it reveals towards the entire colonial cause, an attitude that did almost as much damage to the British armies as did all the musketry of Washington's soldiers.

Goddard was formerly Post Master of Providence and at present owes the Office near One Hundred Pounds lawful Money, he left that place in debt and since has been many times in prison with his *Press* and *Journeymen* and you may rely on it, notwithstanding the publication in Boston, that he is only supported by a Set of licentious people of desperate Fortunes whose sole Consequence, nay even Dependance, is on their fishing in troubled Waters; Men of property both in and out of Trade hold him and his Scheme in the greatest Contempt and Abhorrence, as tending to disturb the public peace and Tranquility of America.

On Friday, the first of April, Goddard was in Portsmouth, New Hampshire, after paying his respects in Newburyport on the way north. The *Boston Gazette* of April 11 inserted a dispatch from Portsmouth dated April 8 telling about his arrival, wishing his mission success, and concluding: ". . . we are informed there is not the Shadow of a doubt of its being warmly patronized by the genuine Sons of Liberty in Portsmouth, who are to meet at Union-Hall this Afternoon—How cheerfully will every well Wisher to his Country lay hold of an Opportunity to rescue the Channel of Public and Private Intelligence out of the Hands of a Power, openly inimical to its Rights and Liberties."

Though Goddard is recorded as not leaving Portsmouth until the thirteenth, he did not stay in this town all the two weeks. Sometime during this interval he traveled up to Casco Bay for a visit to Falmouth, now Portland. His route in Maine took him through the settlements of Wells, Kennebunk, and Biddeford, where no doubt he turned the conversation during the evenings in taverns to his proposals. The northernmost link in his chain of postriders would be Falmouth.

The return trip to Boston took a week. At each town where he had dropped off a letter from the Boston Committee of Correspondence he now picked up a reply. Most of these replies were ready and waiting for him before Goddard actually rode into the town. For example, those of Portsmouth and Newbury are dated April 11. The one from Salem must not have been ready when Goddard reined in his horse there, because this is dated the twentieth, the day of his arrival in Boston. He had been given letters to four mercantile communities but returned with five, Newbury stating its satisfaction as well as Newburyport. Portsmouth in its reply said that the merchants and traders "are now subscribing" for the postal plan. Newbury was "well pleased with the Proposal." Timothy Pickering, as town clerk of Salem, wrote at some length about the financial difficulties of his community. A hospital for smallpox inoculation, costing £1900, had just been built, and the townsmen were in a turmoil over the possible advantages and disadvantages of inoculation. Opposition had been so strong that the town had been forced to close down the hospital. "However, notwithstanding these difficulties, a subscription was begun yesterday."

Edes and Gill inserted in their *Boston Gazette* of April 25 under the Boston date-line an enthusiastic news item about the trip northward as far as Casco Bay:

Last Wednesday [April 20] arrived in this Town from the Eastward, Mr. William Goddard, by whom Letters are received from the Committees of Correspondence of Portsmouth, Newbury, Newbury-Port, Salem, &c. expressive of the hearty Concurrence of the Gentlemen in those Towns with the Proposal of erecting a Post-Office upon constitutional Principles, throughout this Continent. Subscriptions are set on foot in each of them, and they have already succeeded beyond the most sanguine Expectation in all.—The Removal of Dr. Franklin from the Post-Office has added fresh Spirit to the Promoters of this salutary Plan, as several viewed an Opposition to his Interest, at a Time when he had signally served the Cause of America, as a very disagreeable Object; but all Reluctance from that Quarter must now vanish, and all the Friends of Liberty rejoice that they now have an Opportunity of taking up a Gentleman discarded by an *unrighteous* Ministry for the faithful Discharge of his Duty, and placing him above a Dependence on their Caprice, in the grateful Arms of his applauding Countrymen.

The Boston Committee of Correspondence now really got down to work on the problem of how to put the proposal into actual operation. On the evening of the twenty-fifth the first of several meetings was held in the Selectmen's Chamber. Goddard formally presented the replies from the towns he had just visited. Then a subcommittee composed of Samuel Adams, Dr. Benjamin Church, Dr. Thomas Young, Nathaniel Appleton, and Joseph Greenleaff was selected to work out the details. The next evening another meeting was held, and the subcommittee "had leave to sit again." A day later the subcommittee brought forward a proposed draft, only to have the meeting recommit their proposal and put them to work again. Apparently the desired changes were minor since the subcommittee is recorded as reporting again that same evening, though no indication is given in the minutes what action was taken.

In spite of the omission in the minutes of an official approval the Boston group led by Sam Adams started to put its plan into execution on April 30. Subscription blanks headed *"The* PLAN *for establishing a New* American POST-OFFICE" were printed, probably by Edes and Gill. Copies of these were circulated and actual subscriptions taken. The *Boston Gazette* two days later reported: "The second Gentleman to whom it was presented, generously engaged *Fifty Pounds*, Lawful Money, and many others have done as handsomely in proportion to their Circumstances." Of Goddard it was said that he would now be able to set out towards the south, "rejoicing in the great Success which hath attended his Endeavours to rescue the Channel of *public* and *private* Intelligence from the horrid Fangs of ministerial Dependents."

A copy of the subscription form is to be found in the John Carter Brown Library. At the top of the broadside is an inscription in Goddard's graceful handwriting, "To the Gent^n. of the Committee of Correspondence for the Town of Newbury, from their most humble Ser^vt.," and signed W^m. Goddard. The broadside reveals the arguments used and the general outline of the new private postal system as Goddard and the Boston group conceived it.

. . . [By means of the British postal system] a Set of Officers, *Ministerial* indeed, in their Creation, Direction and Dependance are maintained in the Colonies, into whose Hands all the social, commercial and political Intelligence of the Continent is necessarily committed; which, at this Time, every one must consider as dangerous in the extreme. It is not only our Letters that are liable to be stopt and opened by a Ministerial Mandate, and their Contents construed into treasonable Conspiracies, but our News-Papers, those necessary & important Alarms in Time of public Danger, may be rendered of little Consequence for want of Circulation.

Whenever it shall be thought proper to restrain the Liberty of the Press, or injure an Individual, how easily may it be effected! A Postmaster-General may dismiss a Rider, and substitute his Hostler in his Place, who may tax the News-Papers to a Prohibition; and when the Master is remonstrated to upon the Head, he may deny he has any Concern in the Matter, and tell the Printer he must make his Terms with the Post. [Goddard is writing this from personal experience; in fact, he used as one of his arguments this statement: "The sum of fifty-two pounds sterling, Pennsylvania currency, per annum was demanded at the Post Office for the carriage of about three hundred and fifty news-papers, one hundred and thirty miles, payable in weekly payments, as the papers were delivered to the Posts."]

. . . it is therefore proposed. That Subscriptions be opened for the Establishment and Maintenance of a Post-Office; and for the necessary Defence of Post-Officers and Riders employed in the same.

That the Subscribers, in each Colony, shall annually appoint a Committee from among themselves, consisting of seven Persons, whose Business it shall be to appoint Post-Masters in all Places within their respective Provinces, where such Offices have hitherto been kept, or may hereafter be judged necessary; and to regulate the Postage of Letters and Packets, with the Terms on which News-Papers are to be carried; which Regulations shall be printed and set up in each respective Office.

. . . That a Post-Master General shall be annually chosen, by the written Votes of all the Provincial Committees, inclosed and sent to the Chairman of the New-York Committee. . . .

IN Order that the foregoing Plan may be carried into Execution, We the Subscribers do severally promise to pay the several Sums annexed to our Names, to the Chairman of the Committee to be appointed in Pursuance of said Plan, whenever according to the Conditions thereof they shall be called for by him or his Successor in Office.

BOSTON, APRIL 30, 1774.

During this time the newspapers were not inactive. Apparently the keen eye of Isaiah Thomas first noticed in one of the London papers a letter which seemed peculiarly appropriate to the situation. In typical colonial fashion several newspapers reprinted this, including Purdie and Dixon's *Virginia Gazette*, whose readers were given Goddard's activities in considerable detail through the following August. Thomas's *Spy* printed the London letter on April 22, and the Williamsburg paper on May 26, which presented it under a Boston date-line of April 21 after the account of Goddard's return to Boston. Purdie and Dixon prefaced the letter:

To the PRINTER.

SIR,

Be pleased to present to your Readers the following short Address of a prophetick Pennsylvanian [Franklin?] to Lord North, in Consequence of the happy Dismission of Dr. Franklin from the ministerial Post Office in America, extracted from a London Paper of the 5th of February last. I heartily congratulate my Countrymen on this auspicious Event, and am persuaded they will now unanimously join in verifying the Prediction of our absent Friend; and I believe I may say, without any extraordinary Gift of Prophecy, that a CONSTITUTIONAL AMERICAN POST OFFICE will be permanently established in six Weeks from the 21st Day of April, 1774.

A New Englandman.

[Quite possibly the "New Englandman" may have been Goddard; the last clause of this introduction sounds much like him.]

To Lord North

My Lord,

As an American, give me Leave to assure your Lordship that I think the dismissing Dr. Franklin from the Office of Postmaster General in North America, at this particular Crisis, one of the most fortunate Events that could have happened for that Country. It was that Gentleman that brought the Post Office in America to be of some Consequence, and to yield something of a Revenue to the Mother Country. The People there never liked the Institution, and only acquiesced in it out of their unbounded Affection for the Person that held the Office, who had taken infinite Pains to render it convenient to the several Colonies. But what will follow now, my Lord? I will tell you: The Post from Philadelphia to Boston is that alone which produces any Profit worth mentioning; the others, taken together, do not more than maintain themselves; and between Philadelphia and Boston, you may depend on it, the Americans will immediately set up a Carrier of their own, which you, with all your Brethren in Power, together with Lord Hillsborough's Abilities, cannot prevent, and thereby they will entirely starve your Post between these capital Cities; and thus will happily end your boasted Post Office, so often given as a PRECEDENT for raking the Americans.

A PENNSYLVANIAN.

On April 26 Thomas Pownall, former royal governor of Massachusetts, echoed the sentiments of "a Pennsylvanian" during the course of a speech in Parliament when he said that the colonists "now send their letters by couriers, instead of the post, from one town to another; and I can say, your post-office will very soon be deprived of its revenue." Speeches and letters like these, of course, made Goddard's task of persuasion just that much easier.

On the third of May the Boston Committee of Correspondence met again. This time Dr. Young of the subcommittee submitted a draft of a letter to be sent the "Southern Governments," i.e., the Committees of Correspondence of Philadelphia, New York, Newport, and Providence. The minutes read that the clerk was "to provide Mr. Goddard with a Copy" of this letter, which was approved by the meeting. The final letter, as recorded in the minutes, is dated May 5.

In the meantime news of what was happening in New England had reached Philadelphia. Governor William Franklin on May 3 wrote to his father in London: "Your Friends in Boston, as I am told, before they heard of your running any Risk of a Dismission, were encouraging Goddard in his new Post Office, which, if successful, must have deprived you of your Salary as Postmaster General even if you had not been deprived of your Office." As phrased by the royal governor, this was not news to please his father.

Returning to the traveler, we find the *Boston Gazette* reporting Goddard's departure from Boston on May 9: "This Day Mr. William Goddard set out on his Return Homewards, taking Providence, Newport and the principal Towns in Connecticut in his Way. The last mentioned Colony is the only one in New-England who has not greatly encouraged his Undertaking, and there can hardly be a Question whether a Plan, so conservative of American Liberty, will be favoured by that patriotic People or no, when laid before them."

From Boston the Baltimore newspaperman went to Providence, there to deliver one of the letters from Boston and to do what he could to push affairs along. The Providence Committee of Correspondence now showed no reluctance. On May 13 an enthusiastic letter was sent from Providence to the Hartford Committee of Correspondence. The first sentence reads: "We wish this to recommend to you the Business that Mr Goddard is engaged in as highly worthy of your Notice."

On the sixteenth Goddard was in Newport, probably expecting to leave the next day, since we have two letters which he wrote from Newport on that date. One was to Peter Vandervoort, a merchant in New York; the other was to John Lamb. In both letters Goddard asked for certain unnamed articles to be forwarded, presumably subscription forms and the like, to other towns south of New York. In his letter to Lamb, Goddard says that his next stops would be in

Connecticut, where "I shall set out this Day . . . , & as soon as Subscriptions are opened in the principal Towns on the Post Roads & Postmasters nominated, I shall repair to New York, which I hope will be within 10 Days."

A report from a New York newspaper tells us that Goddard arrived in that town on Saturday, May 28. Apparently things had gone well with his proposals in Hartford, New London, and the various towns along the Boston Post Road; in fact, New London had opened up a subscription as early as April 4. By Monday morning he was ready to leave New York since his friends there had already started the operation of the new postal system. A *New-York Journal* article of June 2 defends the "Constitutional Post Office" from its calumniators and indicates that riders were at work on a regular schedule between New York and Philadelphia. When Purdie and Dixon reprinted this article in their *Virginia Gazette* of July 7, they appended as a bracketed and italicized remark (the article had ended with the hope that the new system would "in a few Weeks, be carried into complete Execution"): "*The sooner the better, for the publick Good.*"

"The vast noise and bustle which has lately appeared in almost all the papers relative to the POSTOFFICE in America . . ." opens a letter written from Philadelphia to Williamsburg printed in Mrs. Rind's *Virginia Gazette*, April 21, 1774. Clearly enough, in returning to Philadelphia, Goddard was not on an unknown mission. Though he must have had some difficulties assuaging the feelings of certain individuals, he did succeed in getting his plan into effect. William Bradford apparently as early as April 21 had become the local postmaster for the new constitutional or Goddard's post office, as it was sometimes called. The letter quoted above goes on to imply that the Philadelphia merchants selected Bradford in preference to Goddard, who was not liked, but more likely Goddard was not even a candidate since he had severed his connections in Philadelphia when he closed down the *Pennsylvania Chronicle* the preceding February. At any rate, the new system was already in operation by the time Goddard passed through Philadelphia on his way to Baltimore during the first week of June. Subscriptions had been taken, a postmaster been appointed, and postriders been secured. A Mr. Stinson is spoken of on May 19 as riding the post between Philadelphia and Baltimore. (Stinson may well have been the William Stenson mentioned by Goddard in December, 1773.)

An article signed Amor Patriae in the *Maryland Journal* of June 4 bears all the earmarks of having been written by Goddard. He reveals little specific information but does proudly say: "A complete plan for *establishing* a new American POST OFFICE hath lately been executed at Boston, where, as well as in many other principal towns to the northward, it has been so liberally encouraged and so nobly patronized by a very considerable number of principal gentlemen and others that no doubt seems now to remain of its being very seasonably carried into execution throughout the whole continent."

During the summer months of 1774 Goddard busied himself in extending southward the operations of the Constitutional Post Office. By the first of June, as we have seen, it was a going concern from Baltimore to Falmouth. The first important city below Baltimore was Annapolis. No doubt this continuation southward was arranged so easily by Goddard and the printers of the *Maryland Gazette*, Anne Catherine Green and her son Frederick, that it warranted no discussion in either the Annapolis or the Baltimore papers.

On the second of July Goddard published in the *Maryland Journal* a lengthy article, most of which is a reprint of the subscription form first printed in Boston on April 30. The opening sentences of the article give the present condition of the new system: "The Printer of this Paper, with great Pleasure, acquaints the Public, that his Proposal for establishing an AMERICAN POST-OFFICE, on constitutional Principles, hath been warmly and generously patronized by the Friends of Freedom in all the great commercial Towns in the Eastern Colonies, where ample Funds are already secured, Post-Masters and Riders engaged, and, indeed, every necessary Arrangement made for the Reception of the Southern Mails, which, it is expected, will soon be extended thither—As therefore the final success of the Undertaking now depends on the Public-spirit of the Inhabitants of Maryland and Virginia, it is not doubted . . . but they will cheerfully join. . . ."

Two weeks later another article informed the Baltimore public that the new post offices would soon be in operation "from *Virginia* to *Casco-Bay*." Goddard's activities and plans are revealed: "On the Return of a *particular Agent,* who is just setting off for *Virginia,* the Public will have further Intelligence of the State of the Enterprize in Question, which the Friends of Freedom and their country wish to see compleated by the first of September next, that being the Time appointed for the Meeting of the grand congress at *Philadelphia*—a Body that cannot, with any Degree of Consistency or Safety, intrust or encourage the Tools of those who have forged our Chains, and are striving to rule us with a Rod of Iron." In other words, the system was to be extended to Williamsburg; then what we now call the First Continental Congress was to take over the running of the entire setup.

Before Goddard's visit to Williamsburg there had been much ado in the Williamsburg papers about the proposed post offices. Purdie and Dixon were continuing to reprint many of the accounts from the Boston and New York papers, including the subscription form of April 30. Mrs. Rind in her similarly named *Virginia Gazette* had not printed any of these notices; instead it was in her newspaper that the attack on Goddard of April 21 had appeared. Goddard and Holt may have suspected that Joseph Galloway or someone directly under his influence had written this attack since Holt's *New-York Journal* of July 14 had a contribution from P. Q. censuring Galloway and three other individuals for their assumption of the role of Philadelphia's Committee of Correspondence. Whether Galloway or not, the letter-writer of April 21 continued his campaign against Goddard in Mrs. Rind's July 21 *Virginia Gazette,* asserting that the peripatetic printer had had his proposals rejected in Philadelphia at a "meeting of mechanics."

William Goddard was not the kind of person to take these attacks lying down. In Purdie and Dixon's paper of August 4 he announced in an anonymous letter, dated July 25, that he would set out for Williamsburg "in a few Days" to present in person his proposals to the colony's assembly and the local committee of correspondence. But it was in Mrs. Rind's paper of the same day that he made his counterattack on the letter-writer from Philadelphia. Signing himself "A Lover of Justice," he said the two letters "contain the *grossest misrepresentations* in some parts, and the *most palpab[le]* and *impudent falshoods* in others, which will be made fully to appea[r] whenever the *writer,* or his *correspondent,* shall have the spirit to st[and] forth from their *dark retreat,* and avow those insidious and inhu[man] attempts to injure the reputation of a person who is a stranger in t[his] province."

A few days after July 25, therefore, Goddard rode down to Williamsburg to complete the last link of his chain. (Aware of the sparse population of the Carolinas and Georgia, Goddard was probably little interested in pushing the system farther south. Also, Hugh Finlay in his journal writes at great length about the general inefficiency and sloppiness of the post offices in the Carolinas.) In spite of the campaign against him by the anonymous Philadelphian he was again successful in his attempt, so that the Williamsburg announcement of August 11 is really the announcement of the completion of what Goddard had set out to accomplish just six months earlier. Not only did the Williamsburg Committee of Correspondence approve, but the Virginia colony put itself on record as recommending that the Continental Congress take over the Constitutional Post Offices. It was a similar instruction from the Virginia colony which resulted in the introduction in the Continental Congress on June 7, 1776, by Richard Henry Lee of the resolution affirming independence. The Williamsburg news item of August 11 in Purdie and Dixon's version of the *Virginia Gazette* reads: "Mr. Goddard's Proposals and Plan for establishing an AMERICAN POST OFFICE on constitutional Principles, which appears, by Letters from the Committees of Correspondence and principal Gentlemen of many respectable Provinces and Towns, to have met with the most generous Patronage and warmest Approbation, were agitated at the late Convention of the Representatives of this Colony [from the first to the sixth of August], who justly considered the Object Mr. Goddard is pursuing of great Importance to America, highly worthy the Attention of the General Congress, and as such, particularly recommended it to the Gentlemen appointed Delegates from this Colony." And so a functioning postal system in opposition to the official British one was by this date a going concern from Casco Bay in Maine to Williamsburg, Virginia. No small achievement for the Baltimore printer!

The next and final promotional step was to get the Continental Congress to take over the system. The first attempt made by Goddard was unsuccessful. An entry in the *Journal of Continental Congress* dated Wednesday, October 5, 1774, reads: "An address from William Goddard to the Congress was read and ordered to lie on the table." No other action or discussion is recorded for the First Continental Congress. Apparently the influence of such conservatives as Joseph Galloway was too strong at this time.

During the winter of 1774-1775 Goddard traveled through the colonies again in efforts to expand and strengthen his system. Probably it was on these travels that Goddard was seized in Philadelphia and again placed in the city jail as a debtor. To secure his release, he had to petition the Pennsylvania Assembly and go through the equivalent of bankruptcy. On March 18, 1775, the Assembly passed a bill releasing Goddard, and he was now ready to resume his postal activities. The effectiveness of these activities is evidenced by the notice sent out in March, 1775, by the postmaster general in London to his American deputies. He could no longer give positive directions to them, but they must use their own discretion and judgment since no more was expected of them. A far cry from Foxcroft's arrogant letter of almost a year before.

John Foxcroft as the operating head of the British post office in the colonies inevitably became the target of abuse by Goddard and his supporters. Foxcroft had his headquarters in New York, where John Holt, John Lamb, and several others of the most active and vociferous colonial partisans were also. On May 2 Goddard issued in New York a broadside attacking Foxcroft. The contents of the handbill provide us with little information except how vituperative Goddard could be on occasion.

On May 7 Hartford appointed William Ellery postmaster "to Recive and forward all Letters untill the Business of the Post office shall be regulated by the Continental Congress." By this time more persons than Goddard expected Congressional action. On this same seventh of May Titus Hosmer of Middletown, Connecticut, wrote to Goddard, telling him, "I have seen as many of the Committee as I could conveniently and we have agreed to nominate as a Post-Master for this Town Mr. Wensley Hobby." The next day the Hartford paper published an article on the local appointment, which also contained a list of "Goddard's Post-Offices." This list names postmasters from Cambridge, Massachusetts (Boston was at this time occupied by British troops), to Williamsburg, Virginia. Such doughty patriots as Isaiah Thomas, Thaddeus Burr, and John Holt are included. Postriders are listed starting from Falmouth. Several of these postriders had formerly worked for the British system, such as Peter and Benjamin Mumford, whose activities Hugh Finlay had complained of. Between Cambridge and New York there were different routes for the mails to go. One went from Cambridge to Hartford, probably through Worcester, and then on to New York. Another rider took his way from Cambridge to Providence, to Newport, to New London, and thence to New York. A third rider varied this last route by going through Norwich instead of Newport as a stop between Providence and New London.

The Second Continental Congress started its meetings in Philadelphia May 10, 1775. The battles of Lexington and Concord had occurred the previous April 19, and the mood of this Congress was much different from the first. Apparently in the expectation that the Congress would assume the responsibilities for Goddard's post offices, several of the colonial assemblies now took over the postal operations from the local Committees of Correspondence: Massachusetts on May 12; New Hampshire on May 18. Then on May 29, 1775, the Second Continental Congress "*Resolved,* that Mr. *Franklin,* Mr. *Lynch,* Mr. *Lee,* Mr. *Willing,* Mr. *S. Adams,* and Mr. *P. Livingston,* be a Committee to consider the best means of establishing Posts for conveying Letters and Intelligence through this Continent."

The final action on a report from this committee was taken July 26, 1775, when the Continental Congress adopted a postal system in opposition to the British. Franklin was at the same time elected Postmaster General. Later Franklin appointed his son-in-law, Richard Bache, as comptroller. Goddard was made surveyor, a minuscule post that disappointed him. By its action of July 26, however, Congress ratified and gave status to Goddard's post offices.

The British system continued to operate irregularly and feebly for some time. The remarks made in a debate in Congress on October 7, 1775, imply that the British mails were functioning most in Georgia. This debate was over a motion by Richard Henry Lee that "parliamentary or ministerial posts" should be stopped. Action on this motion was indefinitely postponed, there still being many members of Congress who wanted to offend England as little as possible. The Maryland Assembly finally took matters into its own hands on December 11, 1775, when it passed a motion forbidding the Parliamentary post to go through the province. The effectiveness of the motion is admitted by the announcement officially ending the British system on Christmas Day:

General Post-Office, New-York, December 25, 1775.

Whereas, the Provincial Convention at *Annapolis* has passed a Resolve, "That the Parliamentary Post (as they are pleased to term it) shall not be permitted to suffer or travel in, or pass through that Province with any mail, packages, or letters;" and, in consequence of that Resolve, have taken his Majesty's mail from the Post-Office at *Baltimore*, with the letters contained therein. The Committee at *Philadelphia* having also taken the mail containing all the last packet letters to the Southward, opened many of them, to the great hurt of individuals; and signified to the Postmaster their intention of stopping all others for the future; and other of his Majesty's mails having been taken and obstructed, notice is hereby given to the publick, that the Deputy Postmaster-General is obliged, for the present, to stop all the Posts. They are also hereby desired to take notice, that for the safety of the letters coming by the next or any future packet, they will be kept on board, and the names of those who shall have letters will be advertised, that may either apply themselves, or write to their friends in this city to take them up. An order in writing from the person to whom any letters may be directed will be necessary.

Francis Dashwood, *Secretary*.

More than six months before the Declaration of Independence was promulgated in Philadelphia the channels of communication in the colonies were completely (except, of course, in areas occupied by the British army) under the control of the colonial authorities thanks to the efforts of William Goddard. As Carl Bridenbaugh has phrased it: "Thus occurred the first institutional change of the American Revolution. . . . Indeed, the Colonial Post Office had played a vital role in bringing about American independence; the committees of correspondence could not have succeeded had not communication lanes been so readily available."

BALTIMORE, the scene of William Goddard's activities for almost twenty years, in the 1770's was only beginning to show indications of its future importance. Its population in 1775 has been estimated at 5,934, a figure surpassed by several colonial communities. The nation's first census in 1790 gave the town's inhabitants as 13,503. Though probably few other colonists would have agreed with the Baltimoreans of the early 1770's, we must still be aware of their faith in the town's potential growth. The six thousand burghers could not create the well-nigh metropolitan atmosphere of the Philadelphia of this period, but there was much of the urbane and cosmopolitan about the Maryland town. A building on Market Street was set aside for theatrical performances. Like Philadelphia, Baltimore had not only many German settlers, but it also had on South Charles Street an area called Frenchtown, named after the Acadians who had made their homes there since their forced migration in 1755. In typical Baltimore fashion besides six churches there were three breweries when Goddard first moved into the settlement. The one shipyard and the two ropewalks kept a few families fed, but many other cities along the Atlantic coast surpassed this commercial representation.

Because Baltimore was not the Maryland capital, Annapolis instead had been the scene of printing activity for many years. Since 1738 Jonas Green, great-grandson of Samuel Green of the seventeenth-century Cambridge press, had printed there and had published a weekly newspaper, the *Maryland Gazette*. On his death in 1767, the widow, Anne Catherine Green, took over the business. At the time of Goddard's arrival in Baltimore the Annapolis firm was operating as Anne Catherine Green & Son. The son, Frederick Green, continued as a printer in Annapolis from 1775, when his mother died, until his own death in 1811. The business had never produced a fortune, but the government printing had provided a comfortable living for the Greens.

Though Goddard was not Baltimore's first printer, no one before him had managed to make a go of it nor had anybody even tried to start a newspaper. The first printer was Nicholas Hasselbach, who is supposed to have learned the trade in the German shop of Christopher Sower in Germantown. There is a record of his buying property in Baltimore on July 6, 1765, and the one imprint extant from his shop is dated that same year. Little else is known of his shop's activities. Hasselbach himself died at sea in late 1769 or early 1770 on his way to England, and his wife seemingly made no attempt to continue the business. In 1773 she sold his press and types to Goddard. According to a tradition reported by Wroth, Goddard thought he was buying Caslon type. After he discovered his error, he was able to sell the type to Francis Bailey of Lancaster.

The next printers in Baltimore were Robert Hodge and Frederick Shober. They announced their partnership by an advertisement dated October 31, 1772, in the *Maryland Gazette* of November 5. Only one imprint remains from their shop; they apparently moved to New York by the end of the year.

Isaiah Thomas says that the next printer was Enoch Story, the younger, who ran a print shop from the end of 1772. The three extant imprints all date from 1774 and 1775, so it is possible that Thomas erred by two years. More likely, since Goddard himself carefully read through Thomas's *History of Printing* and wrote down all the errors he noticed and his eye did not catch this as an error, Story did start work in 1772, but no imprint of 1772 or 1773 remains today. Like the widow Hasselbach, Story sold his equipment to Goddard in 1775 and returned to Philadelphia.

The week before Hodge and Shober made their announcement in the *Maryland Gazette*, William Goddard advertised his expectations of opening a print shop in Baltimore. Specifically, the advertisement, dated October 20 (Goddard's thirty-second birthday), proposed the publication of a newspaper to be entitled *The Maryland Journal, and Baltimore Advertiser*. In contrast to the *Gazette*'s twelve and six for annual subscriptions Goddard set his price at ten shillings, the same rate he was charging for the *Pennsylvania Chronicle*. Though Goddard spoke of the encouragement he had "some Time since received from many Gentlemen" in Baltimore, one suspects that the idea of establishing a paper in the Maryland port occurred to him in the afterglow of the 1772 assembly elections, when he had received many votes. Anyway, he said he had "engaged a suitable *Printing-Apparatus*" for work "both in the *English* and other Languages." He hoped to avoid the early Philadelphia financial difficulties by requiring one-half of the subscription costs in advance. The new paper would "contain every material Piece of Intelligence, either *foreign* or *domestic*, with Accounts of the Arrival and Departure of Ships, the current Prices of Goods, the Course of Exchange, Deaths, Accidents, and Events of every Kind, that may be thought interesting to the Publick." Newspapers, pamphlets, and magazines from the other colonies, Great Britain and Ireland, as well as Germany would be received and perused for the benefit of the proposed newspaper. Having his Philadelphia experience in mind, Goddard said that "the Freedom of the Press shall be maintained, the utmost Impartiality observed, and every well-written Piece admitted, without Scruple, that does not tend to destroy or impair our excellent Constitution, injure the Cause of Liberty, disturb the Repose of Society, give Offence to Modesty, or, in any Shape, reflect Scandal on a *News-Paper*."

During the spring of 1773 Goddard must have made many trips between Baltimore and Philadelphia. By May 20 he could advertise in the *Maryland Gazette* that his shop at the corner of South and Baltimore streets was now open for business. The notice is dated May 12, so this is the probable date for the opening of the Baltimore print shop. In the *Pennsylvania Chronicle* of May 31 there is another notice, dated May 26, about the new shop. Mostly it repeats the *Gazette* advertisement, but it does tell us that "WILLIAM GODDARD's *English* and *German* Printing Office is removed from the House of Mrs. *Hasselbach*, to that of Mr. *Jacob Mohler*, Clock and Watchmaker, near the Corner of *South* and *Market Streets*." Both notices requested that subscription agents turn in the names and addresses of the subscribers, so that the new paper might get started. Readers of the *Chronicle* were assured that the Philadelphia paper would be continued "as usual."

Probably during most of 1773 Mary Katherine Goddard supervised the operations of the Philadelphia shop while her brother busied himself in Baltimore. We can also deduce that at this time Goddard had every intention of maintaining the two shops. Though he had not paid off the debts of the old Galloway-Wharton partnership and no longer had any of the Pennsylvania Assembly printing, the *Chronicle* was finally a profitable operation, and Goddard once again was thinking in hyperbole. Later in life he said that he started business in Baltimore with only a guinea of capital—romantic nonsense if ever there was. Though the partnership debts would land him in a Philadelphia jail in early 1775, it was no pauper who started the *Maryland Journal* in 1773. Certainly Goddard did not think of himself as that. He was making what he hoped would be an expansion of a profitable business. Each newspaper would help the other, and together they would provide an increased efficiency. Typical of one helping the other is the notice in the June 14 *Chronicle* asking for a compositor, in both English and German, for the new Baltimore shop. (The continued emphasis on German makes one suspect that Mrs. Hasselbach had made quite a point of this potential business when she sold Goddard her late husband's equipment.)

Finally, on Saturday, August 20, 1773, the long-awaited *Maryland Journal* made its initial appearance, and Baltimore had its first newspaper. Isaiah Thomas in his *History of Printing* described the *Journal* as "handsomely printed on a demy sheet," and John T. Scharf called the presswork "admirable." The coat-of-arms of the Maryland colony was placed in the flag. Tradition (reported in Scharf's *Chronicles of Baltimore*) has it that the engraving of these arms was done by Sparrow at Annapolis. The following December Goddard in a letter (referred to in the previous chapter) to John Lamb in New York inquired after the "Maryland arms that Dawkins was to execute for me." Henry Dawkins must never have done the work since the Sparrow engraving continued in use until 1776, when it was dropped. Underneath the title was a quotation from Horace, "He carries every point who blends the useful with the agreeable, Amusing his reader while he instructs him." (Translation is by Scharf.) No doubt the haste in getting out the issue caused the glaring error of the date-line—Friday instead of Saturday.

On page one there is the usual statement of the printer "To the Public." Not so confident now, Goddard apologized for the delay in starting the *Journal*, blaming it on the difficulty in getting together printing materials, "an inadequate Number of Subscribers," and "several unfortunate Events which have happened to me." The troubles in securing a postrider between Philadelphia and Baltimore were gone into in some detail. But when this problem was solved, he would receive the papers from the other colonies and even the "British and Irish Papers." In heavy capitals Goddard promised his readers that the new paper should be "FREE and of NO PARTY"—a promise he and his sister fulfilled for almost twenty years.

Elsewhere in the opening issue the printer advertised for "An active faithful Man, who can write a tolerable Hand, and keep a fair Account . . . to ride as a private POST or CARRIER between this Town and *Philadelphia*, once a Week." On the same page (three) Goddard inserted a notice requesting ship captains and anybody else having news information to keep him posted. Also there was a pseudonymous letter addressed to Messrs. Chase and Paca and signed Hononcrononthotontologus. It is not difficult to see why this did not become a popular name to sign the innumerable letters published in eighteenth-century newspapers. On page four George Washington had the first of his many advertisements in the *Maryland Journal*. Finally at the end of the paper there was this colophon: "Baltimore: Printed by William Goddard, at the Printing-Office in Market-Street, opposite the Coffee-House. . . ."

In the next issue, August 28, Goddard advertised again for a rider and apologized to his readers for inconveniencing them. He also requested in this same issue the services of "A SOBER LAD, as an Apprentice to the PRINTING BUSINESS." Later, on September 9, he advertised for "one or two sober *Journeymen Printers*, who *can* and *will* work." Obviously he was having troubles with the staff he had recruited from the vicinity of Baltimore.

Unfortunately, the help was not the only problem Goddard had in getting his *Journal* on its feet. During most of the fall the appearance of the paper was irregular, contrasting with the clocklike regularity Mary Katherine maintained for the *Pennsylvania Chronicle*. So often was this true that the November 20 issue featured an apologetic statement by the printer: "The Proprietor of this Paper, who hath been several Weeks on a Tour to the Northern Colonies, for the Benefit of his Health, is *just* returned. . . . The Printing

Business, *in general*, he is determined, under *their* [his customers']
Favour, to prosecute in *this Place*, with the most *persevering Industry*, and the MARYLAND JOURNAL, and BALTIMORE ADVERTISER,
in particular, being so very respectably patronized, shall, *in future*,
be the primary Object of his Care and Attention." The notice concluded with the hope of the publisher to be "able *speedily* and
effectually to remove" all the obstacles to regular publication. Apparently during Goddard's sickness there had been rumors in Baltimore that the printer was more interested in the Philadelphia branch
of the Goddard business and would let the Baltimore paper languish,
and this in spite of the respectable patronage; so Goddard was forced
to explicitly state his intentions.

Difficulties with paper supplies are revealed by the olive-drab appearance of the November 20 *Journal*. A week later the same hue
of the paper caused Goddard to say: "The Printer hereof not having
received a Supply of good fair Paper, which he contracted for and
expected, is, for the present, under the disagreeable Necessity of
using this dark complexioned Sort." Not until December 18 was
the printer able to change from his "dark complexioned" paper.

Ill health, inadequate paper supply, and staff troubles must all
have added up to make the launching of the new Baltimore newspaper a trying time for Goddard. In the *Journal* of November 27 he
advertised for "two Journeymen Compositors, and one Pressman."
Circulation was good, and the commercial activities of Baltimore must
have provided a reasonable amount of job printing. But Goddard
took a drastic step, which he announced in a news item under the
Baltimore date-line of December 9: "The Printer of this Paper has
laboured under the greatest Disadvantages since the Institution of
the Maryland Journal, particularly in being obliged to employ a
worthless Set of Hands, and the most inartificial of the Occupation—
but he has now discharged the whole Knot that infested his Office,
and engaged a regular Set, whereby he hopes to give greater Satisfaction to his Customers in future." For some time afterwards publication was more regular, evidencing either the truth of this statement
or the closer application of Goddard to the business.

As in Providence Goddard was printing the community's first
newspaper. In this role there were many functions that the paper
played in assisting the town's commercial and cultural development.

One can be followed throughout the fall of 1773. Michael Kraus has traced the idea of a private circulating library back to John Mein's twelve-hundred-volume establishment in Boston in 1765. Shortly afterwards Lewis Nicola and Thomas Bradford set up a similar business in Philadelphia. Though Goddard apparently had no hand in the Baltimore institution, he must have followed with interest the activities of Joseph Rathell. Rathell was a schoolmaster in Baltimore who had in the first issue of the *Journal* advertised his services as a private tutor in addition to his duties in the classroom. The self-described "Teacher of the English Language, Writing-master and Accomptant" sought another method of supplementing his income in the *Journal* of October 23. He proposed the establishment of a "Circulating Library in Baltimore-Town." Subscription proposals were to be distributed on the following Tuesday (October 26) at the Coffee House, the Fountain Inn, and the printing office. Other places in the vicinity were also named. These proposals, issued also as a broadside (a copy is to be found in the Maryland Historical Society), constitute the first item under Goddard's name recorded in Wroth's listing of colonial Maryland imprints. The broadside assured its readers that "Libraries have become objects of attention in every polite part of America" and that once a "suitable number of yearly subscribers" was secured, a library of "not less than eight hundred volumes" would be supplied. Catalogues for the convenience of subscribers would be printed. The library itself would include the following categories (a list suggesting the tastes of the potential subscribers): Latin classics, history, poetry, religion, philosophy, physics, agriculture, logic, rhetoric, mathematics, astronomy, geography, chronology, cookery, voyages, travels, adventures, miscellanies (the eigtheenth-century counterpart of today's anthologies), novels, plays, magazines, memoirs, pamphlets, essays, "and every other work of *Merit, Erudition* and *true Humour.*" Additions to the original holdings would be derived from the "newest Publications from *London.*" The method of operation was that each subscriber would pay four dollars a year and have the privilege of taking out as many books as he pleased, one at a time.

The October 30 follow-up advertisement, besides saying that the proposals were already out, included a parenthetical remark about competition from Annapolis: "the Subscription to the *Annapolis*

Library is one Guinea per Annum, besides the Expence of a Dollar a Year for Carriage of Books from thence to this Place by Water." Obviously Rathell was worrying about competition from the Annapolis bookseller William Aikman, who immediately set up a branch agent in Baltimore, Christopher Johnston, advertising this on October 30. All during the month of November Aikman repeated his advertisement, not only for his circulating library, but for the sale of books. How Rathell and Aikman fared in the competition for the trade of the Baltimore readers we do not know, since both discontinued their advertisements, probably for reasons of economy, in the later columns of the *Journal*. But clearly the presence of the new paper and print shop had led to a definite improvement in the facility with which the readers of Baltimore could secure books.

The expansion of business caused Goddard to seek larger quarters. By December 30 he had moved to a new location, only a short distance from the old, indicated by the colophon of that date: "Printed by William Goddard, at the Printing-Office in Market-Street, next Door above Dr. John Stevenson's and two Doors below the Fountain-Inn."

A lighter note for the modern reader and a notice that must have entertained the eighteenth-century Baltimorean as well is to be found in the issue of January 20.

Baltimore, Jan. 18, 1774.

Catherine Treen, the wife of the subscriber, having, in violation of her solemn vow, behaved herself in the most disgraceful manner, by leaving her own place of abode, and living in a criminal state with a certain *William Collins*, a plaisterer, under whose bed she was, last night, discovered, endeavouring to conceal herself, her much injured husband, therefore, in justice to himself, thinks it absolutely necessary to forewarn all persons from trusting her on this account, being determined, after such flagrant proof of her prostitution, to pay no debts of her contracting from the date hereof.

Henry Treen.

As recounted in the preceding chapter, on February 8, 1774, appeared the last issue of the *Pennsylvania Chronicle*, and on February 17 Mary Katherine took over the management of the *Journal*. For almost three years William's energies were bound up with the affairs of the postal system, and the experienced Mary Katherine had to carry on the paper and the business alone. Early in 1774 William, bitten by the bug of his postal scheme, was enabled by the well proved abilities of Mary Katherine to take off on the journey we have already described. During this trip he must have had few worries over the Baltimore shop, knowing her capacities. It would be a pleasure if we could talk about her personality, but we have today none of her personal letters, and, contrary to her brother's practice, she almost never allowed her personal affairs to intrude into her newspaper. A picture of her, the only one we have, appended to her 1783 almanac, shows a not unattractive woman in her mid-forties. The most striking feature is the thin lines of the lips and the fierce, dogged determination they reveal. As publisher of the *Maryland Journal* during all the years of the Revolution she needed whatever determination she could muster.

Soon after she took over the Baltimore paper she ran into troubles which caused the *Journal* to appear with this date-line: "From Thursday, March 10, to Thursday, March 31, 1774." She apologized in a brief note to her readers for the long delay in publication, occasioned by a "Multiplicity of business, respecting the Election now depending." As the war drew near, she frequently had struggles in maintaining any kind of regular schedule for publication—a difficulty she shared with most colonial editors of this period. Insufficient supplies of the usual folio sheets occasionally forced her to print the *Journal* on small-sized sheets. However, we must admit that her carrying on the *Journal* during the entire Revolutionary War was no small achievement.

More than likely the financial difficulties William Goddard was having in Philadelphia in February and March, 1775, caused the temporary removal of a colophon from the *Maryland Journal* starting with the issue of February 6. Until then the colophon read, "Printed by William Goddard." Upon his release from the Philadelphia jail on March 18, Goddard must have made some kind of financial arrangement with his sister. We have no record of this agreement, but on May 10, 1775, the colophon becomes, "Baltimore: Published by M.K. Goddard, at the Printing-Office in Market-Street, next Door above Dr. John Stevenson's." And so it remained for the duration of the war, not only for the newspaper but for all publications issued by the Goddard press.

Among the people in Philadelphia learning of Goddard's being in jail for debt was a printer named Andrew Stewart, who deduced from the Baltimore printer's circumstances that here was an opportunity for him. Who Stewart was we are not sure, but he may well have been the Andrew Steuart who edited the *North-Carolina Gazette* from 1764 to 1766 in Wilmington, North Carolina. Anyway, Stewart advertised proposals in the March 2, 1775, *Rivington's New-York Gazetteer* for a newspaper to be named the *Maryland Gazette and the Baltimore Advertiser*, to start as soon as one thousand subscriptions were pledged. Also, "Advertisements of a moderate length, shall be inserted three times in this paper for Five Shillings" —probably the going rate at the time. No more is heard of either Andrew Stewart or the proposed paper, the vigor with which Mary Katherine pursued her editorial duties no doubt proving an effective deterrent to Stewart's potential subscribers.

The change of the American-British struggle from political to military was recorded quickly in the columns of the *Journal*. The first incomplete news was in the issue of April 26, exactly a week after the Lexington and Concord expedition of the British forces in Boston. This item was date-lined Watertown (Massachusetts-Bay) April 19. That afternoon more complete news came through, and Mary Katherine hustled this into print as a broadside—an extra in the newspaper parlance of today. The note at the bottom of this broadside reveals how the news arrived so quickly: "The above is a true Copy, as received by Express from New-Haven, &c. attested by the Committee of Correspondence from Town to Town." The leaders of the colonial cause considered it imperative that their version of the Lexington and Concord affair reach the ears of the American public before any British account. So effective were they in this attempt that the British never even tried to get their version into print outside Boston, and the colonists had only the committee of correspondence account. The committees were performing the functions conceived for them by Sam Adams.

During the spring of 1775 the colonial struggle was not the only problem for Mary Katherine. Her future competitor, John Dunlap, had learned the printing business from his uncle, William Dunlap. In 1771 he had started the *Pennsylvania Packet*, a newspaper he continued under various names until 1795. He was appointed printer to Congress in 1778. Sometime during the spring of 1775 he set up a branch office in Baltimore and made James Hayes, Jr., its manager. On May 2 this new print shop issued the first number of *Dunlap's Maryland Gazette; or the Baltimore General Advertiser*. Hayes, under the name of Dunlap, continued to run the shop and print the newspaper in competition with Mary Katherine until September 8, 1778, when the pressure of business in Philadelphia probably made Dunlap want to get rid of his Baltimore branch, and so Hayes took over on his own. He continued for almost a year, until July 5, 1779, after which he moved to Annapolis.

The *Journal* of November 8, 1775, carried in its columns an advertisement for linen rags "for the Use of the Paper Manufactory, now erecting near this Town." Probably the proposed paper mill did not go into operation for some time since not until the issue of April 8, 1777, does Mary Katherine announce the *Journal* as printed on paper from the new mill at Elkridge Landing. The Maryland Convention had on May 26, 1776, granted James Dorsett four hundred pounds to set up a paper mill. More than likely this was the mill in which William Goddard had a financial interest and the one that started operations in early 1777.

In the fall of 1775 the administration of the colonial postal system was given by Congress to Benjamin Franklin. Goddard hoped to get the second post in the system—the comptrollership. Instead Franklin made his son-in-law, Richard Bache, comptroller. Goddard was offered the postmastership at Baltimore or the surveyorship of the system. He accepted the low-paying position of surveyor, no doubt feeling greatly chagrined at the turn of events. Mary Katherine was made the postmistress of Baltimore, and a notice regarding the "Constitutional Post-Office" in the *Journal* of October 11, 1775, is signed M. K. Goddard. Thereby she became, as far as we have any record, the first postmistress in the colonies and the only one in an important position under the new government after July 4, 1776.

Goddard's duties in his new position required that he travel about the country checking the routes, etc. Ezra Stiles records a meeting with Goddard in Wrentham, Massachusetts, on November 21, 1775. The conversation that evening, centering on which members of the Continental Congress would likely vote for independence, showed how much the minister and the printer and obviously many other colonial leaders supported the break with England almost eight months before its eventual promulgation. Stiles calls Goddard "very much acquainted with the principal characters of the present day." Then he entered into his diary the probable vote of each member along with the presumed wealth of most. At the end Stiles summarized the estimated vote by colonies as ten for and three against (New York, Pennsylvania, and Maryland). As early as November, 1775, there were many in the colonies who were not only talking about independence but were confidently expecting it to take place. (Why the discussion should have included the wealth of the members is hard to tell now, since no economic determinism either for or against independence is discoverable from the figures in Stiles's diary. Of course, that may have been the point.)

Though he doubtless had other convivial evenings of talk before tavern fireplaces besides the one in Wrentham, Goddard was quite unhappy in his position as surveyor of the postal system. He felt that his accomplishments in 1774 and 1775 deserved much more consideration and reward. Also, no love was lost between Franklin and Goddard. As a result, on June 21, 1776, while in New York, the postal surveyor wrote a memorial to Congress petitioning for a commission in the army. Goddard said how much he had suffered financially in order to set up the colonial postal system in opposition to the British. His position as surveyor maintained him, but that was all. More important, the preliminary work of getting the system going was now finished. Since the country needed men in its army, could he have one of the field grade positions in either of two regiments currently without a colonel as commanding officer? The petition was read by Congress on June 24 and referred to the Board of War. This board, without comment, then referred it to Washington. On July 29, 1776, Washington made his reply. Unfortunately for Goddard, the commander-in-chief was doing his best at this time to accept as few political appointees to his army as he could; therefore he strongly recommended that no commission be awarded. One of his aides, Colonel Parsons, spoke with Goddard and assured him that there were too many experienced officers who deserved promotion before such a political appointment should be made. Goddard had too few friends in Congress for any attempt to be made to overrule Washington's decision, and so he remained in the postal service, much disgruntled.

His travels took Goddard through the colonies a great deal. On September 15, 1776, Ezra Stiles refers to his being in Newport after leaving New York a week before. This time their conversation was on military prospects. On November 20 he was in Baltimore; an affadavit of that date, now in the Maryland Hall of Records, bears his signature as a witness. By the winter of 1776-1777 Richard Bache was postmaster general in place of his father-in-law, who had departed for France, but Goddard was not promoted.

Inevitably Bache and Goddard quarreled and the latter resigned. In a letter to John Hancock, as president of Congress, dated January 18, 1777, Bache reported that Ebenezer Hazard of New York had been appointed to the surveyorship. Goddard "whilst in Office, did Business in a very careless, slovenly Manner." Bache then narrated the incident precipitating the resignation: "Immediately upon my receiving the late Resolve of Congress to establish more frequent, the Current of Intelligence between the Armys of the Northern and Middle Departments and the Congress, I sent off the late Surveyor of the Post Office to carry this Resolve into Execution, he got as far in his Journey as Hackensack, where he found the Army under General Washington retreating, he thought proper to retreat along with it as far as Newark, where he staid for some Time, and then came back again to Philadelphia desponding, and appearing to me, as if he gave the whole American Cause up; I was a good deal chagrined at his Return, & as he had frequently threaten'd to resign his Office, I thought this a proper Time for him to do it." This letter is the only account we have of the resignation, and from this distance it is impossible to judge the merits of one side or the other. No doubt Goddard's dislike of the Franklin family did not make him a satisfactory employee, and it was better to sacrifice Goddard than the influential Bache. Though it has not been preserved, probably Goddard's side of the incident was given in a petition to the Continental Congress, read on January 10, 1777. It was referred to the Board of War, so that Goddard must have been again trying to get a commission in the army in spite of the aspersions cast on the printer's courage and loyalty by Bache. No other record of this petition is to be found; obviously nothing came of it.

Shortly after the first of the year Goddard was back in Baltimore helping his sister get out the *Maryland Journal*. Mary Katherine had recently taken on the business of bookbinding in addition to her printing and bookselling, as an advertisement of December 11, 1776, informed her customers. All during 1776 she had had much trouble with her paper supply. In Philadelphia Goddard had numbered his pages consecutively through each annual volume. Until July 3, 1776, Mary Katherine had continued this practice in the *Journal*, but this made only too obvious the irregularity of publication, and therefore was discontinued. Life as a printer in the midst of the Revolutionary War was difficult, but she was managing to keep things going. In issues of February 25 and March 4, 1777, she did snipe at the statements of a competitive bookbinder, William Pritchard, but otherwise Mary Katherine refused to be drawn into the disputes her brother could never avoid.

This serenity was interrupted by the violent quarrel William had with the members of a Baltimore organization calling itself the Whig Club—a quarrel which threw the whole Maryland community into a turmoil. To understand this turbulent affair, we should go back to May 29, 1776, when George Somerville called on Mary Katherine at her printing office. As she described the call in a letter to the Baltimore Committee of Safety, he "abused her with threats and indecent language on account of a late publication in her paper." On June 3 the committee met to consider her letter and, "conceiving it to be their duty to inquire into everything that has a tendency to restrain the liberty of the Press," ordered Somerville to appear before them that afternoon at three o'clock. At first Somerville ignored the summons, but, the committee promptly sending soldiers out for him, he found himself before them not too many minutes after three. He was reprimanded severely, made to apologize, and released on good behavior. Evident throughout the entire incident is the committee's assumption of the importance of the "liberty of the Press."

Another bit of background is supplied by William Eddis, the surveyor of customs for the British at Annapolis. He reported on May 31, 1776, that within Baltimore a group calling itself the Whig

Club had been organized. Eddis thought the aim of the group was to seize the royal governor, then on a ship (along with the port surveyor) in the Chesapeake Bay. Though nothing came of this purported scheme, the Whig Club of Baltimore continued to function. During the winter months of 1776-1777 the club became more active as it acquired new members from the men on leave from Washington's army. The club's method of operation was to send individuals whom it suspected of Toryism into banishment by means of anonymous notes signed "Legion." On January 9, 1777, the Maryland Council of Safety warned the Baltimore County Committee of Observation about the Whig Club's activities as "contrary to the twenty-fifth section of the Declaration of Rights." The local committee, four days later, replied that they did not know who the members of the club were, but that Mr. Edwards of the town guard had received one of the notices of banishment. To show its respectability, the club on February 11, 1777, published in the *Maryland Journal* a statement of purpose and a set of rules.

The president of the Whig Club at this time was Captain (acting Commodore) James Nicholson. In March, 1776, while in command of the state ship *Defence*, he drove a British sloop, the *Otter*, out of the Patapsco River and recaptured a prize from her. After this one naval exploit Nicholson rested and never thereafter sullied his record by anything as plebeian as combat. Instead, he became the Revolutionary counterpart of today's briefcase-carrying Pentagon admiral. In June, 1776, he was appointed by the Continental Congress to superintend the building and the fitting out of the *Virginia*. Not until 1778 did this ship leave harbor, and then on March 31 it was captured by the British without a round of shot having been fired from her guns. In spite of this record so successful was the brave commodore in his forays into Philadelphia that the Continental Congress in October, 1776, named him number one in the order of seniority among naval captains. In this position Nicholson not only continued his efforts not to fight the British but thwarted almost everybody else's attempts to contact the enemy—and succeeded rather well in both enterprises. John Paul Jones may have beaten the *Serapis*, but he could not prevail against the senior captain of the United States Navy in the halls of Congress. In disgust Jones left this country in 1783, never to return. Another exploit of the commodore resulted in a reprimand from the Maryland Council of Safety. As "Captain Snug-in-Harbor" he found it necessary to maintain a full complement for the unfinished *Virginia*. Privateers and ships not involved in Nicholson's seniority were known to have attacked British ships, and the seamen of Baltimore did not want to sail under the distinguished stay-at-home. As a result, Nicholson's officers resorted to press gangs in the streets of Baltimore. Within Maryland there was much criticism including the reprimand mentioned, but Nicholson fought his usual successful holding action within Congress, and nothing except a short temporary suspension came of the various appeals to that body by governors, councils, and private citizens. It was Goddard's misfortune to run afoul of the commodore's brand of patriotism, always the concern of those "snug in harbor," not of those at sea.

Samuel Chase, one of the Maryland signers of the Declaration of Independence, was worried about the seeming receptivity shown by many Americans to the peace offers made by the British. As part of a campaign against these offers, in the February 25, 1777, *Journal* he published two short articles, which soon threw all Baltimore into an uproar, at least after the Whig Club had read them. Chase had given the articles to Goddard, who in turn gave them to his sister for publication. The first anonymous paragraph appeared on page two:

To the Printer.

Through the channel of your Paper, I take the liberty to congratulate my countrymen on the important intelligence, this day received by Congress.—The terms of peace offered, by General Howe, to America, manifest the magnanimity, generosity, humanity, and virtue of the British nation. The offers of peace, and, in return, to require *only* our friendship, and a preference in our trade and commerce, bespeak the ancient spirit and love of liberty, which was once the acknowledged and boasted characteristick of an Englishman. My soul overflows with gratitude to the patriotic virtuous King, the august incorruptible Parliament, and wise disinterested Ministry of Britain. I am lost in the contemplation of their private and public virtues. I disbelieve and forget, nay will readily believe every assertion, that the monarch of Britain is a sullen and inexorable tyrant, the Parliament venal and corrupt, and the Ministry abandoned and bloody, as wicked and base calumnies. I am not able to express the feelings of my soul on the prospect of immediately seeing my native country blessed with peace and plenty. I am almost induced to complain of Congress for concealing one moment these glad tidings; however I will anticipate the pleasure, and claim thanks from all lovers of peace, for thus early communicating what may be relied on as literally true.

Yours, &c.

TOM TELL-TRUTH.

Baltimore, Feb. 20, 1777.

Directly opposite, on page three, was this implied comment on Tom Tell-Truth:

For the MARYLAND JOURNAL.

Many and various Stratagems have been already practised by the insidious and wicked Court of Britain, and her artful Agents, to deceive and divide the open, generous, unsuspecting Americans. One more Attempt is made. A Report is industriously circulated, that the Commissioners of Britain, Lord and General Howe, through General Lee, have offered to Congress honourable Terms of Negociation. Be not deceived my Countrymen. Expect nothing but Fraud, Force, Rapine, Murder, and Desolation from the Hands of the Tyrant of Britain, and his base and bloody Partisans. Neglect not one Moment to collect your Forces, to drive the Enemies of Peace, Liberty and Virtue from your Country. Shun any Connexion with the People of Britain, as with a common and infected Prostitute. The Sun beholds not a more perfidious, corrupt and wicked People. My Soul detests them as the Gates of Hell.

I have it not in my Power to communicate the Letter from General Lee to Congress. I have seen his Letters to his Friends, to whom he writes, "That by Permission of Lord and General Howe, he had wrote to the Congress, requesting them to depute two or three Gentlemen to New-York, to whom he wishes to communicate something, deeply interesting not only to himself, but, he thinks, the Public."

"Timeo Danaos, et Dona ferentes."

I suspect the Commissioners, nay, their *most conciliating* OFFERS.

CAVETO!

According to Goddard the irony of Tom Tell-Truth so thoroughly eluded the members of the Whig Club that some of them came to Chase for advice about what to do to Goddard. Chase, not taking them seriously, said that Miss Goddard should be tarred and feathered. The reaction of Chase makes clear that neither he nor the two Goddards had any expectation that what was written as irony would be taken literally, a miscomprehension by no means unknown in the history of irony; but events dramatically proved them wrong. On the evening of March 3 the club met at its usual meeting place— David Rusk's tavern. As a result of the deliberations it was determined to find out the name of the author of Tom Tell-Truth.

(Caveto was ignored.)   Lieutenant-Colonel Nathaniel Ramsay and George Turnbull called on Mary Katherine to divulge the author. She referred them to her brother as the deliverer of the article at issue. On asking Goddard the same question, the two club members received a resounding refusal. Back to Rusk's tavern Ramsay and Turnbull went to reveal the results of their mission. More deliberation and Captain John Slaymaker was sent to Goddard with a handwritten note requesting him to attend the next evening's meeting, at six o'clock, of the Whig Club. The note was signed Legion.

At six o'clock on the evening of the fourth Goddard was not at Rusk's tavern, so a delegation of six, some armed, was sent to his house to bring him forcibly to the meeting. One of the print shop's workmen, Justus Brown, was with Goddard at the time and accompanied the group to the tavern. Upon arrival Brown was refused admittance to the club room and had to spend the evening at the bar. Apparently there was a bit of a struggle before Goddard would go, but the six, combined with the printer's rheumatism, were enough to make any delay perfunctory. In the club room Commodore Nicholson was in the chair. Goddard was again asked who the author of Tom Tell-Truth was and again refused to name him. The meeting with Goddard lasted until nine-thirty, long enough for everybody to become insulted and insulting. The net result was that the Whig Club, on one of the different occasions when Goddard, still under guard, was shunted out of the club room into the bar, voted to banish the printer from Baltimore. The written notice was handed to him about ten o'clock by Captain David Plunket after Goddard had returned to his living quarters with Brown. This notice, again signed Legion, said that banishment from the town was to be effective by twelve the next morning (later Goddard poked fun at this timekeeping) and from the county in three days.

Rheumatism momentarily forgotten, Goddard did leave town the next day, his destination the state capital Annapolis. There he wasted little time in preparing a memorial, dated the sixth of March, addressed to the Maryland Council of Safety delineating his troubles, excoriating the members of the Whig Club, and requesting the protection of the laws and the censure of the club. The council referred the memorial to the state assembly then in session. On March 7 the legislature considered the matter and referred it to its

Committee of Aggrievances to find out the truth in the affair. This report was ready by the tenth, and on that date an account favorable to Goddard was submitted. The conclusion of the Committee was "that such proceedings [of the Whig Club] are a manifest Violation of the Constitution, directly contrary to the Declaration of Rights . . . , and tend in their consequences . . . to the overthrow of all Regular Government."

Content with this state of affairs for the moment, Goddard returned to Baltimore only to be greeted by a broadside, dated March 11, from the Whig Club defending its actions. No copy of this broadside has survived, but fortunately for us Goddard reprinted it in his pamphlet less than a week later. The gist of the defense is contained in a word placed in large capitals—*recommended*. Goddard was recommended to leave Baltimore; to the club's *"gentle entreaty* and *mild argument* Mr. *Goddard* opposed the most *mulish obstinacy* and *brutal impoliteness."* No mention was made of Caveto on page three of the by now well-known issue of the *Maryland Journal* of February 25; only Tom Tell-Truth came in for more denunciation.

Goddard was never one to take such comments quietly. So he busied himself in his rooms over the print shop preparing his defense; instead of a broadside he wrote a twenty-page pamphlet. This appeared with the date March 17, so Baltimoreans did not have long to wait for the next installment of the Whig Club affair. This pamphlet, entitled *The Prowess of the Whig Club, and the Manoeuvres of Legion,* had the appropriate couplet from Swift on the titlepage: "These Demoniacs let me dub/ With the Name of LEGION-CLUB." Of course, Goddard gave his version of the events and embroidered them with his choicest epithets. The members of the Whig Club were "a motley crew of *extortioners, military pettifoggers,* and *petty clerks, amphibious heroes,* and deluded *artists"*— and these terms were footnoted to indicate their accuracy. More to the point Goddard gave *in toto* his memorial to the Maryland Council of Safety, the note from the Whig Club banishing him from Baltimore, and the report to the assembly of the Committee of Aggrievances. In an appendix were included the Whig Club broadside of March 11 and the two articles from the pen of Samuel Chase which had started all the uproar. Earlier Goddard had stated that the articles were "written by one of the Delegates to Congress." It should not have been too difficult for the local readers to deduce the figure of Chase behind the pseudonym of Tom Tell-Truth, though apparently not too many of them were so observant. Goddard concluded the main part of the pamphlet with this threatening N. B.: "A KEY to the *names* and *characters* of the *Legion*, who have become so *famous* by their expedition against *Tom Tell-Truth*, will be published, as soon as it shall appear necessary."

For several days the community remained superficially calm while *The Prowess* was read by everybody, including the members of the group presided over by Commodore Nicholson. But this latter group of readers became more and more uncomfortable as they heard the jibes of the people of Baltimore. Finally on Tuesday, March 25, the Whig Club erupted into action and caused one of the first of the many riots for which Baltimore was notorious. From the various depositions made a few days later we can reconstruct the events of the day in some detail.

Between ten and eleven in the morning of the twenty-fifth, headed by Commodore Nicholson, several men armed with sticks and cutlasses came up the street towards the Goddard printing establishment. They first surrounded the building, so that no one could escape from within. Then the Commodore, armed with a stick, ran up the staircase to the workroom where Goddard was and grabbed hold of the printer to force him downstairs. One of the workmen shut the door, only to have it immediately pushed open by others of the Whig Club, who then joined in the struggle. One of the workmen, Justus Brown, later said that he was much bruised on the arms and back by the fight and thought it best, when Goddard was inevitably dragged away, to spend the afternoon in the country. Another of the workmen was thrown downstairs by Benjamin Nicholson and badly hurt. Goddard, who, according to Brown, had been under a physician's care for his rheumatism, after getting his face bloodied, was forced down the stairs and outside. Here his pockets were searched by several of the club members. The commander of the *Virginia* started to hit Goddard with his stick but was stopped from doing so by his compatriots. Instead, grabbing the printer by the collar, he pushed his victim down the street towards Rusk's tavern. Henry Sheaf, a friend of Goddard's, was standing in the doorway of Hayes's print shop as the procession passed. Captain James Cox, one of the Whig Clubbers, greeted Sheaf with this sneer, "Where are your fifty men to support Goddard?" To this remark Commodore Nicholson added, "You damned rascal, I will fifty men you," and swung his stick menacingly.

While Goddard was being escorted to the club room at Rusk's tavern, Mary Katherine was doing her best to help her brother. First, she requested Andrew Wilson to go to the captain of the town guard, William Galbraith, and ask his assistance in quelling the riot and preventing the threatened loss of her brother's life at the hands of Nicholson's mob. Captain Galbraith's reply was that he could do nothing without the specific orders of the chairman of the Baltimore committee. (Probably he meant the committee of observation.) To prove his point, Galbraith produced his orders, but he did dispatch one of his corporals, Murdock Kennedy, to Nathaniel Smith, captain of the troops stationed in Baltimore. Smith, a member of the Whig Club, was at Rusk's tavern awaiting the arrival of Nicholson and his motley crew. He told Kennedy that Galbraith could have part of his men, but he would not command them or order them in any way; in fact, "he would sooner lay down his commission than order his men to fire on such a body of gentlemen." Smith then went up in person to the guardhouse and repeated his sentiments to Galbraith, adding that "there was not above two or three words to be said to Mr. Goddard and then he would be dismissed." With this comment Smith returned to the tavern not to miss the "two or three words." Meanwhile Miss Goddard had gone herself to Captain Galbraith to find out why nothing was being done. He read through his orders to her to prove his hands were tied. A boy was then sent to the committee chairman, James Calhoun, followed shortly by Mary Katherine. Calhoun, apparently not knowing what was afoot, in reply to the boy's request for orders for Captain Galbraith said that he had none. Miss Goddard then appeared on the scene and demanded that Calhoun dispatch orders to Galbraith. He responded, "Captain Galbraith's Guard [was] very insufficient for that purpose, and might only occasion her brother being worse treated than he otherwise would be and should give no orders about it." As a result, in spite of all this running around by various people nothing was done by anybody constituted to maintain

law and order in the community. (Because of the unsettled conditions of the Revolution there were no magistrates functioning as
yet.)

In the meantime two of the Whig Club members, Daniel Bowley
and David McMechan, prepared for the arrival of Goddard at
Rusk's tavern by getting a horse and cart belonging to Andrew
Stigars and placing them in front of the tavern. Seemingly they
had in mind to tar and feather Goddard after he had ridden the rail
out of town.

The procession led by Commodore Nicholson eventually arrived
at Rusk's tavern with its captive. (There had been talk of including
Justus Brown in the party, but Brown had pleaded his injuries.)
They went into the meeting room of the tavern, where a discussion
about what to do with Goddard ensued. After sending the printer
outside the room, the group concluded that their captive should de-
part from Baltimore immediately. Unbeknownst to Goddard but
perhaps known to Nicholson and his cohorts, some thirty or forty
people had gathered near the Market House to put an end to the
mob rule of Baltimore. The presence of this group may have deterred the Whig Club from making any use of Andrew Stigars'
horse and cart. Anyway, after some discussion between Nicholson
and Goddard it was agreed that the printer would return to his home
and prepare himself for departure that night. Accordingly Goddard was then released.

The thoroughly alarmed printer, who had at no time in the
entire proceedings ever yielded his basic principle to the mob, went
back to the print shop and prepared for his departure. As part of
his preparations he printed a broadside directed to Mr. David
Rusk, the owner of the tavern used by the Whig Club. Eighteen
of the participants were named and described as a "gang of Ruffians."
Goddard announced his intentions "as expeditiously as possible, to
proceed to *Annapolis*, where I shall solicit the Legislature of this
State for Protection against the Miscreants, who have been guilty of
the flagitious Practices by which I am now suffering; and that I
shall do my utmost to bring them to condign Punishment." Not
exactly the words used on such an occasion by a Milquetoast. Probably very shortly after this broadside was issued Goddard took himself over to the guardhouse for the protection of Captain Galbraith's

company that night. At noon the next day Galbraith saw to it that Goddard was able to ride out of town safely on his way to Annapolis. Galbraith, worried about his role in the affair, at the same time sent off two accounts of his actions to the Council of Safety. In fact, probably a good many persons in Baltimore began to have second thoughts on the twenty-sixth about their activities of the day before.

Two days later Goddard prepared a memorial to the Committee of Aggrievances giving his version of the events of the twenty-fifth. On April 2 the committee met and took depositions from several persons, including Goddard himself. Not until April 11 was the legislature ready to act on the case of the Whig Club of Baltimore, though the committee had made its report, including the various depositions, on the afternoon of April 2. At the session of April 11 Samuel Chase, the unknown author of the original articles, was present in the assembly and, in fact, was the guiding spirit in the events of the day.

Thirty-five years later Benjamin Galloway, one of the members from Ann Arundel County of the Maryland Assembly in 1777, described what took place in the legislative halls in Annapolis. The sergeant-at-arms had been sent to Baltimore to bring before the house as many of the members of the Whig Club as possible. Therefore, during the day's proceedings these men (neither Galloway's letter nor the printed *Votes and Proceedings* provide us with any of their names) "were placed at the bar of the House of delegates, charged with *high crimes* and *misdemeanors*." But let Galloway tell us the story:

After a discussion and a very animated and *truly interesting one it was* [in the course of this discussion a resolution that "Mr. Goddard's memorial and letter be returned to him, and that he be desired in future to give this house no more trouble" was voted down 51 to 6]: during which, *no* attempt was made *by any* member of *that Whigg House* of Delegates, to suggest *an idea even,* that could be considered as intended to operate on the PUBLIC MIND as a *justification* of so singular, and abominable a proceeding as the Whigg Club was, as *every side* of *that House, agreed* to have been *guilty of,* towards said William Goddart; but, *more especially* said proceeding was animadverted on and reprobated by divers members, of the house, in loudest tones of the *sort of patriotism* by which the *virtuous* portion of the *real* Whiggs of that *eventful* day, *were moved*: as a *most alarming, daring usurpation* of *the powers* of *government* by *the Whigg Club*. A *feeble* attempt was indeed made, for the purpose of offering *a quasi apology* for said misbehaviour on the ground, that tho irregularity was discoverable *in the mode*, yet the *act done ought to be overlooked*, as it was an *ebullition* of *Whiggism*. But, *Old S Chase*, with *that manly, that unbending firmness*, and *ardent love* and *attachment* to *Law* and *Order*, scouted, *yes*, he scouted the *Idea*, that *it could*, in *any* degree, in *any* situation, while the General Assembly were in Session, be *tolerable, by that Body, to wink at such an enormity! no! not even when our army had been just beaten, kicked from Pillar to Post, from Dan to Bersheba*: and the *most alarming* circumstances seemed to (*too well*) *justify* a *serious* apprehension by every one who was in possession of *our real* situation, that these United States would in a few months, be reduced to the *miserable* condition of a *conquered* people. The Whigs of July 4th 76, *well knew*, that if *they suffered such shameful doings*, and usurpings to *pass uncensured by them, instanter*; the *fundamentals of our free government, must be overturned*. And, what I pray, did They do? Why! a motion was preparing by S Chase Esqr in the H of Delegates (I was sitting with him at the Clerk's Table) he was drafting a number of Resolutions, to be adopted by the House of D. and to be sent to the Senate for their concurrence, requesting *Governour Johnston* to direct the Attorney General to prosecute the persons who composed the said Club, with the *utmost rigour* of Law. But, it being intimated to S Chase Esqr and by him communicated to the House, that the characters belonging to said illegal meeting, *The Whig Club*, who were then *in custody at the bar of the House, were duly sensible* of the nature of the *heinous offences* that they had committed, were *willing* and *ready* to make *any* acknowledgment, and render *all* the *satisfaction in their power, to* the *insulted* and *injured Sovereign* of the state: *The People*: which *was accepted*, after *due* deliberation, by the house of delegates: but accompanied, with and by, an *express*, the *most positive, unqualified declaration, asseveration*, in their capacities, as the *guardians* and *vindicators* of the *rights* and *liberties* of a most *grossly insulted*, and *offended free people, That*, such like conduct, would *never again* be *so lightly passed over by the ruling powers*; The *acknowledgment*; The *Constitution*; and The *solemn promise* of *Amendment*, contained in a paper as placed thereupon in *glowing* language by S Chase Esqr and adopted by the General Assembly *was pronounced* by the *Chairman* [obviously Commodore Nicholson was among those present] of the offending Club, the members thereof, being placed to his right and left hands, (The Ball Room, was the *Locus in quo*) couched in language *humiliating*, and well calculated to make a durable impression on the popular mind—His [Samuel Chase's] conduct on that occasion alone entitled him to a monument, to be placed on the State House Hill. The Whig Club were liberated from their state of imprisonment, and told to return to Baltimore and by their future course of conduct, afford a *satisfactory proof* of the sincerity of their *declared deep sorrow* for *their past offence*, as *part* of the *very illegal* and *dangerous* combination, called The *Whigg Club*. They so did: but Governor Johnson by recommendation of the Gen Assembly [by a vote of 49 to 5] *issued instanter*, a proclamation grounded on said gross misbehaviour of said *red-hot, wou'd be thought Whiggs*.

The governor, Thomas Johnson, did not issue his proclamation *instanter*, as Galloway remembered, but waited until the seventeenth. Goddard became impatient, particularly since he was advised not to return to Baltimore until the governor released his proclamation. On the fourteenth Goddard wrote a letter to the governor telling his situation and requesting not only the statement but the prosecution of the members of the Whig Club, a list of whose names he enclosed with his letter.

The *Maryland Journal* of the fifteenth printed the resolutions of the assembly passed on the eleventh directed against the Whig Club and requesting that the person and property of Goddard be given the protection of the law. Finally the governor issued his proclamation on the seventeenth, and Goddard could return to Baltimore. The next day he released a broadside giving both the assembly resolutions and the governor's proclamation. Also he released a postscript to *The Prowess of the Whig Club* dated April 18. Three versions of this postscript exist, two in Goddard's hand and the other in print. In the John Carter Brown Library is the probable first of these to be written. Never printed, this version is by far the most vituperative, directed as it is primarily at Commodore Nicholson. Goddard labeled this manuscript, thirty-four pages long with additional inserts, "Part 2." The next version, also in Goddard's hand, is at the Library of Congress. Entitled "Part of the Whig Club," it is only eight pages long and much toned down. What is likely the final version is a four-page printed text, dated April 18, 1777, at the American Antiquarian Society. Two of the four pages are taken up by the assembly resolutions and the governor's proclamation. The last page is a list of the most active Whig Club members, thirty in all, leaving only one page of text written by the printer. Probably Mary Katherine was the person responsible for the condensation and softening of the tone. The first thirty-four-page text must have been written in Annapolis while Goddard was waiting to return to Baltimore. No doubt he appeared at Mary Katherine's print shop with Part 2 in hand wanting to have it set up immediately, but then the sister did her persuading. The copy in Worcester has marginal notations and corrections by Goddard, indicating he had in mind later expansion, but as far as we know nothing came of this.

The Council of Maryland on April 23 sent a formal letter to the various justices in Baltimore County enclosing copies of the assembly resolutions, memorials, and various depositions. The letter ended: "I have the utmost Confidence that you will give Mr Goddard every Protection, warranted by Law, in your Power."

Goddard, now on top of the Whig Club, could not let matters rest. Still smarting from the mob actions of March 25, he wrote on May 26 a memorial to the Continental Congress relative to the various officers in the army and navy who had been active in the Baltimore mob—seven were named. Presumably Goddard was expecting to demand disciplinary action, but at the moment all he requested was permission to send proofs of his accusations. The Congress did nothing about Goddard's memorial, and so ended the Whig Club affair.

EVEN though William Goddard, thanks to the assist from Samuel Chase, had most of his own way with the Whig Club, the conclusion of the case found him unhappy and discontented. How much of this discontent was caused by his rheumatism aggravated by his struggles with Commodore Nicholson is, of course, impossible now to say. But for a year or so after the March, 1777, riots Goddard went around with a chip on his shoulder. Indicative of his attitude was a letter he wrote on August 30, 1777, to his old friend Colonel John Lamb in New York. Placed in brackets at the end of the letter (written to introduce a Dr. Fallon to Lamb) as a kind of afterthought is this sentence: "I am too much dissatisfied with my present Situation, to say any thing relative to myself further than that I think I have been most infamously treated both by Whig & Tory." Instead of viewing the Whig Club affair as a victory for freedom of the press—which it was—Goddard sullenly retreated into his own shell, adopting the attitude that everybody was against him. He must have at times much annoyed the busy, energetic Mary Katherine as she ran the print shop, got out the *Journal* fairly regularly each Tuesday, and administered the daily affairs of the Baltimore post office.

Finally in February, 1778, Goddard reached the depths of his despair. Through his mind had been running past sufferings, including his frustrations about the postal system, for which he had done so much and received so little. The animosity he always bore Franklin came to the fore, and he conceived the design of publishing a pamphlet attacking the then minister to France. In pursuit of this design Goddard wrote to his former mentor and partner John Holt, now in Poughkeepsie, telling him his proposal and requesting information and advice. Holt, horrified at Goddard's idea, wrote a fourteen-page letter in reply, dated February 26, 1778. Holt stated his agreement with Goddard's sentiments but disagreed violently with his tactics. To emphasize his dislike, Holt compared Franklin's attitudes to "a Thief's cutting the Throat of the Man that saved him from the Gallows." Holt thought because of the doctor's role in the Stamp Act crisis that "he was either unfriendly to the American Cause, and took an active part against it, at that Period, or at least was totally inactive in its Favour." Holt went on to examine the actions of Franklin and his son William in some detail. Summing up his opinion, he wrote: "As to his private Character, I always greatly respected the Doctor . . . ; and as a natural Philosopher, I have the highest Opinion of him; but I have long thought his publick Conduct mysterious and suspicious, and have been obliged to consider him as a dangerous Person." But as to Goddard's proposed attack, Holt doubted that it would cause Franklin's dismissal anyway and suggested that publicizing such criticisms of the minister to France might harm the American cause. Also, Goddard's many enemies would take an opposite position from whatever Goddard took. About the Whig Club scandal Holt said: "Tho' you undoubtedly had the better in it, and, every one allows, were right in opposing their arbitrary proceedings; yet, as it is generally supposed that they meant well and were actuated by a laudable Zeal, tho' it transported them beyond their Knowledge,— and that they were desirous of accommodating the Matter upon amicable Terms, it has been thought by some of your real Friends, was rather too severe and publick a Mortification to them; and too expensive to yourself, in the Loss of so many Friends, who might have been serviceable to you and the Publick. . . . I happened to be at Philadelphia at the Time when your Narrative of the Affair, made its first Appearance at that Place. . . . The sarcastic Strooks of Wit and Humour it contained, never failed to produce a Laugh, at the Expense of the poor Whig Club—But yet the Writer was thought severe, and as little friendly to the American Cause, as to the Whig Club." (This criticism of his role in the recent affair must have hurt Goddard very much. Probably it was this more than any other argument that persuaded Goddard to give up his proposed attack.) Towards the end of the long letter Holt asked Goddard, should he go ahead with the publication, not to mention Holt's name in any connection with it. Fortunately for Goddard he followed the advice of the Poughkeepsie printer and dropped his design of attacking Benjamin Franklin.

What slowly pulled Goddard out of his doldrums was the sheer necessity to work. Getting out a newspaper during the Revolutionary War was no easy task, and the editress needed all the help her brother could give. The *Maryland Journal* had one of the best publication records of the wartime newspapers. Conscientious as Mary Katherine was, she could not by herself solve the most urgent problem for the Revolutionary printer—paper. This item became more and more scarce as the war went on. As early as 1773 the American Philosophical Society had shown its awareness of the problem by offering prizes for the collection of old rags for the paper mills. During the war journeyman papermakers were usually declared exempt from military duty because of the importance of their craft. While still working as surveyor in the postal system, apparently Goddard had started his plans to build his own paper mill in the Baltimore vicinity. These plans bore fruition as early as April 8, 1777, while William was still in Annapolis awaiting the proclamation to be issued by Governor Johnson. As mentioned before, Mary Katherine announced under the Baltimore date-line in this issue, "The Paper on which this Journal is printed was manufactured at a Mill lately erected at Elk-Ridge Landing." Beyond a doubt the existence of this mill was one of the most important reasons why the *Journal* could maintain its publication more nearly regularly than its competitors. For example, Frederick Green had to stop completely his *Maryland Gazette* in Annapolis because of the paper shortage.

But starting a paper mill and keeping it going were two different things. Two problems made difficult the continuous operation of the mill. One was the supply of rags, particularly linen rags. A notice in the *Journal* of May 26, 1778, shows this vividly. "The Stoppage of the *Paper-Mill*, near this Town, for the Want of a Supply of Rags, and the enormous Prices demanded at the Stores here for PAPER, constrains us to print the *Maryland Journal* on this dark and poor Sort, which our Readers will, we are persuaded excuse, for one Week at least, when they are assured, that rather than deprive them of *the important Intelligence of the Times*, by the Discontinuance of our *Journal*, we have given from *Forty* to *Fifty Pounds* a Week for the Article of Paper *alone*, an equal Quantity of which, might, formerly, have been purchased for *Eight Dollars!*"

Later, Adam Waybill, likely the mill's foreman, advertised for thirty thousand pounds of rags at one time.

Of even more trouble to the owners of paper mills was personnel. To become a skilled papermaker demanded a long and arduous training. Wartime conditions were not conducive to this training, and the armies occasionally took away some of the journeymen. Therefore it is not surprising to find frequent advertisements in the *Journal* for apprentices and skilled craftsmen. By November 30, 1779, the desperateness of the situation is shown by a notice in the *Pennsylvania Packet*. By this time Goddard was in partnership with Eleazer Oswald, and the two were running the mill while Mary Katherine continued the *Journal*. The advertisement requested the services of a papermaker, whose desire for security was appealed to by this N. B.: "A German, with a small family, would be very agreeable. There is a house and a pretty meadow contiguous and belonging to the mill."

One of the inevitable economic results of the Revolutionary War was a tremendous inflation. Frequently Miss Goddard had to raise her subscription prices. Rates in 1773 were ten shillings a year. On July 8, 1777, this price was doubled. By October, 1778, the rate was set at fifty-two shillings a year, only to be doubled six months later. By another six months, October, 1779, a charge of ten pounds was announced. No doubt, the advertising rates went up with the subscription costs, but these were not published. The difficulty in collecting is revealed by a notice in the December 15, 1778, *Journal*. Payment could be made either in cash or "country produce." This latter term included: "Beef, Pork, or any Kind of Animal Food, Butter, Hog's Lard, Tallow, Bees-Wax, Flour, Wheat, Rye, Indian Corn, Beans, Buck-Wheat, Barley, Hops, Oats, Vegetables, Flax Seed, Wood, Charcoal, tann'd Sheepskins, brown Linen, Linsey Woolsey, Feathers, Linen and Cotton Rags."

In spite of paper shortages and inflation Mary Katherine Goddard managed a printing coup—the running off on her press of the first copy of the Declaration of Independence with the names of the signers attached. This was done in the latter part of January, 1777. The colophon at the bottom reads: "Baltimore, in Maryland: Printed by Mary Katherine Goddard." A copy of this imprint, now in the

Maryland Hall of Records in Annapolis, is certified by the signatures of Charles Thomson and John Hancock.

On October 13, 1778, Mary Katherine announced that she had added to her shop "a complete and elegant Bookbinding Room." A bookbinder had been engaged, and obviously she hoped to supplement her income by this means. Thereafter she regularly advertised for tanned sheepskins, as in the list of "country produce," for the use of her bookbinder. She had carried on this business before, but only in a small way. Also she was actively pushing her bookselling operations. For example, in the February 2, 1779, *Journal* she printed a long list of books, headed by a Greek Bible, to be sold at her shop, "cheap, for cash."

Too easily we tend to think of the life of the Americans during the Revolution as restricted to activities related to the war. This, of course, was not true, yet the events of the war occupied the minds of the people in a way that no later war this country has fought in ever has. All this is well shown by a notice in the March 16, 1779, *Journal*. A three-day horse race meeting was to be held with purses of £500, £250, and £150. The promoters of the meeting thought it necessary to preface their announcement with a rather apologetic note: "The present War, in its dreadful Progress, hath not only proved destructive to the human Species, but, amidst a Variety of distressing Calamities, hath deprived this Continent of an immense Number of its best Horses: particularly such as were suitable for Cavalry—And as it is an acknowledged Fact that RACES under proper Regulations and Restrictions, are conducive to the Pubic [*sic*] Good, having a Tendency to promote and encourage the raising a valuable Breed of that most useful and noble Animal; under that Idea a Number of Gentlemen from Motives the most disinterested and Public-spirited, have determined, occasionally to pay Attention to an Object of that manifest Importance; and this they mean to do in such a Way as shall not do Violence to the strictest Laws of Morality, or in any Shape contravene the wise Purposes of the Rulers of our State."

In 1779 William brought into the Baltimore scene Eleazer Oswald, and it was in conjunction with him that Goddard roused the ire of another Baltimore mob. Oswald, fifteen years younger than Goddard, had come to the colonies from his native England in

1770. Shortly after his arrival he was apprenticed to John Holt, and eventually married Holt's daughter. Influenced by Holt, he became an ardent patriot, joining the military forces of the Revolution in 1775. In the army he served first under Benedict Arnold (where he became a friend of John Lamb, Goddard's associate in the postal campaign in 1774) and later under Charles Lee. Perhaps partly because of his displeasure at Lee's court-martial and also because of a seniority dispute over his rank, he resigned his lieutenant-colonelcy at the end of 1778. Oswald's acquaintance with Goddard dates at least from latter 1778, since in a letter to Colonel John Lamb dated Philadelphia, October 15, he speaks of his intentions to go to Baltimore to visit the printer and his regrets at "his [Goddard's] not being here as I promised myself much Satisfaction in his conversation."

On June 8, 1779, Goddard and Oswald announced their new partnership in a notice in the *Maryland Journal*. They were going to "carry on the PRINTING, BOOKSELLING, and STATIONERY BUSINESS." The paper mill at Elk-Ridge Landing was under their control. They had it "in Contemplation" to print an edition of the Bible. But this new firm was not to interfere "in the smallest Degree" with that of Mary Katherine Goddard, "who, it must be acknowledged, hath supported her Business with Spirit and Address, amidst a Complication of Difficulties." Thus to the truculent, embittered Goddard was added the martial, also disappointed Oswald. (Later Oswald acquired some notoriety for his feud with Mathew Carey.)

Next to enter the scene was General Charles Lee. A soldier of fortune who early espoused the colonial cause, he was one of the few experienced officers Washington had during the first part of the war. After various ups and downs in his military career he was court-martialed for his role in the Battle of Monmouth on June 28, 1778. (For the details of this affair the reader can consult the biography of Lee by John R. Alden.) Very much embittered by his treatment, Lee retired to his plantation in Berkley County, Virginia, there to nurse his grudges.

As early as December 8, 1778, the *Maryland Journal*, along with many other newspapers, had published a lengthy statement defending his position, written by Lee. As a matter of fact, Mary Katherine had merely clipped the defense from the December 3 *Pennsylvania*

Packet. But it was with the issue of July 6, 1779, that all hell broke loose. At his country estate Lee had written a series of twenty-five rhetorical questions, which he called "Some Queries, Political and Military." First he tried to get them published in a Philadelphia newspaper, but met with no success. Then he turned to Goddard. In a letter, apparently written before he knew that the partnership between Oswald and Goddard had been formed, dated June 7, Lee sent the Queries to Goddard for publication in the *Journal*. Even then the Queries were not rushed into print, publication being delayed almost a month, and there must have been several conversations among William, Mary Katherine, and Eleazer Oswald before agreement to print was finally reached. But appear they did on page one of the issue of July 6. The Queries asked pointed questions about the conduct of the war by Congress and Washington, including Lee's own court-martial. Washington was especially castigated, as in Query IX: "Whether it is salutary or dangerous, consistent with or abhorrent from, the principles and spirit of Liberty and Republicanism, to inculcate and encourage in the people an idea, that their welfare, safety and glory depend on one man? Whether they really do depend on one man?" Though printed anonymously, the Queries were given a Philadelphia date-line.

Two days afterwards, late in the evening of Friday the eighth, a group of men (Goddard said thirty) headed by some officers of the Continental army—Thomas Cromwell, John Bayley, and Stephen Shermandine—rushed into Goddard's bedroom and demanded that the printer immediately come with them to the local coffee house, where the main body of the objectors were. This time there was no hesitation about proceeding directly to William, and no question was asked of his sister. After a struggle, which Oswald joined in, a compromise was reached. Goddard promised to go to the coffee house the next morning at nine o'clock, there to be questioned in broad daylight.

The next morning Goddard, accompanied by Oswald, went for protection to the four magistrates of Baltimore (appointed since the Whig Club fracas)—William Spear, George Lindenberger, Abraham Van Bibber, and James Calhoun. The first two agreed to help maintain law and order, Lindenberger making the condition that Goddard be unarmed. Van Bibber refused to have anything to do with the affair, alleging his inexperience and youth. Calhoun, the former chairman of the Baltimore committee who had refused to issue any orders on the occasion of the Whig Club riots, peremptorily refused even to talk with the two partners. Returning to his house, Goddard divested himself of his pistol and walked down the street to the coffee house. Just opposite this he observed Calhoun standing with Spear in the doorway of the former's house and walked over to them. Calhoun's reaction was to order Goddard and Oswald away, and Spear, noticing that his son-in-law Colonel Samuel Smith was heading the mob, now in the street, turned away.

In the middle of the street in front of the coffee house an impromptu trial was held. A cart stood ready and waiting complete with an adequate supply of rope. Van Bibber was among those who testified at this trial about the lack of patriotism shown by the printer. A search of the print shop was made to secure incriminating evidence, but nothing was found. Completely overpowered by the mob and seeing no help from any direction, Goddard yielded to their wishes. First he admitted Charles Lee to be the writer of the Queries. Next, he was forced to sign a statement including, "I have transgressed against truth, justice, and my duty as a good citizen." After agreeing to publish all this in the *Journal*, Goddard was released and allowed to go home. Still in the company of his partner, he quickly saddled his horse and set out for Annapolis.

As a supplement the next week's *Journal*, dated July 14, published what the mob had won from Goddard. His signed statement was given, along with two letters from Charles Lee, one of June 7 enclosing the Queries and the other of June 17 wishing the two members of the new partnership success in their undertaking and referring again to the Queries.

Though in Baltimore the mob of the ninth (almost conspicuously none of the leaders of the former Whig Club were active in the General Lee affair) seemed to have things its own way, Goddard and Oswald busied themselves in Annapolis. Goddard presented a memorial, dated July 13, to the governor and the council requesting the protection of the law for himself and the impeachment of the four magistrates of Baltimore. Mary Katherine Goddard followed up this memorial by a letter of the fifteenth, in which she named ten witnesses, including Oswald, who would appear in Goddard's behalf at any hearing. As a result, on the seventeenth the council sent out notices of a hearing to be held on the twenty-sixth.

Content with this stage of affairs, Goddard apparently returned to Baltimore to prepare his memorial for publication in the *Journal*. Almost the entire first page of the July 20 issue is taken up with it together with a short introduction calling the members of the mob "vermin" and a brief statement by Oswald attesting to the truth of Goddard's memorial. On the next page is a cryptic sentence: "Mr. Goddard's extorted Acknowledgment, and Negative VOLUNTARY Counter-Declaration, with an Introductory Letter to the Printer, came to Hand too late for this Day's Paper."

All this, except the last sentence, was then printed verbatim in an Annapolis *Maryland Gazette Extraordinary* of July 25. In addition, an exchange of letters between Colonel Eleazer Oswald and Colonel Samuel Smith, the leader of the Baltimore mob, was printed. The exchange started on July 11, when Oswald challenged Smith to a duel after loading him down with insults. Smith in a reply the next day refused the challenge. He stated that if Oswald had been defending his own rights, he would have felt obligated to participate in a duel; but since Oswald was defending the rights of his partner, he would not allow himself to be involved. Oswald then threatened to publish the correspondence. Smith asked for a delay to consider the matter, but Oswald terminated the reconsideration by this exposé. The exchange was concluded by some remarks of Oswald describing Smith's character as "a worthless one."

No record was made of the hearing of July 26. Presumably the council sent everybody home on his good behavior in return for his silence. No mention later was made of the hearing by any of the participants, even though Goddard filled a good many columns of his sister's *Journal* relative to the affair. Seemingly the result reasonably contented Goddard, because he returned to the fray even more sure of himself than before.

However, Goddard retained some tact, which we can see in his handling of a letter from Charles Lee. Lee had written to him on July 14 a followup to the original Queries. This letter, less severe in its strictures on Washington but more stringent on his subordinates, Goddard, perhaps at the insistence of his sister, refused to publish.

He must have recognized that another publication from the pen of General Lee would add new fuel to the fire of the Baltimore mob's resentment and incite its members to more activities directed against him. (Within a few weeks the Lee epistle was sent to various Philadelphia editors, all of whom promptly rejected it.)

The statement promised in the July 20 *Journal* appeared on schedule a week later. Goddard signed this at Annapolis on July 17. The key passage vigorously denied the forced recantation previously published. "By publishing certain 'QUERIES, Political and Military,' in the *Maryland Journal*, on the 6th instant, I have NOT 'transgressed against Truth, Justice, or my Duty as a good Citizen,' and, as I have never given just cause of offence to 'His Excellency General Washington, or the good people of this town,' I have NO '*reparation*' to make them, or '*pardon*' to solicit." Probably it was a good thing this far from obsequious notice appeared after the council hearing on the twenty-sixth.

The following week's *Journal*, August 3, had two articles on the affair. A brief one on page three was a purported "Extract of a Letter from a Gentleman of Distinction, in a neighbouring State, to the Printer." This letter defended the importance of the liberty of the press. Referring to the Baltimore situation only by implication, the anonymous writer (quite possibly Goddard himself) concluded: "Restraints on the Press in any Cases, except Libels and Treason, narrow and debase the liberal Sentiments of the Soul, and curb the rising Efforts of Genius: It is a Mockery of the Understanding to call that Country free, where this Restraint is tolerated, approved of, and supported."

Though somewhat hidden on an inside page, this statement could well have served to introduce the featured article on page one. Joseph Reed, the President of Pennsylvania, felt himself insulted by the original Queries and wrote a letter to Goddard defending his role in the Lee court-martial, etc. This letter was promptly printed in the *Journal*. Thereby Goddard in practice defended the right of the press to print not only the unpopular but the remarks of those disagreeing with the editor. Many years before, the Peter Zenger case had resulted from the printer's publishing articles critical of the established authority but agreeable to the popular taste. And in the Maryland of 1777 and 1779 the Baltimore printer won his case.

Since those stalwart days more lip service than practice has been applied to this aspect of freedom of the press, but the concept has actively survived.

In the columns of the *Maryland Journal* the matter rested there, but General Lee had not been vindicated by the affair and continued resentful. In a letter dated August 1, 1779, to the French Consul in Baltimore Lee referred to the Baltimore mob as "low-bred ruffians" and "banditti." On August 24 Lee's aide, Major John S. Eustace, wrote to Lee telling of his efforts to place two of Lee's defenses in the Philadelphia papers. He had failed to do so in spite of the help of Goddard and Oswald, who happened to be in the city. Lee then wrote to Joseph Reed, challenging him to assist in their publication "as a gentleman and one embarked in the common cause of the liberties of mankind (of which the freedom of the press is the basis)." As late as October 24 Benjamin Rush wrote to Lee about the refusals of the Philadelphia printers and asked for Lee to be patient since the "Summer flies that now din our ears must soon retire."

The one long-lasting result of the Charles Lee affair for Goddard was the friendship that sprang up between the retired general and the printer. On December 24, 1779, Oswald in a letter to Lee said that Goddard intended to pay Lee a visit at his Berkley County seat. Thereafter Goddard must have made the trip south and west to Lee's estate, Hopewell, frequently, because Lee in several letters used Mary Katherine Goddard in Baltimore as his mailing address. In 1781 Lee was trying to fulfil Goddard's request for a good riding horse, but had to write his friend that at the moment all he had on hand was "a worn out full Brother of Rosinante."

Though Lee had a sufficiency of land and money in England, he found himself short of ready cash in America now that his pay as a general had ceased. Therefore he made an attempt to sell his 2800-acre Virginia estate. This transaction enabled Goddard to render Lee a much appreciated service. On November 10, 1780, Lee entered into a contract with Edward and Ezekiel John Dorsey to sell his property. In the original agreement, Goddard acting as go-between, a price in hard cash was stipulated with a six months' forfeiture if the remainder of the money after the down payment was not given to either William or his sister. Basically the dispute which followed resulted from the attempt of the Dorseys to pay for the land in depreciated currency, which would have given Lee almost nothing. General Lee was not extricated from his difficulties until early in 1782, but eventually he was, thanks to the efforts of Goddard. Mary Katherine and William were given powers of attorney to act in the affair by Lee, and with this authority Goddard managed to persuade the Dorseys to accept the refunding of their down payment, cancel the original contract, and return the land to Charles Lee. As the nineteenth-century editor of *The Lee Papers* for the New-York Historical Society put it, Lee's *"Berkley Estate* was snatched like a Brand out of the Burning fire by the Exertions of Wm Goddard." In the final settlement Robert Morris of Philadelphia was used as a banker. The net result was not the complete saving of Lee's American fortune but an increase in the ties of friendship between the two men.

In September, 1782, Lee, on his way to Philadelphia, stopped for a few days in Baltimore to visit the Goddards. He went on to Philadelphia, where he died October 2. Ironically, considering the general's pronounced deism clearly shown by one of the clauses in his will, the body of Charles Lee was buried in Christ's Church Burying Ground. He had written: "I desire most earnestly, that I may not be buried in any church, or church-yard, or within a mile of any Presbyterian or Anabaptist meeting-house; for since I have resided in this country, I have kept so much bad company when living, that I do not chuse to continue it when dead."

For Goddard a more important clause in the will was Lee's bequeathing of his Berkley County estate. This was divided into three parts, the first two of which went to Jacob Morris and Evan Edwards, former aides of Lee's, and the third equally divided between Oswald and Goddard. At first, it looked as though this bequest would not amount to anything since Lee had left a good many debts, including money lent to him at various times by the Continental Congress. Lee's sister, Sidney Lee, learned of the dilemma of the four would-be recipients and sent to America £4500 to cover the debts, so that the intent of Lee's will could be fulfilled. She was able to do this because his English property had greatly increased in value during the Revolution. Eventually, probably in 1785, the estate of Hopewell was sold and Goddard received his share.

By this time Goddard was in partnership with Edward Lang-worthy and the two men were printing the *Maryland Journal*. Into Goddard's possession had fallen the various papers of General Lee, and the Baltimore printer was, in effect, serving as the literary executor of the estate though no mention was made of this in the will, but from a comment Goddard made in a letter Lee and the printer had talked over eventual arrangements for the general's papers. Inevitably the partners decided to publish in book form a selection from these papers. A general plan was sketched out and proposals drawn up on that basis. But first Goddard, a bit more aware of the necessity for tact than he had been six years before, thought he had better write to George Washington and inform him of the plans since obviously many of the published papers would be critical of Washington's conduct in Lee's court-martial. In this letter, dated May 30, 1785, the Baltimore newspaperman asked Washington whether he had "any particular request, respecting the said Work." He enclosed a copy of a possible title page and prom-ised to send one of the subscription proposals when it was printed—a promise he fulfilled two weeks later. The title page revealed that three volumes were proposed. Letters both to and from the general were to be included as well as miscellaneous writings. Also a biography of Lee, written presumably by one of the partners, was to be incorporated.

Washington did not receive this letter until June 8, nine days apparently then being required for the transit of a letter between Baltimore and Mount Vernon. Therefore it was not until June 11 that he wrote his answer. For him, Goddard's "own good judg-ment must direct you in the publication of the manuscript papers of General Lee. I can have no request to make concerning the work." Washington's feelings at this time are well given in his own words: "I am gliding down the stream of life, and wish, as is natural, that my remaining days may be undisturbed and tranquil."

On July 15, 1785, the *Maryland Journal* advertised the sub-scription proposals for the three volumes of the "Miscellaneous Collections, from the Papers of the late Major-General Charles Lee." No actual printing was to take place until enough subscrip-tions had been received to make the project a paying proposition— all this in typical eighteenth-century publishing fashion. The price of the three octavo volumes was to be one guinea, half on subscribing and the other half on delivery. Subscriptions were to be received not only by the Baltimore printing firm but by Frederick Green in Annapolis and George Richards in Alexandria.

No doubt the printed proposals were circulated vigorously but the hopes of the partners were not fulfilled by the number of half guineas coming in. So there was never a Baltimore printing of the papers of General Lee and there the matter rested for several years.

Goddard and Langworthy soon parted company, but the latter took with him copies of many of the manuscripts and continued on his own to write up a brief biography of Lee. Finally he secured the publication of this volume, entitled *Memoirs of the Life of the Late Charles Lee, Esq.*, in London in 1792. This volume included a varied selection from the general's writings prefixed by Langworthy's biographical account, dated Baltimore, March 10, 1787. Then in retirement, Goddard did not receive a copy of this publication until the end of 1793. Incensed at the book, he wrote to Washington to clear his own name of any connection with it, since after the 1785 proposals inevitably readers would have suspected his connivance. Also, though Goddard said nothing of this, the originals of the Lee manuscripts were still in his possession. In a mellow mood Goddard talked about his "departed Friend," General Lee, and his desire in the 1785 proposed three volumes to include nothing "that would wound the Feelings, or excite the Disapprobation, of a single worthy Person, or cast the least Blemish upon the Reputation of General Lee." Revealing his Federalist approval of the President, Goddard stated his desire "to exculpate myself from an Imputation of Disrespect to a Character—for whom, with applauding Millions, I feelingly accord my humble, tho' sincere, Tribute of grateful Veneration."

Even though it is not part of the biography of William Goddard, it is appropriate to tell the final outcome of the Lee papers that the printer kept with him during all his years in retirement. Eventually the grandson of the truculent printer, Colonel William Goddard, gave permission to the New-York Historical Society to print them in four volumes as *The Lee Papers* in the society's *Collections* during the 1870's. Not too many years later the originals of the papers were lost, and we are now dependent upon the printed versions as edited by the society's nineteenth-century editors.

WILLIAM could stew all he wanted to over the affairs of General Charles Lee, but Mary Katherine had to keep the kettle of the print shop boiling regularly—and this she did in her own unobtrusive way. In early 1779 she witnessed the demise of her only competing newspaper in Baltimore, the *Maryland Gazette* of James Hayes, Junior, who had taken over the shop of John Dunlap in 1778. Even Frederick Green in Annapolis was forced by the shortage of paper to discontinue his newspaper for four months. Obviously the Goddard and Oswald monopoly of paper manufacturing in Maryland was paying off for the *Maryland Journal*.

Business for the Baltimore woman printer was undoubtedly not too bad in 1779. Though the Lee affair may have cost William some assorted bruises and increased rheumatic pains and Mary Katherine no small loss of sleep, the circulation of the newspaper quite likely expanded. In a notice in the November 2 *Journal* the editress said it "circulates as extensively as any Paper in the Continent." She was trying to maintain a regular Tuesday publication and requested advertisers to have their copy in by ten o'clock Monday morning.

Of similar import is the announcement in the *Journal* of October 5 of the imminent publication of *The Maryland Almanack For the Year of our Lord, 1780*. Later advertisements reveal that the calculations for the almanac were done by the Philadelphia astronomer, David Rittenhouse. Almanacs were too dependable a source of revenue to be overlooked as long as there was paper available. They were priced at ten shillings a copy or twelve dollars a dozen. Besides her own almanacs Mary Katherine sold those printed in German by Matthias Bartgis in Fredericktown, Maryland. The sales of the 1780 almanac must have been satisfying, because the 1781 almanac was printed as early as September 28, according to a notice in the September 26 *Journal*. Now called *The Maryland, Delaware,*

Pennsylvania, Virginia, and North-Carolina Almanack, and Ephemeris, For the Year of our Lord, 1781, this version of the annual best-seller featured the calculations of the Baltimore mathematician, Andrew Ellicott. Though one may wonder how many sales there were in North Carolina, apparently the financial returns of the almanac, as well as succeeding ones, were more than adequate.

The grim days of the Revolution did not cause everybody to lose his sense of humor. Thomas Jones in an advertisement of May 2, 1780, closed his notice of the availability of the services of his bull Pluto, who "will propagate . . . for one barrel of Indian corn," by this Shandean display of wit and erudition. "PLUTO is supposed to be descended in an ⸺ line from the infamous 10, for whose pedigree, I would refer the curious inquirer to the old Roman poet OVID, who will satisfy him fully on that head." The influence of Pope instead of Sterne can be seen in the couplet (the rhymster may well have been William) appended to a notice by Andrew Davidson in the February 6, 1781, *Journal.* He had the not infrequent advertisement about a deserting wife with the usual warning not to trust her financially. And then:

> And if a wedded woman put to sale,
> Deal not with her unless she brings her male.

The relative prosperity of the Goddard press may have been the cause for Mary Katherine's moving her print shop and post office next door to "a more convenient Situation," as the announcement in the March 20, 1781, *Journal* read. More important than the moving is our first evidence of strain between Mary Katherine and William. The Baltimore printress inserted over her name almost a column-long article on April 3. This "To the Public" stated that she had heard there were designs to establish another press in Baltimore "in Opposition to hers, with a View to diminish her Business, and compel her to quit the same." This notice may have been a method of maneuvering against her brother, who had been discontented with his background role during these years. Mary Katherine had been unhappy over William's difficulties in both the Whig Club and the Lee affairs and was, no doubt, a bit weary of being involved in troubles caused by someone else. All in all, she did not feel any necessity of allowing William's desires to interfere with her own hard-earned prosperity. Forestalled by his sister's article of the third, a week later Goddard, with his partner Eleazer Oswald, proposed to set up a press limited to the printing of inexpensive editions of European writers, such as Sterne, Goldsmith, and Junius. Though the advertisement by the partners is long and fulsome, it bears evidence of being hastily written, or perhaps rewritten under pressure. Mary Katherine must have argued her brother out of his plans for another press, for the net result was that the firm of Goddard and Oswald continued to run the paper mill and never did any printing, and the two partners gradually resumed their assistance in Mary Katherine's print shop. However, from now on there is a distinct coolness between the brother and the sister, who had done so much for so many years for the Goddard family fortunes. It must be given in William's favor that his notice did say that the partners would have "no Concern with any NEWS-PAPER, nor any Profit therefrom; for they . . . wish the Printress of the MARYLAND JOURNAL, &c. may meet with that Encouragement from the PUBLIC, which her Assiduity and Care shall merit."

The surrender of Cornwallis and his forces at Yorktown on October 19, 1781, and the subsequent limitation of the war to a stalemate around New York City relieved many of the wartime pressures on Baltimore. As early as June, 1781, Thomas Wall was presenting theatrical entertainment under the guise of a "Lecture on Heads" or a "Dissertation on Noses," and the printing of play handbills was added to the shop's business. But it was in December that we can more readily see evidence of the effects of the Battle of Yorktown. For example, the *Journal* of December 18 is distinctly whiter in color than its predecessors had been for several years. A week later the regular listing of ship arrivals and departures in the port of Baltimore was resumed. The commercial activities of the city began to revert to a peacetime basis. This peacetime relaxation and equanimity appear in a letter, signed Philo-Theatricus, published in the March 19, 1782, *Journal*. This letter is interesting as one of the few extant pieces of theatrical criticism we have from the eighteenth century. The performance discussed was the ever popular *Venice Preserv'd*. Noteworthy about the letter is its limiting of its comments to the acting performance with nothing said about the virtues or non-virtues of the play itself.

During the later part of 1782 and early 1783 Americans were

very much concerned over the negotiations going on in Paris between the American and British commissioners. As a result, the demand for news was greater than ever. Also, the increasing mercantile and manufacturing activities of the port on the Chesapeake demanded more advertising space than before. Once-a-week publication being now insufficient, on March 14, 1783, Mary Katherine announced that the *Maryland Journal* would add a Friday edition to its regular Tuesday appearance. Given as an immediate reason was the now twice-a-week postrider between Philadelphia and Baltimore, but the unmentioned probable reason was the opening by John Hayes of a new print shop in Baltimore. Within a couple of months Hayes began to print on Fridays the *Maryland Gazette*, but by now the community of Baltimore had expanded enough to maintain two newspapers.

For over two years after what was more than likely a bitter quarrel between the brother and sister over his proposed press William remained in the background. After Oswald had departed for Philadelphia probably about the end of 1781, Goddard was left with the paper mill at Elk-Ridge Landing which must have provided him with a fairly comfortable income. Then in latter 1783 we again become aware of his presence in various small ways. A notice in the July 15 *Journal* for a broadside of a public letter from Washington tells the readers that purchase can be made of "W. Goddard, at the Printing-Office adjoining the Dwelling-House of Dr. JOHN STEVENSON." On September 12 another notice in the name of William Goddard advertised for a miller to run a "merchant-mill." The printing hand of Goddard is apparent in various minor changes in the typography of the *Journal* in latter 1783. Typical of these is the obituary of John Hancock printed on December 2 and enclosed at top and bottom with lines of skull and crossbones.

Finally, on January 2, 1784, the name of William appeared in the colophon of the *Maryland Journal*, which read: "Printed by William and Mary Katherine Goddard, at the Post-Office, in Market-Street." Four days later the colophon was: "Printed by William Goddard, (in Dr. Stevenson's Warehouse, adjoining his Dwelling House) in Public-Alley, near Market-Street." What kind of agreement William entered into with his sister we do not know. From subsequent events it is apparent that Mary Katherine did not think herself well treated by her brother. She continued as postmistress of Baltimore and proprietress of a bookstore but no longer had any connection with the print shop and newspaper unless she continued silently to draw out some of the profits for her share of the business. That Mary Katherine had been prospering reasonably well is shown by a notice in the March 21, 1783, *Journal* revealing the theft of a trunk from her. The trunk was "covered with black Leather, and ornamented with Gold-Leaf." Among the contents were fourteen guineas and a half, four half-johans (a johan was a Portuguese coin worth about nine dollars), thirty or forty dollars, and bank notes for fifty, forty, and ten dollars. Mary Katherine had not done badly as proprietress of the *Maryland Journal*. But even though she was not suffering financially, the former editress never again resumed friendly relations with her brother. Perhaps prosperity made both Goddards arrogant and unforgiving, but Mary Katherine deserved more from her brother, even if the more was merely brotherly affection.

Mary Katherine's methods as a newspaper editor contrast with those of her brother. She was dependable and he brilliantly erratic. She never allowed her personal affairs to intrude into her newspaper; William's various quarrels were always intruding, even into Mary Katherine's paper. The impersonal quality of her editing convinces us that she was an excellent newspaperwoman but leaves little concrete or personal to say about her, no letters or other such material of hers having survived. We do find in both *The Partnership* and *The Prowess of the Whig Club* that in the 1770's William went out of his way to compliment his sister's competence and loyalty.

William was riding high. The next decade was by far the most prosperous one of his career. For so long had he been a "struggling printer" that he too easily yielded to various grandiose schemes for wealth, but he did continue to give Baltimore a well-edited newspaper. In his notice "To the Public" announcing his sole assumption of control of the *Journal* Goddard assured his readers that he had new printing materials of many kinds and could do whatever was requested of him.

During these flush times he tried his best to make investments that would bring in a profit. One of these had its origins as far back as January 26, 1779, when an advertisement in the *Journal*, signed

Wm. Goddard and Comp., stated the new company's expectations of setting up a printing office in Alexandria, Virginia. Shortly thereafter Eleazer Oswald came along, and Goddard dropped for the moment the Alexandria scheme. (The *Journal* of January 26 exists at the Maryland Historical Society in two variants, one having the advertisement referred to and the other omitting this in favor of a strayed horse notice. This may indicate that the 1779 proposal was mostly a feeler to try out public sentiment in the Alexandria vicinity.) But Goddard did not forget his scheme. In the *Journal* of May 28, 1782, there was an announcement, dated May 20, that a new printing office had "just opened" in Alexandria under the aegis of George Richards and Company. A year and a half later proposals were given to start a newspaper to be called *The Virginia Journal and Alexandria Advertiser*. (Note the similarity of the title to *The Maryland Journal and Baltimore Advertiser*.) On February 5, 1784, the first issue of this paper appeared. It continued to July 4, 1789, when Richards' death ended the enterprise. Many years later, in a letter to Isaiah Thomas giving various corrections to *The History of Printing*, Goddard specified his own connection with the Alexandria firm. He had loaned a press and types to start the business and from time to time had given money to Richards, who was a "relative." Before Goddard could get any return on his money, Richards died and the Baltimore printer was out five hundred pounds, according to his own statement. It is possible, though there is no evidence to support this, that Goddard in the 1780's lost more money in similar investments. The *Norfolk and Portsmouth Journal* in Norfolk, Virginia, may, for example, have had Goddard as one of its financial backers during its brief career.

Unfortunate as Goddard was in his choice of printers to back, he did make his Baltimore shop into very much of a going concern— not that Mary Katherine had not turned over to him in January, 1784, a quite successful business. The *Journal* continued to appear twice a week and had a generous quota of advertisements of all sorts. One of these, in the issue of October 26, 1784, must have amused many of its readers. "ABRAHAM SITTLER, requests that the Woman, by the Name of SALLY, who, some time ago, lived with him, and now resides about Eight or Nine Miles from Baltimore-Town, would return and live with him again."

Of more importance to Goddard than Abraham's Sally in October and November, 1784, was the annual almanac. Regularly since the 1780 one calculated by David Rittenhouse Mary Katherine had published each year her *Pennsylvania, Delaware, Maryland, and Virginia Almanack* (North Carolina was dropped from the title after 1781). After the first one Andrew Ellicott had done the calculations. In the settlement between the brother and sister apparently each assumed he was to have the privilege of publishing the annual almanac. This misunderstanding resulted in the appearance in November, 1784, of two almanacs with identical titles except that one is *William Goddard's . . . Almanack* and the other *Mary K. Goddard's . . . Almanack.* Unfortunately for the relations between the two William was offended by the threat to his almanac monopoly and leaped into print with an attack upon his sister's publication, to which Mary Katherine took great umbrage; she never forgave her brother. William in his attack said, "Observing a spurious Performance, containing a mean, vulgar and common-place Selection of Articles . . . I find myself obliged to inform the Public, that the above-mentioned spurious *double-faced Almanack,* is only a *Pennsylvania* one, under a *Baltimore* MASK, or Title-Page, and which was printed in *Philadelphia,* and sent to this *Market,* by a certain *hypocritical Character,* for the dirty and mean Purpose of FRAUD and DECEPTION." No wonder Mary Katherine felt hurt at the attack! As far as we know, never again was there anything but bitterness between the two for the rest of their lives. Mary Katherine did occasionally advertise the wares of her bookstore in the *Journal* after this and official notices under her name as postmistress appeared, but otherwise the two avoided each other.

Still seeking to expand his business, Goddard on January 25, 1785, announced his partnership with Edward Langworthy. The latter had been a member of the Continental Congress from Georgia and claimed to be a well-read scholar, later proposing to write a history of Georgia. Langworthy's partnership was secured for two purposes. One was the editing of the Charles Lee papers discussed in the last chapter. The other was revealed in the announcement of the partnership. A new magazine, *The American Spectator,* was to be founded as soon as there were sufficient subscriptions. It is much to be regretted that the plan did not go through because part of the original prospectus called for "the History of every COLLEGE, ACADEMY or SEMINARY" in this country. Such a series of accounts would be invaluable to the cultural historian. Neither the proposal to print the Lee Papers nor *The American Spectator* coming to anything, the partnership was abandoned after a year's duration in January, 1786, Langworthy becoming the head of the newly founded Baltimore Academy.

By comparing an itemized receipt for advertising with the actual newspaper we can deduce the space rates of the *Maryland Journal* in these days of its "extensive circulation." We have such a receipt preserved at the Maryland Historical Society made out to Archibald Moncreiff for various insertions in 1785. For advertisements repeated between three to six times there is a uniform rate of two shillings and sixpence. (Seven and six was then computed as equal to a dollar.) Each advertisement is one column wide and about an inch long. Most of these contain line drawings of ships, but a few do not, and the rate is the same with or without the drawings. (The line drawings were from a generous supply of stock cuts, such supplies being essential for any newspaper of this period.) These rates are undoubtedly higher than those of most papers of the 1780's since the *Journal* had such a large circulation.

During all his career as a printer Goddard was a great traveler up and down the Atlantic seaboard. His postal duties had, of course, provided a reason for the many journeys, but these trips were continued long after he had quarreled with Bache and quit his job as surveyor. One of his favorite trips was through New England, particularly to his old home in Providence. John Carter, who had bought the *Providence Gazette* from Sarah Goddard, continued as one of William's best friends. Baltimore, in spite of the almost twenty years of Goddard's stay, never was home to him as Providence was; probably the Baltimore mobs of 1777 and 1779 intensified this feeling. As a quite eligible bachelor of forty-five and a rather prosperous one, Goddard found the attractions of Miss Abigail Angell of Providence most appealing. And so we read in the May 27, 1786, *Providence Gazette* this news item: "Thursday last [May 25] was married at Cranston (by the Rev. Mr. OLIVER) WILLIAM GODDARD, Esq; of Baltimore, Printer, to Miss Abigail Angell, eldest Daughter of the late Brigadier-General ANGELL; a Lady of great

Merit, her mental Acquirements, joined to a most amiable Disposition, being highly honourable to her Sex, and are pleasing Presages
of connubial Felicity." Abigail Angell was the daughter of James
Angell and was born December 3, 1758. Her father had died in
1785, and now as a twenty-seven-year-old heiress and belle of one of
Providence's oldest families (her great-great-grandfather Thomas
Angell had been one of the original settlers of Providence in 1636)
she provided one of the most important weddings of the social year
in Providence.

The day after John Carter published his account of the wedding
in his newspaper he sat down and wrote a charming letter to Mary
Katherine Goddard telling her of the events and expressing the hope
that the affectionate qualities of Abigail would serve to bring together
the brother and sister. As an old friend and a courteous eighteenth-
century gentleman, he felt he could take certain liberties that someone else could not.

Dear Miss Katy
. . . The marriage took place at Col Bowen's Villa, three miles from
town, on Thursday afternoon, the 25th, at two O'clock. The morning
had been appointed, but it being Ascension Day, the Reverend Mr. Oliver,
who joined their hands, was under a necessity of devoting the forenoon
to duties of a more sacred and indispensable nature. There were present
. . . [a list of twenty-seven guests, including John Carter, is given].
The Bride was clad in an elegant white Lutestring, and made a
charming appearance: she behaved *like herself* on the occasion, though
the solemnity of the ceremony caused a momentary embarrassment. The
motto for the Ring, having been directed by the Bride, I must give you,
as it evinces her elegance of mind, and good judgment, *"This joins in
blissful bands consenting hearts."*—Col. Bowen's good lady being out of
health, the pageantry of a public celebration was purposely avoided; but
though the guests were few in number, mirth and conviviality prevailed.
Excepting my own, it was the most pleasing scene of the kind I ever
attended, your absence being the only alloy. On the two following days
they were visited by all the genteel inhabitants of Providence, and to-
morrow they leave Col Bowen's to reside by invitation at Mr. Whitman's
[Mrs. Whitman was a sister of Abigail] till their departure for Baltimore,
which will take place too soon.
Brigadier-General Angell having left four sons and two daughters,
and having lived long on his paternal estate, retired from business, the
fortunes of the ladies are consequently not large. The part assigned to
Mrs. Goddard is estimated at about 2500 Dollars; but was she destitute
of a shilling, *such a wife* would prove a fortune in herself; and your

Brother, in the opinion of every one here, is amply compensated for remaining so long a Bachelor. . . . Friends may differ, and the fell demon of discord intrude to interrupt the felicity of families, but I will never for a moment believe that Miss Goddard can be implacable. . . . Allow me to enjoin, with all the warmth of my heart, an immediate settlement of every matter in dispute between you and your brother. . . . Mrs. Carter joins in congratulations and compliments.—She has procured a small portion of the wedding Cake for Miss Goddard's pillows, which shall accompany the present hasty scrawl, and we hope may induce pleasing dreams. . . .

Miss Katy was not reconciled though her bitterness undoubtedly mellowed from what it had been in 1785, when she was reported to have in one day instituted five law suits against her brother.

Abigail at first found Baltimore a bit difficult to adjust to, especially the diet. She wrote to John Carter soon after her arrival about her first reactions to the city. Carter in his reply of July 24 teased her for complaining of "the want of fish" and told her to "be a good girl, bear in mind the interesting word *obey*, eat your 'hominy and pone' with a contented mind." We can safely assume that these worries were trivial, and Abigail soon adjusted to eating Baltimore's crabs and snapper turtles.

Courtship and marriage had kept Goddard away from Baltimore so much during the first half of 1786 that he found it necessary in the August 18 *Journal* to assure his readers the editor "now conducts his Business in Person, and gives the most constant Attendance."

John Hayes, publisher of the *Maryland Gazette* in Baltimore, had watched with considerable envy Goddard's tremendous success with his annual almanacs, and so he resolved to try to break the Goddard monopoly. He first hired away Andrew Ellicott, who had been doing the calculations for Goddard, and then published *Ellicott's Maryland and Virginia Almanack, and Ephemeris, For the Year of our Lord 1787.* Goddard, of course, quickly learned of this defalcation and turned to Benjamin Workman of the University of Pennsylvania faculty to prepare his own almanac, which Goddard prefaced by a bitter attack upon his imitators. Finally, Edward Langworthy, who may have been nursing a grudge against his former partner, joined in the fray in the November 7 *Maryland Gazette* with over a page of attack, which he signed Juvenal. The fight was on, and Baltimore in November and December of 1786 witnessed a tremendous struggle between the two printers for the almanac trade. No holds were barred as the two newspapers filled their columns with invective for several weeks. The new bride must have had several doubtful moments about the gentility of the newspaper profession as she read some of these scurrilities. There is, however, one difference in the exchange of abuse between Hayes and Goddard and the dirt-shoveling Goddard had participated in before. The competitive fight for the almanac trade, no matter how bitter it was, did not affect the personal friendship between the two printers. The almanac wars of the eighteenth century are comparable to today's ritualized feuds among radio and TV comedians. The conventionalized quarrels in both centuries deliberately seek to drum up more trade. Practiced as Goddard was by this time in exchanges of personal invective, he could turn to impersonal exchanges with some adroitness. And, in fact, we find in this campaign some of Goddard's best-written abuse.

The first blow was struck by Goddard in the preface to his almanac. But even before this was released for publication, Langworthy in the *Gazette* under his pseudonym of Juvenal poured the coals of fire on Goddard's head. Obviously neither printer could keep any trade secrets from the other, and so on the same day Goddard said in the *Journal* that some kind of vituperation was to be expected from a "DIVINITY-HUNTER, the *Reverend* and—— *worth*, NEDDY CROCODILE," who had been working on his attack for two weeks. The printer continued his defense by assuring his readers that several thousand copies of his almanacs had already been sold, including one order for three thousand.

During the next weeks of the campaign Juvenal was joined by somebody signing himself J. C. and by Ellicott, who printed a list of errata in Goddard's almanac. Goddard was assisted by A. B. and by an Impartial Observer. The *Journal*'s two appearances a week compared to the *Gazette*'s one gave the older paper some advantage because most of the time the quantity of mud was more important than the quality. Hayes got sidetracked from the main issues of the struggle by a personal vendetta with one James Mann, and these two laid it on thick. Goddard called on the aid of Lex Talionis and Jack Retort before he was through, rightly figuring that the Baltimoreans of the 1780's would not be familiar with the exchanges of abuse in Philadelphia twenty years earlier. The *Journal* of December 19 featured a play in four scenes, whose chief characters were Crocodile (Langworthy), Tycho (Ellicott), and Jack Turnspit (Hayes).

Perhaps two samples of the Goddard abuse should be given. The first one is an alleged advertisement in the *Journal* of November 28:

Literature

Preparing for the Press, and will be speedily published, if sufficient Encouragement should be given by the *deeply-interested* Public, An *Improvement* on *Chesterfield*;

AN ENTIRE NEW WORK,

ENTITLED,

MODERN ELOQUENCE;

OR,

The *Phrase* in *Fashion.*

COMPRISING,

A Variety of *profound, moral, graceful, liberal,* and *truly urbane* EXAMPLES, for the *Improvement* of the rising Generation, and more particularly to *adorn the Manners, refine the Taste, ornament the Style,* and *mend the Hearts* of the Author's *Pupils* in Town, and his young *Hearers* in the Country;—or, to speak more *intelligibly,* to prepare them for "*active Life,*" by teaching them how *to throw Dirt scientifically, give the Lie emphatically,* and to intersperse their Conversation and Writings with all the *fine Tropes* and *Figures* of the *Billingsgate Seminary,* where the Author received his *refined* and *most sublime* Education.

By EDWARD CROCODILE,

Haberdasher of Pronouns, and *Auctionier of Divinity—pro Tempore.*

The Author flatters himself that he need not attempt to illustrate the *vast* Utility of the above Work, as it must be obvious to all whose Minds are *moderately* illuminated by *similar Rays of Science*—and as a *Proof* of his *transcendent Abilities,* he need only, *he* is persuaded, refer to his Performances, under the Signature of *Juvenal,* which have lately *dignified* Mr. *Hayes*'s Gazette, the *Poignancy* of which, he *verily believes,* have "pierced," through and through, and *done, quite done* for, the *tough Vitals* of "*Will. Goddard.*"

N.B. If the above Essay of CROCODILE's *masterly Genius* should be patronized, he will, it is thought, bring forward some other Works of

equal Worth, with which, it is said, he is now *heavy ladened.*—Pro
Bono Publico.

"No Crab more active in the *dirty Dance,*
Downward to climb, and *backward* to *advance.*"

The quotation from Goddard's favorite "Dunciad" appropriately
leads us to the second sample of the printer's writing abilities. This
was a poem printed in the January 2, 1787, *Journal.* After this
date no more attention was given to the dispute in either of the two
Baltimore newspapers. Probably the determining factor in ending
the exchange was not so much the efficacy of the poem but the normal
dwindling of almanac sales with the start of the new year. The
Marquis of Queensberry rules for an almanac war were those of
almanac sales and newspaper circulation, and the rules were rigidly
adhered to. But let us turn to Goddard's poetic strictures on the
occasion:

A Description of Scandal

Around the world [?] Sprite
Speeds undiscern'd to poison pure delight:
Amidst the foremost of this haggard band,
Unwearied poster of the sea and land,
Wrapt in dark mists, malignant Scandal flies,
While Envy's poison'd breath the buoyant gale supplies.
Tho' *Sheridan,* with shafts of Comic wit,
Pierc'd, and expos'd her to the laughing Pit,
Th' *immortal hag* still wears her *paper crown,*
The dreaded Empress of the idle town:
O'erleaping her prerogatives of old,
To sink the noble, to defame the bold;
In chase of worth to slip the dogs of strife,
Thro' all the ample range of public life;
The Tyrant now that sanctuary burst
Where happiness by privacy is nurst,
Her fury rising as her powers increase,
O'erturns the altars of domestic peace.
Pleas'd in her dark and gall-distilling cloud,
The sportive form of Innocence to shroud:
Beauty's young train her baleful eyes survey,
To mark the fairest as her fav'rite prey.
For Scandal, restless fiend, who never knows
The balmy blessing of an hour's repose,
Worn, yet unsated with her daily toil,
In her *base work* consumes the midnight oil.

O'er fiercer fiends, when heavy slumbers creep,
When wearied AVARICE and AMBITION sleep,
SCANDAL is vigilant, and keen to spread
The plagues that spring from her prolific head:
On TRUTH's fair basis she her falsehood builds,
With *tinsel sentiment* its surface gilds;
To nightly labour, from their *dark abodes*,
The *Demons* of the *groaning Press* she goads;
And smiles to see their *rapid art* supply
Ten thousand wings to every INFANT LIE.

In January, 1787, Benjamin Franklin made an attempt through a Baltimore agent to collect the sixty-pound bond of almost twenty years before that Goddard and his sister had signed. Considering the circumstances of the printer at the time, the reply of Goddard to Franklin's agent, David Lenox, is rather equivocating. While objecting to paying the heavy burden of accumulated interest, he promised his good intentions for the future, though he pointedly reminded Lenox of the Pennsylvania Assembly act of March, 1775, releasing him legally from all debts prior to that date. In spite of his statement, "I shall ever consider myself *morally* bound to pay my Debts," Goddard probably had little if any intention to pay this particular debt, despising Franklin as he did.

The publication of the 1788 almanacs by the Hayes and Goddard presses in the fall of 1787 led to another exchange between the two editors. But the 1787 fight lasted only a short while and was never as violent as the one a year before. The only exception to this was a remark by Andrew Ellicott (the principal attacker of Goddard) about the Baltimore printer's marriage "on the wrong side of forty." Perhaps this hurt him and his recent bride more than he would admit since beginning about this time the couple began to think more and more of retiring from the printing business and returning to Providence. Goddard in his notices "To the Public" every so often refers to his having given the "prime of his life" to the people of Baltimore. And Abigail was probably encouraging her husband in this attitude. Perhaps she never entirely overcame her lack of enthusiasm for "hominy and pone."

During latter 1787 and early 1788 the leading topic of discussion in all the states was the ratification of the new constitution proposed by the convention held in Philadelphia. Among those seeking ratification in Maryland was William Goddard, who printed several essays in the *Journal* in support of his opinion. On April 26, 1788, Maryland became the seventh state to ratify, and Baltimoreans decided this called for a celebration on Sunday, May 1. The inevitable parade meandered through the main streets of the city, featuring a band followed by representatives of forty-five different trades. Among the trades was printing with both John Hayes and William Goddard walking, who had gotten together for a float topped by a figure of Gutenberg. Alongside the two editors "Mercuries" distributed copies of the new constitution to what the *Journal* estimated as three thousand people witnessing the parade. In the middle of the procession the place of honor was held by the crafts associated with the sea. Leading this group was a miniature, fifteen-foot-long fully rigged ship on wheels, called *The Federalist*. The procession ended on a hill, ever since that day known as Federal Hill, where speeches were made. At the conclusion of these Commodore Joshua Barney, who had superintended the building of *The Federalist*, launched the vessel. That evening there was a huge bonfire and a banquet on Federal Hill and a ball at Starck's Tavern. Commodore Barney, later to acquire fame in the War of 1812, afterwards sailed the vessel to Annapolis, where more festivities were held. From the capital he sailed *The Federalist* down the Chesapeake and up the Potomac River to Mount Vernon, where he docked on June 9 in time for breakfast with Washington, to whom the ship was presented.

The banquet on Federal Hill, attended by four hundred persons, was under the supervision of Goddard and George Salmon, first president of the Bank of Baltimore. William Evans, afterwards proprietor of the Indian Queen Hotel, served as caterer for the occasion. His bill for £200 included such items as 560 pounds of bacon and ham, 9½ gallons of peach brandy, 15½ barrels of beer, a separate barrel of beer "for the committee," and more miscellaneous beer, grog, and "teddy." Obviously Goddard, active as he was on this occasion, was regarded as one of the city's leading citizens.

In 1789 Goddard started to move his financial interests from Baltimore to Providence. James Angell, Abigail's younger brother, had been in Baltimore since latter 1786 and had interested himself in the printing business. On July 24, 1787, he announced the setting up of a print shop, though we have no record of any im-

prints from his shop. Angell made himself a part of the
Baltimore community by marrying Mary Barney, sister of Joshua, on
Christmas Day, 1788. A letter to Moses Brown, executor of General
Angell's estate, on April 7, 1789, reveals the plans being discussed
by James and his brother-in-law. James Angell was turning over
to Goddard all his property in Rhode Island in exchange for a
partnership in the Goddard press in Baltimore. The letter actually
said that the veteran printer was about to set out for Providence to
settle the arrangements there. This visit lasted for two months
since a letter dated June, 1789, to Horatio Gates, a friend acquired as
a result of the Lee affair, speaks of his recent return from Rhode
Island, along with his expectation of visiting Gates at his Virginia
estate. Doubtless Goddard set a good price for a partnership, because the June 26, 1789, *Journal* says it "hath the most extensive
INLAND and SEA-COAST Circulation of any Paper in the United
States." Finally, on August 7, 1789, the Goddard and Angell partnership was announced. In the announcement Goddard referred to
the "Labours of an OLD SERVANT." He was weary of his many
struggles.

During the next few years Goddard and his wife spent almost
as much time in Providence as they did in Baltimore. They stayed
with her relatives, such as the Jacob Whitmans, or with his friends,
such as John Carter. On one of these trips in June and July of
1790 the first child of Abigail and William died after a long illness
while the family was visiting the Whitmans. On November 29
of the same year the first of the five children to live to adulthood
was born—Ann Elizabeth.

In 1790 Christopher Hughes and Leonard Harbaugh engaged
in an epistolary exchange of insults through the columns of the
Maryland Journal. Commonplace as such exchanges were in the
eighteenth century, this one would not merit our mention here but
for two things. One is that Goddard and Angell were taken into
court for printing one of the letters—for which they were promptly
acquitted. And the other is that a broadside was printed during the
course of the controversy with this colophon: "Printed at P. Hassen-
clever's Iron-Works." Goddard in an attempt at anonymity was
reviving memories of his role in the turbulent days of the Stamp
Act struggle and the *Constitutional Courant,* for which Lawrence

Sweeney had given the New York authorities the iron-maker's name as the source.

While William was becoming more involved with his friends and interests in Providence, Mary Katherine had been operating her bookstore and running the Baltimore post office. Ever since 1775, when the Continental Congress took over her brother's Constitutional postal system, she had served as the only woman postmaster in this country, thereby giving her a certain claim to posterity. She was among the most efficient of the various postal officials of her day. Ebenezer Hazard, then postmaster general, in a 1786 letter to General Horatio Gates described her extreme punctuality in remitting her accounts to his office. During the Revolution postmasters were fortunate if at the end of each quarter they did not have to dig into their own pockets. Not until peace and more settled conditions did the post office in communities such as Baltimore start to provide any income for those in charge. In 1789 the new government under the presidency of Washington was busy setting aside many of the appointees of the days of the Articles of Confederation. Ebenezer Hazard found himself replaced as postmaster general by Samuel Osgood, who then proceeded to appoint his own postmasters. Towards the end of October, 1789, Mary Katherine was much surprised during the course of a seemingly routine visit to Baltimore by Burrell, the assistant to Osgood, to receive a note telling her to turn over her office to John White. The postmistress was enough of a Goddard not to take this lying down. She first objected probably in person to Burrell, who told her she was replaced because a person of more physical vigor was needed who could ride horseback frequently and superintend the postal activities of the states below Baltimore, it being intended to make the city a regional headquarters. (Even if seriously suggested, which is doubtful, nothing was ever done in this direction.) Then Mary Katherine, as an experienced newspaperwoman, gave her case verbal publicity in Baltimore, and soon a petition signed by more than two hundred of the leading businessmen of Baltimore was sent to Osgood. This petition to retain Miss Goddard in her old position, dated November 12, 1789, was signed by several of the former attackers of Goddard in 1777 and 1779. Apparently the sister was held in greater affection than the brother. On December 23 no reply from Osgood yet forthcoming, she addressed a memorial to President Washington. Washington replied on January 6, 1790, that he would not interfere with the affairs of any department and had referred the matter to Osgood. Osgood defended his position in a reply to the Baltimore merchants on January 7. Five days later Mary Katherine petitioned the United States Senate, asking that she be restored to her former position. On February 18 receipt of this petition was recorded in the Senate *Journal*, but no action was taken. And so Mary Katherine lost her place as postmistress.

Mary Katherine Goddard continued to reside in Baltimore for the rest of her life. The 1790 census records her as owning four slaves and having one "other free person" in her household. For many years she continued her bookstore (William never resumed this branch of the business after the separation of the two in January, 1784). In 1803 she moved her shop from 80 Baltimore Street to smaller quarters at 28 Chatham Street. About 1809 or 1810 she retired from her business, and the 1810 Baltimore directory lists her as a gentlewoman at the latter address. She died on August 12, 1816, at her last home at 18 Conewago Street. Her will makes no mention of her brother, from whom she had so long been alienated. During the last years of her life she had lived alone except for a Negro slave, Belinda Starling. As a reward for the years of care and affection Mary Katherine gave Belinda her freedom and "all the property of which I may die Possessed all which I do to recompence the faithful performance of duties to me." No other person is mentioned in the brief will, made on May 21, 1816. Seemingly these last years of her life were lonely ones for America's first postmistress and editress for practically a decade of Baltimore's first newspaper.

In seeking to comprehend the life of our Federalist ancestors, we find many difficulties. They had refinement, elegance, taste, and discrimination, but their practice of these qualities was much different from ours. For instance, today's Baltimore *Sun* would probably not carry such an advertisement as did its predecessor, the *Maryland Journal*, on November 12, 1790. "James Bryden, Hair-Dresser and Perfumer, at the Civet-Cat, in Market-Street, Baltimore, has imported, in the last Vessels, from London, a large and general Assortment of Perfumery, &c. &c. . . . Also just received, from

Kentucky, A large and fresh quantity of Bear's Grease, which is much esteemed for its efficacy in thickening and hastening the growth of the hair, nourishing its roots, and preventing its turning gray, at 1s. 10½d. and 3s. 9d. per bottle." James Bryden and Elizabeth Arden may have many things in common, but bear's grease is probably not one of them.

The *Maryland Journal* continued to be the most popular newspaper of its day. At one time Goddard spoke of sending out each week "Seven Reams of this Journal." However many customers this means, the *Journal* during the early days of Washington's administration became one of the staunchest supporters of the Federalist party in its struggles against the anti-Federalists. Douglas Southall Freeman in his biography of Washington comments, "Highly esteemed also for conspicuous gallantry in the crucial years [was] . . . William Goddard's important *Maryland Journal* at Baltimore."

Publication of an almanac continued each year. For his 1792 almanac Goddard, with much ado, called upon the astronomical services of Benjamin Banneker. In Evans's *American Bibliography* there is a note about this 1792 almanac. "The first publication of Benjamin Banneker, a free negro, born in Baltimore County, fifty-nine years of age at this performance, which he accomplished, unaided, from books loaned to him by the Ellicott family—themselves remarkable for scientific achievement. The Publishers' preface makes clear that in selecting Banneker's calculations for their Almanac, which they did at the instance of James M'Henry, they were actuated by a mingled feeling of deference for Mr. M'Henry, and Mr. David Rittenhouse's opinions, of philanthropy, and for the business effect it would have on the sale of the Almanac." Regular advertisements in the *Journal* informed the readers about Banneker's efforts as the Goddard and Angell firm pushed the sales in its usual vigorous fashion.

For some time now Goddard and his wife had found the management of their Rhode Island properties requiring more and more time-consuming trips in spite of the assistance of their friend Moses Brown. There were now two girls in the family—Mary Angell Goddard having been born May 24, 1792—and Abigail's importunities to quit the hurly-burly printing business carried more weight than ever before. That the abruptness of Goddard's retiring is apparent and not real comes out in a letter the Baltimore printer wrote to his old friend and fellow craftsman in Providence, John Carter, on November 26, 1791. Goddard had just returned from Philadelphia and wrote primarily to felicitate Carter on the recent marriage of his daughter. Afterwards he added: "In the Spring I shall, probably, see you at Providence—but whether to take up my 'permanent Residence' there, or in its vicinity, I cannot, as yet, conclusively determine—It depends much on the Punctuality of Mr. Angell—in a certain affair now on the Tapis." Apparently what precipitated the retirement was a speculation, in what we don't know, of twenty-five hundred pounds. Goddard lost on the speculation, and in order to repay the person who had backed him he sold his interest in the *Journal* to his young partner, James Angell. Though Goddard was not quite as poor as his announcement of his retirement in the August 14, 1792, *Journal* implied, he still took away from Baltimore very little capital. The twenty-five hundred pound loss added to the five hundred lost a few years before to George Richards & Co. did not leave the Goddard family wealthy, yet the parents obviously saw their way clear for future sustenance and a graceful old age. Goddard wrote his farewell to the readers of the *Maryland Journal* at some length. He requested those who owed him to make payment so that he could have "a Pittance wherewith, in humble Mediocrity, I may cultivate my little Farm." He concluded his article by revealing that his "little Retreat" would be "near the Town of Providence, in the State of Rhode-Island." Among those who heeded the request to pay their back bills was the French consul in Baltimore, Chevalier d'Anemours, who accompanied his payment with a letter wishing Goddard "every sort of happyness; and [the Chevalier] assures him —it will contribute to his own to hear—that he has found it in the alluring occupations of a rural Life." The much mellower, much less truculent, Goddard of the 1780's and 1790's made many more friends than the fierce defender of his rights in the 1770's. Though Goddard's name was not dropped from the colophon of the *Journal* until February 22, 1793, the Goddard family sailed for Rhode Island shortly after the August announcement, and William Goddard thus ended his thirty-year career as a printer and newspaperman.

UNTIL this point the task of writing William Goddard's biography has been one of recording events, actions. Now the manner of living changes. With many people the placid Indian summer of life after pronounced activity is brief and decidedly anticlimactic. Not so with Goddard. He still had over twenty-five years of a contented existence to live. His two extant portraits, now in the drawing room of the home of Mrs. C. Oliver Iselin in Providence, graphically show these two manners of living, each meaningful in itself. The first painting—the one almost always reproduced—reveals a relatively young man not much past forty who stubbornly stares at the viewer from the canvas. The unknown painter has brought out an implacable, confident character with certain overtones of gentleness. The second portrait, done by James Frothingham, is that of a gentle, genial soul whose eyes twinkle in enjoyment. The implacability is now only the overtone to a basic contented confidence instead of the previous urgent self-assurance. Frothingham's portrait, painted probably when Goddard was in his late sixties or early seventies, reveals the person whom a fellow printer, William McCullough, could describe in these terms in a letter to Isaiah Thomas: "Goddard, whom you also mention, was truly facetious. He was the soul of conviviality, at a dinner of friends, and had a fund of laughable entertainment. I have heard some of his jokes, but they would scarcely be thought modest in print. He was a poet."

We are fortunate in having still standing the house in which the Goddard family lived near Providence for the next eleven years. Called the Clemence-Goddard-Irons house, it is now owned by the Society for the Preservation of New England Antiquities and is located at 38 George Waterman Road in Johnston. Now surrounded by rows of suburban homes, the house in 1792 was the focus for a two-hundred-and-fifty-acre farm. This farm had belonged to General Angell, and a year after his death Abigail and James purchased the shares of the other heirs for £398. Then in 1789, probably as part of the partnership agreement, James relinquished to his sister his interest in the farm. Thus the way was prepared for Abigail, William, and the two children to settle there in August, 1792.

The house was old even then, having been built about 1680 (and 112 years do lend a patina of age to any house) by Thomas Clemence, a friend of Roger Williams. A simple, unostentatious, weathered saltbox, it would have provided comfortable, though not luxurious, quarters for the growing family. The outside dimensions are only approximately 24 by 27 feet, but in 1792 there may have been an additional leanto besides various buildings not now standing appropriate to the maintenance of a farm. Almost all of one end wall of the dwelling is a huge fieldstone chimney, which provided a large cooking fireplace for the kitchen-dining room and another similarly large one for heating purposes in the parlor. The first floor consists of four rooms—the kitchen-dining room, in size about 15 × 15; the parlor or front room, about 9 × 15; a bedroom, about 9 × 15; and a second bedroom, about 9 × 9. A steep stairway in one corner of the kitchen leads up to a loft running all the way across the house. There is also underneath the entire building a cellar entered by a trap door in the parlor. Without difficulty we can visualize the retired printer and his family spending most of their evenings in what I have called the kitchen-dining room watching logs burn in the huge fireplace as the father reminisced about his past experiences to the children or to the not infrequent visitors, most of whom would have had their after-dinner port or brandy in the parlor.

In this relaxed mood Goddard on August 17, 1793, wrote to his friend General Horatio Gates, the conqueror of the British army under Burgoyne at Saratoga, now living on his Virginia plantation, Traveler's Rest. Gates and his wife were invited to visit the Goddards in their Johnston retreat, where, as Goddard phrased it, "I expect to pass the remaining days that may be allotted me by Divine Goodness." In comparison with the bustling scene in Baltimore, he hoped "to enjoy the happiness of more tranquil scenes amongst the affectionate Friends & Companions of my youth." Gates happened to be then near New York, and so Goddard reminded him of the packets which "furnish such convenient & delightful Means of passing from New York to Providence."

For the next few years Abigail was busy with her expanding brood of children. To the two daughters born in Baltimore a son, William Giles, was added January 2, 1794, and then two girls, Abbie Angell, in early 1795, and Sarah Updike, June 9, 1796. Caring for five children and acting as hostess for her convivial husband would have kept Abigail busy.

For William there was the round of activities necessary to the management of the farm plus some properties within the city of Providence, particularly a group of lots across the street from the Baptist church. The stature of Goddard in the community is indicated by his joining a Providence merchant, Cyprian Sterry, as sureties for the "Sum of Twenty Thousand good Spanish milled Dollars" to provide a bond for William Peck as district United States marshal. In 1797 the town meeting of Providence appointed a committee, probably favorable to Goddard since it included Moses Brown, to "enquire into the Title which William Goddard possesses to a certain Lot of Land situated at the North End of this Town and now in the possession of Simeon Thayer." In 1798 the three lots at the corner of North Main and Thomas streets had a taxable valuation of $1660, $1500 of which pertained to the lot at 79 North Main, where there were some store buildings. Occasionally William traveled down to Baltimore to see about liquidating his various interests there in the press and the paper mill. One such trip is mentioned in a letter to Moses Brown in June, 1799, and Goddard wrote to his brother-in-law, Jacob Whitman, Jr., that he had used some of the proceeds of the sale of his Baltimore establishment for the purchase of property in Providence. So it is not surprising to find the 1800 census listing not only the seven members of the Goddard family but including four other persons, probably farm hands or tenants, under the household of William Goddard.

But Goddard was not really a farmer, and the isolation of the farm must have drastically limited the number of guests who could be entertained. Also, the children were growing up and needing more space than the picturesque old farmhouse could provide. No doubt, Abigail wanted to see more of her Providence friends and relatives now that the children no longer demanded intimate supervision. So the Goddard family in 1803 moved from the Johnston farm to a larger dwelling at the corner of Main and Thomas streets. There were three bedrooms now plus a loft containing a spare bedstead. The dining room, or keeping-room, was separate from the kitchen, and Abigail would not have to worry about the grit and smoke from the fireplace getting into her damask table linen. The front parlor now had room for a Pembroke table, two card tables, and ten chairs, so that the father could entertain his friends after dinner much more spaciously. Though the Goddards were not living in anything like plush circumstances, still they were comfortable and could take their place among the Providence gentry with few qualms.

Among these gentry of Providence were the Carters. One of them, Dr. Benjamin Carter, had in 1804 asked Goddard if he wished to invest any money in a trading expedition to Canton, China. Goddard had to turn down this opportunity, not having, as he described it, the "Mexican Means." In spite of this refusal he still ordered luxuries such as silk and China tea. "Should you remain at Canton, as you intimated, I may possibly have a Chance of sending you a few Dollars—equal to the Purchase of a Piece of Silk, of the first Quality, for my Wife and Daughters, *or* a Coat for myself & Son, with a handsome Tea Cady filled with *Imperial*." Three years later, in 1807, Goddard wrote again to Dr. Carter, then in Canton, about a desk he had ordered.

One of the close friends in these calm days was Moses Brown. The Brown brothers were the leading merchants and property owners of the city of Providence. Moses, the most active in business of the four brothers, had been one of the two executors of the estate of Abigail's father. Afterwards he served as a kind of financial adviser to the Angell and Goddard families. In this era merchants frequently performed the functions of banks for their customers. And so it was with Moses Brown for the various Angells and Goddards. Therefore we find many memoranda going back and forth between the merchant and the retired printer. Most of these notes, frequently undated, relate to routine items of business. Sometimes Goddard takes the liberty of an old friend and asks Brown to make sure that the financial affairs of a relative are in order. An example of this is a letter, dated May 27, 1812, written after Jacob Whitman, Jr., had died, and Goddard wanted to make sure the wife's affairs were properly settled. But quite apparently the relationship between Moses Brown and William Goddard was more than business. At some time (the note from Goddard to Brown relative to this is undated) Moses must have tried his hand at printing, perhaps solely as a means of saving his firm money, and he called on the old printer's assistance as technical adviser. The note implies that Goddard was searching among his possessions for stray bits of printing apparatus to send to the old Quaker merchant. Probably the most important service Brown rendered the Goddard family was on July 24, 1813, when he canceled the remainder of a mortgage he held against Goddard in return for some old and not too valid claims against him. Brown's friendly generosity did much to make the last years of Goddard's life and his widow's (she lived until 1845) more comfortable.

John Carter was another of the Providence friends of Goddard, if not the closest of them all. William Giles Goddard, William's son, many years later spoke of this "truly fraternal" friendship. Almost every day, now that the Goddards were living in Providence, Goddard made the short walk over to the Shakespeare's Head printing shop of Carter, and the two friends would talk about the present affairs of the *Providence Gazette*, founded by William so many years before, and exchange reminiscences and maledictions on that terrible Mr. Jefferson or Mr. Madison, staunch Federalists that both printers were.

Through John Carter the former acquaintanceship with Isaiah Thomas was revived. On March 29, 1800, Carter wrote to Thomas, and Thomas enthusiastically responded a few days later, suggesting that Carter and Goddard come together to visit him in Worcester. Whether this particular trip was made or not, many other trips back and forth between Worcester and Providence were made by all three men and their families. Thomas, whose acquaintance with Goddard went back to the days of the Constitutional post offices, in his reply to Carter on April 5, 1800, mentioned that the three of them were New England's only surviving printers from pre-Revolutionary days. Thomas had turned over the running of his large printing establishment to his son and was beginning to interest himself in other affairs. One result of this freedom was the publishing in 1810 of his *History of Printing in America*. Obviously many of the conversations among the three veterans of the printing wars during the years before 1810 were about the materials to go into the book. As so frequently happens with individuals in Goddard's situation, antiquarian interests provided a genuine zest for living. Thomas in his preface acknowledged the help of four "elder brethren of the type, WILLIAM GODDARD and JOHN CARTER, esqrs. of *Providence*; and mr. THOMAS BRADFORD, and the late mr. JAMES HUMPHREYS, of *Philadelphia*." Because of Thomas's close connection with Goddard his character-sketch of the retired printer merits attention: "Goddard, although considerably advanced in life still retains his *naiveté*, and the pleasantness and facetiousness of his disposition, which qualities render him a remarkably pleasant companion."

Thomas must have let his friends soon know that he was hoping to collect new material along with corrections to the old for a revised edition of his *History of Printing*. (This second edition was not to be published until 1874.) Goddard busied himself in writing down in letters what he could for his Worcester friend. One of these was a revealing letter of April 15, 1811. To understand, we must remember first the Stamp Act crisis of 1765, when Goddard as a vigorous patriot distrusted Benjamin Franklin's role in that affair. The *Pennsylvania Chronicle* quarrels had added to Goddard's personal animosity towards the successful Philadelphian, which was increased by Goddard's sojourn as surveyor of the postal system under Franklin and Richard Bache. After Franklin's death his name became a symbol of liberal anti-Federalism, and the Federalist Goddard found this role as repulsive to him as the real Franklin had ever been. In 1778 Holt had discouraged him from printing a pamphlet against the elder statesman, but now he was not to be deterred from expressing his dislike in a private letter to the Worcester editor. Franklin had entered into a "conspiracy" with Galloway and Wharton to overturn the old proprietary government in Pennsylvania so that they could acquire *"Wealth & Power* for themselves & Connexions." When this plan failed, "from a *Royalist* he insidiously turned into a *dark Republican*. . . . When he arrived in America [in 1775], he was considered a suspicious doubtful character —and Mr S. Adams, & other Patriots, asked me my opinion of him, at Philadelphia being very suspicious of him. I told them if they could convince him that it would redound to his INTEREST to support the American Cause, he would soon declare himself in its Favour, and not otherwise. This they did, & Franklin became, as they advised me, *an unsuspected confidential* PATRIOT." The letter continues with an account of Franklin's "sinister" maneuvering in the postal system and pushing of Goddard aside for his son-in-law, Richard Bache. Concluding the commentary on Franklin is this sentence: "After all, as I have said before, as applied to John Calvin by the celebrated Dean Berkeley, afterwards Bishop of Cloyne 'To give the Devil his Due'—Doctor F. 'was a very great Man.'" The old rancors were still in Goddard after all these years of peaceful retirement.

A few letters now at the Rhode Island Historical Society, mostly undated, show the affectionate father and husband. When his children were away for visits of a few days to relatives Goddard wrote his beloved Eliza, Mary, Sally, Abby, and William entertaining notes filled with the chitchat of a fond parent. To Eliza and Mary he says, "Your Absence hath demonstrated your great *Importance* in our Family." Another time he writes to " 'my Mary' and 'my Sally' " a note teasing them about the possible date of their return from Dedham and enclosing four dollars. A letter written September 5, 1814, to "My ever dear Abigail" starts out, "Tho' you have been absent but a few *Hours*, yet the *Days appear* to have *lengthened*, occasioned by the want of your Presence and Society—so essential to my Happiness." With this letter one of the daughters had written a brief epistle, to which the father added this wry remark, "Ann Eliza's *Proof Sheet*, carefully revised and corrected by an *old Corrector* of near 74."

William Giles Goddard, the only son, attended Brown University, from which he graduated in 1812. In October the recent graduate paid a three-day visit to Isaiah Thomas. Arrangements were probably made then for young Goddard to study law in the office of Francis Blake in Worcester. On the first of November the prospective lawyer arrived for his longer stay in Worcester. William Giles found the pull of a newspaper, aided no doubt by the friendship of Isaiah Thomas, too strong and he began working on the *Worcester Spy*, then published by Thomas's son. In early

1814 he returned to Providence, where he joined a three-way partnership in publishing the *Rhode Island American*. The former newspaperman reported in obvious pleasure and pride in his letter to Abigail of September 5, 1814: "William is steadily labouring in his *Vocation*, and I am pleased to find 'bears his Faculties meekly.' About 7 this Eve, I read a Proof of his 2d Page, to facilitate his Business, and I hope he will be able *seasonably* to repose alongside his watchful anxious Father."

During all these years of retirement the papers of General Charles Lee remained in Goddard's possession. In 1810 he must have felt as though a skeleton were being dug out of a closet when Daniel Carthy of New Bern, North Carolina, wrote to him. Carthy was trying to prove that the unknown author of the famous Junius letters was Charles Lee. Goddard sent Carthy a box of Lee's manuscripts pursuant to the North Carolinian's request and argument that if Lee's authorship could be proved the manuscripts in Goddard's possession would become valuable. The only result, of course, was a correspondence and the acquiring of a new friend. Carthy in a letter to Major Thomas Coles, a Providence mutual acquaintance, on March 21, 1811, talked about Abigail's qualities: "You give me such an high idea of the literary taste, talents, and accomplishments of Mrs. Goddard, that, although I should dread her censures, I could wish to be near her, that my work might receive the preenings of her criticism and the stamp of her approbation." Later Carthy revealed his current literary enthusiasm: "Last fall a friend of mine was going to New York. He asked me the common place question, whether I had any commands. I answered none, unless he should meet Diedrick Knickerbocker in his travels, in which event, I entreated him not to forget to present my respects and acknowledgments for the very great pleasure I had received from a perusal of his incomparable History of New York, my native Country." Earlier Carthy had published an open letter to Knickerbocker in the *United States Gazette*. Washington Irving must have enjoyed the open letter and would have appreciated the compliments for Diedrich Knickerbocker.

At this stage of his life Goddard took much pleasure from his membership in the American Antiquarian Society, founded by Isaiah Thomas in 1812. At the meeting of the Society on September 29,

1813, fourteen people were added to the membership rolls, including William Goddard, Yale's President Timothy Dwight, and the renowned scientist, Benjamin Silliman. Goddard became quite interested in the Society's activities and wrote many letters to Thomas with suggestions for new members and the like. All this did much to take away the sting of the loss he felt in the death of John Carter on August 12, 1814. The removal of such a close friend made the old printer aware of his own age and declining strength.

The affairs of another old friend intruded themselves on Goddard's attention during these last few years. Evidently while still in Baltimore he had become acquainted with Lighthorse Harry Lee, of Revolutionary War fame and the father of Robert E. Lee. Lee had been badly mauled by a Baltimore mob in 1812 and never recovered his health thereafter. In search of relief from physical pain in 1816 and 1817 he was in various islands in the Bahamas. His eldest son, Charles Carter Lee, was a student at Harvard, and the father wrote many letters of paternal advice to his son in care of William Goddard in Providence, vessels from the Rhode Island port putting in frequently for salt near where Lee was staying. On August 29, 1816, Lee wrote directly to Goddard telling him of his current activities and hopes for surcease from his constant pain. Lee also requested Goddard to suggest the name of a school near Providence for the crippled son of a friend of his in the Bahamas. Since Lee sent three copies of this letter by various vessels, Goddard forwarded one of these to Carter Lee at Harvard.

But time was running out for the old newspaperman. On September 25, 1817, Isaiah Thomas spent the night with the Goddards and recorded in his diary that his friend was "very infirm." On Tuesday evening, December 23, 1817, the seventy-seven-year-old printer died. William Giles Goddard had the filial duty of writing his father's obituary for the *Rhode Island American*. In the brief notice he appropriately said at one point: "The first years of his long life were passed amid the turmoil of useful activities—the last in the bosom of domestic quiet." Three days later the weary bones of William Goddard found their last rest in the North Burying Ground in Providence.

In perspective, the major personal flaw of Goddard is, no doubt, the quarrel with the reliable Mary Katherine. Because this is so crucial to a full comprehension of both brother and sister, it would help us to have at least some tangible evidence at this point on the attitudes of the two. As a result of this lacuna we are forced to suspend our judgment. We do know from the remarks of various people that as a person Goddard was jovial, affectionate, and fond of telling a good story. What these contemporaries called his naïveté we would term his refreshing enjoyment of the life immediately around him. Perhaps this sense of wonderment contributed to the abrupt bellicosity he presented so often to the world's view. Goddard had the ability to organize something new, be it the postal system or another newspaper, but too frequently his chip-on-the-shoulder attitude lost him all that he had or might have gained.

However much we speculate about why Goddard was tactless at the very moments when tact was most needed, we must not ignore his quite genuine achievements. He did succeed in doing exactly what he set out to do—supplant the existing British postal system with another one that the Continental Congress could take over. Granted that some of the success came from the manipulative and propagandistic skill of Sam Adams and other members of the Boston committee, still the original idea was Goddard's and he did the work to get things going. For this accomplishment he deserves an important place in the history of the beginnings of this country. Our present postal system descends directly from the Goddard or Constitutional post offices. But more important than this descent is the advantage early control of communications gave the colonists in the Revolution. Many of the factors involved in the struggle—armed forces, morale, sentiment of the people—balance out roughly equal between the two sides. In contrast, the propaganda war was one-sided, not only because of the skills of Paine and others like him but because of the virtual disappearance of the British postal system in latter 1774, thanks to the efforts of the young printer from Baltimore.

Nor should we forget Goddard's contributions as a printer and newspaperman. His knowledge of and skill at the craftsmanship of his trade make him one of the outstanding printers in eighteenth-century America. Besides having good typography and layout of the page, he edited well-run newspapers. In his era this meant having, as Goddard so frequently phrased it, "extensive correspondence." The coverage of the *Pennsylvania Chronicle* was one of the most thorough in the colonies, both in quantity and quality. Though Goddard was on the defensive in both the Whig Club and Charles Lee affairs and on neither occasion did he exhibit tact, the principle successfully defended each time merits his having an important niche in the history of American journalism.

What might be called the rhythmical pattern of the career of William Goddard makes us wish we knew more about the human personality. Approximately between the ages of twenty-five and thirty-five he was most affirmative in his actions. From then on his role is more often defensive. Yet both cycles are active, not passive, with the possible exception of the winter of 1776-1777. So easily the final phase of a life like Goddard's could have been tawdry and squalid, but instead he mellows, becomes the affectionate and loving husband and father, and finds contentment in simplicity. No doubt Abigail contributed a good deal to this final phase, yet we must admire and envy the personal resources within Goddard that made this possible. Yes, being a listener to the raconteur William Goddard in front of his fireplace in the old farmhouse is a pleasure we would love to have shared with Abigail and the children. Then we could have summoned up remembrances of the patriotic founder of our postal system, the militant defender of freedom of the press, and the belligerent editor of newspapers—yet there would have lingered with us an intensely human personality.

NOTE ON SOURCES

The most important sources for this book have been the files of the *Providence Gazette* in the Rhode Island Historical Society, the *Pennsylvania Chronicle* in the Historical Society of Pennsylvania, and the *Maryland Journal* in the Maryland Historical Society. Before such a biography as this could be written, the listing of imprints in each colony and state had to be done. Fortunately here I was able to call upon the work of John E. Alden, *Rhode Island Imprints, 1727-1800* (New York, 1949); Charles R. Hildeburn, *A Century of Printing: the Issues of the Press in Pennsylvania, 1685-1784* (Philadelphia, 1885-1886); Lawrence C. Wroth, *A History of Printing in Colonial Maryland, 1686-1776* (Baltimore, 1922); Joseph Towne Wheeler, *The Maryland Press, 1777-1790* (Baltimore, 1938); and A. Rachel Minick, *A History of Printing in Maryland, 1791-1800, with a Bibliography of Works Printed in the State during the Period* (Baltimore, 1949). That Maryland's printing history has had the most thorough coverage and that each of the three volumes named devotes a chapter to the Goddard press have been of tremendous value.

The bulk of the manuscript letters to, by, and about Goddard are to be found in the collections of the John Carter Brown Library (the most important single source), the Rhode Island Historical Society, and the Maryland Historical Society. These three libraries also possess copies of most of the Goddard imprints.

A word of appreciation should be expressed here to Lawrence C. Wroth, whose work on Maryland printing in 1922 first pointed out the importance of Goddard not only as a printer but as a founding father of our postal system. Dr. Wroth's meticulous research has made the task of the Goddard biographer much simpler. His book, *The Colonial Printer*, 2nd ed. (Portland, Maine, 1938), is the best presentation of everything the title implies. The printer is here seen not only as a follower of a particular trade but as a human being affecting social, economic, political, and cultural conditions of his day.

Two volumes that have been much pored over in the course of the research for this book are Clarence S. Brigham's *History and Bibliography of American Newspapers, 1690-1820* (Worcester, 1947).

CHAPTER II

Information about Giles Goddard and his forebears is to be found in the manuscript by Kingston G. Hadley, "Giles Goddard and His Descendents," at the New-York Historical Society and in various records at the New London Historical Society. The diary of Joshua Hempstead has been published in the *Collections of the New London Historical Society* (1901). Dr. Alexander Hamilton's journal was edited by Carl Bridenbaugh, *Gentleman's Progress: the Itinerarium of Dr. Alexander Hamilton 1744* (Chapel Hill, 1948). The church records are in Wilkins Updike, *A History of the Episcopal Church in Narragansett Rhode Island Including a History of Other Episcopal Churches in the State*, 2nd ed., edited by Daniel Goodwin (Boston, 1907). Two articles by Beverly McAnear in the *New Jersey Historical Society Proceedings*, LIX (1941), on James Parker provide information on Parker's activities in the 1760's. The letter to Isaiah Thomas is in the library of the American Antiquarian Society. Isaiah Thomas's *History of Printing in America* (Worcester, 1810, and 2nd ed., Albany, 1874) tells us much about Goddard's activities in these early years, including his journeyman work for Samuel Farley. That Goddard himself assisted Thomas in the preparation of the *History of Printing* makes the book particularly valuable for our purposes.

CHAPTER III

The sketch of Gregory Dexter is summarized from Bradford F. Swan, *Gregory Dexter of London and New England 1610-1700* (Rochester, N. Y., 1949). The £120 figure comes from Worthington C. Ford, ed., "Letters from James Parker to Franklin," *Proceedings of the Massachusetts Historical Society*, Second Series, XVI (1902), 186-232. For an estimate of the role Goddard's new press played in Providence, see Lawrence C. Wroth, "The First Press in Providence, a Study in Social Development," *Proceedings of the American Antiquarian Society*, n.s., LI (October, 1941), 351-383. The remark by the Providence printers of 1907 is found in *Printers and Printing in Providence, 1762-1907* [Providence, 1907], p. 9. The printed records of the Rhode Island Colony and the archives in the state capitol in Providence provide some of the material upon which this chapter is based. The letter to Josias Lyndon is in the Peck MSS, Rhode Island Historical Society. The comparative printing figures between Goddard and his Newport competitors are based on a study of records in the state archives, for which the assistance of Miss Mary Quinn was valuable.

CHAPTER IV

The Parker letters and Isaiah Thomas's *History of Printing* are helpful for the New York period. Goddard's name as a member of the Sons of Liberty is to be found in the Belknap Papers, 1745-1776 (120), in the Massachusetts Historical Society. Goddard's *Constitutional Courant* is reproduced in Albert Matthews, "The Snake Devices, 1754-1776, and the Constitutional Courant, 1765," *Publications of Colonial Society of Massachusetts*, XI (December, 1907), 409-453. This is supplemented by a now lost letter by Goddard given by William R. Staples, *Annals of the Town of Providence*, in *Collections of the Rhode Island Historical Society*, V (1843), 542-544. The data given by Staples are corroborated by a letter from Goddard to Isaiah Thomas reprinted in Clarence S. Brigham, *Journals and Journeymen: A Contribution to the History of Early American Newspapers* (Philadelphia, 1950), p. 101. The Goddard letter to Parker is in the Franklin Papers at the American Philosophical Society, XLVII, 30.

CHAPTER V

The most important source for the Goddard-Galloway story is William Goddard, *The Partnership: or the History of the Rise and Progress of the Pennsylvania Chronicle* (Philadelphia, 1770). The William Bradford 1766 broadside is in the collections of the New-York Historical Society. The David Hall Letter Book 1764-1767 at the American Philosophical Society provides much material, Hall's letters to Strahan coming from that source. The letter from William Franklin to his father is in the Franklin Papers at the American Philosophical Society, XLII, 3. The April 14 letter from Franklin to David Hall exists at the Salem County Historical Society, Salem, New Jersey. For calling attention to this letter, gratitude is expressed to Dr. Whitfield J. Bell of the American Philosophical Society. The Nathaniel Shaw letter to Wharton is reproduced in the *Collections of the New London Historical Society*, II (1933), 191. The career of Benjamin Mecom is discussed in Carl Van Doren, *Jane Mecom* (New York, 1950), *passim*. The records of the Pennsylvania Assembly of this period are in *Pennsylvania Archives*, 8: VII and VIII. The original of the letter from Sarah Goddard to her sisters is at the Providence Public Library. Though actual quotations are from the manuscript Minute Books in possession of the Library Company of Philadelphia, the story of Goddard's printing of the Company's book

labels derives from Edwin Wolf, "The First Books and Printed Catalogues of the Library Company of Philadelphia," *Pennsylvania Magazine
of History and Biography*, LXXVIII (January, 1954), 45-55. The
letters from Goddard to John Smith of Burlington are in the Library Company of Philadelphia. Strahan's 1772 letter to Franklin is in the American
Philosophical Society's Franklin Papers, III, Part II, 117. Valuable
material on the colonial newspapers of this period is supplied in Arthur M.
Schlesinger, *Prelude to Independence: The Newspaper War on Britain,
1764-1776* (New York, 1958).

CHAPTER VI

The most important sources for the story of Goddard's post offices
are the Minute Books of the Boston Committee of Correspondence now
in the Manuscript Collection, New York Public Library. The dating
of Goddard's trip north so closely is possible because of these papers and
the many items appearing in the newspapers as he went along. Hugh
Finlay's journal, now in the National Archives, is available as *Journal
Kept by Hugh Finlay, Surveyor of the Post Roads on the Continent of
North America* (Brooklyn, 1867). For the early history of our postal
system, see Wesley E. Rich, *The History of the U.S. Post Office to the
Year 1829*, Vol. XXVII of *Harvard Economic Studies* (Cambridge,
1924). Peter Force's *American Archives* (Washington, 1837-1853)
reproduces several informative newspaper clippings. The letter to John
Lamb is in the Lamb Papers at the New-York Historical Society. John
Foxcroft's letter to his superior is from the Public Records Office, London.
The Titus Hosmer letter is in the Yale University Library.

CHAPTER VII

The early printing history of Baltimore derives from the account given
by Wroth in *A History of Printing in Colonial Maryland, 1686-1776*.
Valuable in spite of its undigested quality is John T. Scharf, *Chronicles of
Baltimore* (Baltimore, 1874). The statement by William Eddis is in
his *Letters from America, Historical and Descriptive; Comprising Occurrences from 1769, to 1777, Inclusive* (London, 1792), p. 304. The
Whig Club account is based, in addition to the broadsides and newspaper
stories mentioned in the text, on official records, some published, in the
Hall of Records, Annapolis, and on depositions at the same place and at

the Maryland and Rhode Island Historical Societies. The original of the letter from Benjamin Galloway is also at the Hall of Records.

CHAPTER VIII

The Holt-to-Goddard letter is to be found at the American Antiquarian Society. The best modern biography of Charles Lee is John R. Alden, *General Charles Lee: Traitor or Patriot?* (Baton Rouge, 1951). *The Lee Papers* were collected and published as volumes IV to VII of the *Collections of the New-York Historical Society, 1871-74* (New York, 1872-1875). As with the Whig Club affair, records and depositions found at the Hall of Records and the Maryland and Rhode Island historical societies provide much of the story. Lorenzo Sabine on the basis of the Whig Club and Charles Lee incidents included Goddard (pp. 326-328) in *The American Loyalists, or Biographical Sketches of Adherents to the British Crown in the War of the Revolution* (Boston, 1847). I hope the accounts given in this book will make any need for defending Goddard from this imputation superfluous.

CHAPTER IX

Copies of the almanacs mentioned in the chapter may be found at the Maryland Historical Society. The originals of the letters from John Carter to Mary Katherine and Abigail Goddard are at the John Carter Brown Library. The account of the Federal Hill episode is based on papers at the Maryland Historical Society. The various petitions to the government by and about Mary Katherine Goddard's plea to retain her postal position are now in the National Archives. A copy of her will is in the Hall of Records, Annapolis.

CHAPTER X

The final phase of Goddard's career derives primarily from letters in the possession of the Rhode Island Historical Society and the John Carter Brown Library and records in the Rhode Island State Archives. The William McCullough letter is at the American Antiquarian Society, as are the letters from Goddard to Isaiah Thomas. The letters to General Gates were printed in *The Lee Papers,* as were those from Daniel Carthy.

The correspondence with Lighthorse Harry Lee was partially printed in Henry Lee, *Memoirs of the War in the Southern Department of the United States*, rev. ed., by Robert E. Lee (New York, 1869). One unpublished letter in this correspondence is at the Henry E. Huntington Library and Art Gallery. *The Diary of Isaiah Thomas, 1805-1828* was published by the American Antiquarian Society (Worcester, 1909).

INDEX